S0-ACD-597

# HOW TO
# HELP HURTING
# PEOPLE

## Edited by
## Dr. Colleen Birchett

A  Publication

urban ministries, inc.
Chicago, Il 60643

Publisher
Urban Ministries, Inc.
1439 West 103rd St.
Chicago, Illinois 60643
(312) 233-4499

First Edition
First Printing
ISBN: 940955-08-3
Catalog No. 9-2733

Copyright © 1990 Urban Outreach. All Rights Reserved. No part of this publication may be reproduced, stored in a retrieval system, or transmitted in any form or by any means, electronic, mechanical, photocopy, recording or otherwise except for brief quotations in printed reviews without prior written permission from the holder of the copyright.

Scripture quotations are from the King James Version of the Bible. Printed in the United States of America.

I dedicate this book to
my mother,
Esther Bernice Birchett

# CONTENTS

# ACKNOWLEDGEMENTS

We wish to thank the following churches, church organizations and social agencies whose representatives completed the questionnaires which provided the data we used to select the topics to be covered in this book.

(Churches and Church Organizations)
Allen Temple Baptist Church of Oakland, California
Bible Community Baptist Church of Detroit
Liberty Temple Full Gospel Temple of Chicago
Operation PUSH Minister's Alliance of Chicago
Rock of Ages Church of Chicago
Trinity United Church of Christ of Chicago
Westlawn Gospel Chapel of Chicago
(Christian Counseling Centers and Rescue Missions)
The Center for Life Skills of Chicago
Circle Family Care of Chicago
The Social Services Department of the
Salvation Army of Chicago
The Pacific Gardens Mission of Chicago
The TV 38 Counseling Hot Line of Chicago
(Prison Ministries)
Good News Ministry of Chicago
(Social Service Agencies)
Family Focus of Evanston, Illinois
Social Services Department of the Circuit Court of Illinois
(Bible Colleges, Christian Service Departments)
Manna Bible College of Philadelphia
Philadelphia College of the Bible of Philadelphia

We also wish to acknowledge the contributions of Mrs. Sara Hennings who transcribed tapes and typed most of the manuscript. Then of course, we wish to acknowledge the outstanding contributions of the Publications Manager, Shawan Brand and Mary Lewis, Copy Editor. We also wish to thank Word Processor, Cheryl Wilson for her tireless efforts. Last but not least, of course, we wish to thank Media Graphics Corporation and Dickinson Press.

# PREFACE

During childhood, I experienced the presence of the Lord on a number of occasions. I experienced His presence when I stood on the pew beside my mother, watching the "Loftoneer" choir of Rev. Lofton's church marching in, and listening to Eula Jean singing the descent of "Tell It, Sing It, Shout It, Everywhere!" I experienced His presence while listening to my Uncle Billy's sermons, and I experienced His presence while reading the story of the death, burial and resurrection of Christ, sitting on my grandmother's bedroom floor.

However, it was during the summer of 1960, at one of the most traumatic periods of my family's history, when I consciously made a decision to accept Jesus Christ as my personal Saviour, and to live a Christian life. I then began to observe the transforming power of the Lord at work in my family and in myself. My father had been hospitalized after a nervous breakdown, and my mother, at 34 years of age, was left with eight children to raise alone. About a year later, my youngest brother, Derrick would be born retarded. During this time, every member of our family was hurting, particularly my mother.

As a family, we did not reach out to any social agency for advice. Instead, we reached out to the Lord and to the Community of Faith--the only help we knew. Our experience as a family would have been overwhelming if it had not been for the Lord and for the nurturance of the Community of Faith. I was old enough, at that time, to observe how this worked. I observed Sister Ellis, the church secretary of the little storefront church near our home (Bible Community Baptist Church), become a friend of my mother and provide emotional support as my mother got her "bearings."

I observed the leadership of Rev. George Gooden as one member of my family after another made conscious decisions to accept Jesus Christ as their personal Saviour. Then I watched as such members as Gilford Baker and Robert Boyd befriended my father and my brothers and encouraged them in the Christian faith. The nurturance of the Lord and His people made the difference in my family's lives.

Many changes have taken place in our family since that time. Family members now belong to a variety of church families, including Greater Grace Temple of Detroit, Christ Temple of Marion, Indiana, Christ Temple of Detroit, Trinity United Church of Christ in Chicago, and Emmanuel Temple of Rochester, New York. The Black church has continued its healing ministry in my family's lives, and most of us are leaders in Christian ministry. Last summer we had a reunion in Marion, Indiana where my brother, Elder David Birchett pastors, and we all shared our testimonies. We told the story of "how we got over" and that story has become the motivation for the design and the content of this book.

**Purpose of the Book.** The book is designed for people who are concerned about helping hurting people. It is designed for people in local churches who come into contact with hurting people. Every day thousands of hurting people reach out to churches throughout the country. In the Black community, the Black church has played a special role in this respect. In some communities, the Black church may be the only institution of hope still standing. Therefore, it is the purpose of this book to provide the types of insights into hurting people that will cause people in local churches (Black churches in particular) to be able to minister to hurting people more effectively.

**Objectives of the Book.** Upon completion of this book, the reader should be able to use the principles presented to help people suffering from a variety of emotional crises. The reader should be able to recognize and discuss 12 different emotions commonly experienced by Black people who are hurting. The

**8**

reader should be able to describe the types of situations giving rise to these emotional crises, and should be able to apply guidelines presented to more effectively minister to the hurting person. The reader should also be aware of signs when the hurting person should be referred for professional counseling of a professional counseling agency. The book can be used for personal study, for group study, and in church training sessions.

**The Content.** The introductory chapter contains a transcript of a sermon by Dr. Jeremiah A. Wright, pastor of Trinity United Church of Christ. Introducing the sermon are statistics on some of the sources of pain in the Black community. Each of the remaining chapters addresses a different emotion, experienced by Black people who reach out to the Black church for help, during times of crisis. The emotions covered are: Abandonment, Anger, Anxiety, Depression, Fear, Frustration, Grief, Guilt, Insecurity, Loneliness, Low Self-Esteem, and Powerlessness.

The emotions were selected based on a survey distributed to counselors and social workers at a variety of social agencies and churches servicing hurting people. Ninety-three counselors and social workers completed questionnaires. Each respondent listed the twelve emotions most commonly experienced by Black hurting people who come to them for help. From the emotions listed by the ninety-three counselors, the twelve most frequently named emotions were selected. Then a chapter of the book was assigned to each emotion.

Christian counselors, pastors, Christian social workers, and Christian psychologists were invited to author these chapters. The authors represent a wide range of Christian experience and professional expertise. The book also includes a bibliography of books about counseling, the role of the Black church in counseling, and on ministering to people experiencing the various emotions covered. Quite a few of the books, dissertations and periodical articles contained in the bibliography are by Black authors.

**The Organization of the Book.** With the exception of the introduction, each chapter is divided into two parts. Part One begins with a short vignette (or case study) of a person who is hurting from the emotion covered by that particular chapter. Then a biblical character who experienced this type of emotional crisis is presented. The emotion is defined, the types of situations evoking that emotion are discussed, and guidelines for helping people who are hurting from this emotion are presented.

Part Two of each chapter contains a case study which allows the reader to apply principles covered in the chapter. Each case study contains three types of exercises: "fill-in-the-blank/discovery exercises", "summary exercises" and "personal applications".

Short biographies of each author are presented at the end of the book, near the bibliography.

**Uses.** This book can be used for private as well as group study. It can be used during Sunday School, as an elective. It can be used during training hour, to train all church workers and "bench members". It can also be used during weekday Bible Studies as a Bible study guide, and it can be used in family devotions. In fact, it may also be used as a foundation for a church-wide retreat.

**Private Study.** If used as a private devotional guide, it might be useful to spread the material out over weeks or perhaps months. Select a different chapter each week or month. Then select different exercises each day until the exercises for a given chapter are exhausted.

Once all of the chapters are completed, it might be useful to read additional books and periodical articles from the bibliography at the end of the book. These books can be used to extend a group study, or can be used in private study. They can provide additional information and support as you continue to minister to the hurting.

**Group Study -- 90-Minute Sessions.** The book is designed for a two-part group study session. Part I would be a time when

**10**

participants, under the direction of a group leader (or minister) study Part One of the chapter, along with the scriptural passage presented. This initial study session would require about 30 minutes. Then the group leader would begin the laboratory session. In the laboratory session, the group would, collectively, investigate the case studies presented at the end of each chapter.

The group study session is designed so that every person can contribute something to the understanding and application of the principles covered in the chapter. This process would begin as the group leader divides the larger group into five smaller groups. Each small group would be assigned a separate exercise from the set provided with the case study.

A small group leader would be appointed (or elected) for each small group. Within the small groups, the small group leader would assign one question (or two, depending on the size of the group) to each participant. In the event that there are more participants in the small group than there are questions, then people might work on questions in two's, three's (or more).

About ten minutes should be allowed for each small group participant to answer the question assigned to him/her. Then another 10 minutes should be allowed for participants to present their answers to the questions to the small group of which they are a part. Then the remainder of the time should be spent allowing the small group, to discuss the "summary question" which is the last question of each exercise.

At the end of the small group discussions, the smaller groups would convene with the larger group again. In the larger group, a spokesperson from each of the five smaller groups would summarize their small group discussion. Then the larger group, under the direction of the original leader, would discuss the final "Summary Exercise" and the "Personal Application" at the end of each chapter.

**Group Study -- 60-Minute Sessions.** In shorter periods, it might be necessary to use part of a given chapter as a stimulus for discussion during the group meeting itself. Then the other part of the chapter might be used as a "homework" assignment or for private devotional study.

**Family Devotions.** During the week preceding the study of a given chapter, all members would read a given chapter privately, along with the "Case Study" at the end of the chapter. Each member would select a different related "fill-in-the blank/discovery" exercise and, on the basis of it, prepare a short presentation for family devotions.

The devotional period would begin with a discussion of the points the author makes in the chapter. Then the case study would be read. Then each member would present insights they have based on the exercise (related to the case study) that they completed during the week. After each member has contributed, then the family, together, would discuss the "Summary Exercise" and "Personal Application" at the end of each chapter case study.

In summary, the book can be used in many ways. However, the main purpose is that Christians everywhere become more sensitive to the needs of those in our families, Community of Faith and communities who are hurting and who are in need of a closer relationship with the Lord Jesus Christ.

# INTRODUCTION

*People hurt when they experience pain. Today racism and poverty are injecting enormous doses of pain into African American lives. Physical and emotional pain are felt when a son or daughter becomes the victim of police brutality. It is felt when a plant moves to another country and causes hundreds of families to fall into poverty. It is felt when a baby dies in infancy, and it is felt when hard won civil rights are again taken away. Statistics by the United States Center for Health Statistics indicate that, for large numbers of African Americans, racism and economic oppression have become lethal.*

*Racism became lethal when, in January of 1989, a white police officer in Miami killed a Black motorcyclist, apparently for no legitimate reason. It became lethal again, when, in New York, during the same year, white youths chased a Black youth and murdered him because they suspected that a white girl from their neighborhood had dated a Black man.*

*In the same year, Bernard Goetz received only a one year sentence after shooting four Black youths on a subway train, saying that their presence made him feel insecure. In the same year national network news carried pictures of a white police officer pushing the head of Don Jackson through a motorcycle shop window. Why? Because he was arguing with them over whether he was speeding.*

*During the same time period, the Supreme Court removed many civil rights protections of African*

13

Americans. In June of 1989, the Supreme Court determined that the 1866 Civil Rights Act could not be used to sue local and state governments or private industry for violations of civil rights. This action will soon add to physical and emotional pain resulting from discrimination.

Economic and political oppression become very personal when the physical and emotional pain from these realities expresses itself as a disease within one's physical body. Poor physical health is one of the byproducts of poverty and emotional stress. Throughout the Black community, people are constantly suffering from physical disease, emotional disease and the loss of loved ones.

For example, the most recent vital statistics of the United States reflect that nearly three times as many Black infants die during childbirth as white children. Moreover, while the life expectancy for Black Americans remained at 69.4 years (with the life expectancy of Black men at 65.2), the life expectancy for white Americans rose from 74.6 to 75.6.

The Center for Disease Control reports that, for every 1,000 Black Americans, 35.3 are diabetic, compared to 27.4 per 1,000 for white Americans. The number of Black Americans who die of diabetes is slightly more than twice the number of white Americans who die from the disease. Twice as many Black Americans die of liver diseases and, of Black Americans diagnosed as having cancer, only 37% survive beyond five years, compared to a 50% survival rate for white Americans. Nearly six times as many African Americans die of homicides and violent crimes as the number of white Americans who die in this manner. All of these diseases add to the emotional pain felt by the victims.

**14**

*African Americans are also dying of AIDS. The most recent statistics of the Center for Disease control reflect that, during 1988, hospitals reported a total of 90,990 cases of AIDS. Of that total, 58% had died during the year. That was an increase of 34% since 1987. Twenty-seven percent of these people were African Americans, even though African Americans constitute only 12% of the population. The reality of the AIDS epidemic has added immeasurable emotional pain both to the victims and to their families.*

*In July of 1989, the National Research Council reported, that although Black Americans made economic and political gains during the past 50 years, the gains had stagnated during the 1970s and 1980s, with most still remaining separated from the mainstream of American life. The NRC reported that, while major gains for African Americans had taken place during the 1940s, 1950s and 1960s, the standard of living, education, housing, personal earnings and participation in the political arena had, in the main, stagnated. According to the Department of Labor, throughout 1989, the percentage of African Americans who were unemployed remained at about 12%, compared to 5% for White Americans. Unemployment is another source of emotional pain in the Black community.*

*Consequently, there is a disproportionate amount of pain in the Black community today. The above facts would suggest that this pain may increase with the entrance of the 1990s and the approach of the 21st century. However, in spite of this, African Americans have hope. Physical and emotional pain is not new to the Black community. It has been a part of African American life that dates back at least as far as the date that the first African was snatched from the shores of Africa and brought to America against his/her will.*

**15**

*However, throughout African American history, hope and healing have been found in Jesus Christ. In this way, people who hurt have been able to uncover a source of power in tribulation that comes from Jesus Christ alone.*

*The following sermon, delivered by Dr. Jeremiah A. Wright, Jr., reminds hurting people that there is hope. He calls attention to the fact that pain can become a source of power. God has prepared a palace for each of us, that we can only enter, if we don't give up on God when we are in pain.*

*This sermon is a good introduction to the subject of this book, helping hurting people. It can serve as a mental framework for people who minister to hurting people, and for those of us, from time to time, who hurt.*

## "The Power That Comes From Pain"

*By Dr. Jeremiah A. Wright, Jr.*

A person has to have lived through something to get a sense of the power that comes from pain. The first verse of Andre Crouch's well-known masterpiece, "Through It All," contains a truth which is profound in its implications and which is addressed in Second Corinthians 4:7, 8 and 9. The first verse of this song says, "I have had many tears and sorrows. I have had questions for tomorrow; sometimes I didn't know right from wrong."

The author is describing a painful situation. "I have had many tears and sorrows" (pain!). Sadness and heartbreak mean pain. "I have had questions for tomorrow." Uncertainty about serious situations brings pain. "Sometimes I didn't know right from wrong!" Ethical and moral quandaries create a tension within the soul that spills over into spiritual chaos and causes pain.

The author is describing a three-fold, triple whammie of a painful situation. One of my friends right now is telling me about a child whose natural daddy is sexually molesting that child. This type of situation brings on questions about pain: What do you do? Do you keep a child away from the parent? The author of the Andre Crouch song is talking about pain, but he doesn't stop there. He says, "But"--and we will come back to this--"But", he writes, "in every situation, God gave this blessed consolation; your trials only come to make you strong!" He's saying that there is a certain strength that comes from pain.

Your trials only come to make you strong. He's saying that "Trouble," in the words of A. L. Patterson, "only comes with God's permission. Trouble only comes with God's purpose." All things work together for good to them that love the Lord. Your trials only come to make you strong. Trouble only comes with God's protection. The Bible says, "I will never leave you nor forsake you!" (Hebrews 13:5). The Lord has told us that in this world we will all have some trouble, but to be of good cheer because He has overcome the world (John 16:33). He never puts more on us than we can bear. Again, Andre Crouch's song says that trials only come to make us strong.

There is a particular power that comes from the experience of pain and only the predicament of pain can produce this particular power. John R. Claypool loves to tell the story of the girl who was his classmate in high school. She was living proof of that power that comes from pain. This girl was normal in every way except for the fact that she had been born without any arms. Her parents early on, after the shock of seeing their perfectly formed infant in every other aspect lying there helpless in the hospital, her parents decided very early that we only have one of two options. Either we can teach her to face life feeling sorry for herself, and that gives her the vantage point of pity, or we can teach her to face life using what she does have to make up for what she doesn't have. Psychologists like to call that compensatory skills, using what you've got and not worrying about what you

**17**

don't have.

Her parents reasoned, if we exercise this second option that will give her the vantage point of power instead of pity. So they set about teaching her to do everything that other folk did with their hands, from the time she was a toddler on, with her feet. By the time Claypool got to high school, he says this girl was a living legend. She could write. She could draw. She could eat. She could even drive a car!

It was incredible, a phenomenon, but, what was even more powerful was what she would say to people (most often strangers) whom she would catch looking down at her empty sleeves. You know how people do when they discover a handicap or a special condition and a special citizen? They would reach to shake her hand upon being introduced only to have that look come on their face when they realized that they had blown it.

Sammy Davis, Jr. talked about that look and blowing it in a similar fashion when he and Ray Charles were both playing a gig together in Las Vegas at the same hotel. Sammy said he went to Ray's room to relax after the show one night, and after having gone to his own room first to shower and freshen up after performing, he got over to Ray Charles' room about forty-five minutes after their final curtain; and when Ray opened the door to his suite it was pitch black in there, and Sammy said, "Hey, Man, what you doing sitting up in here in the dark with all the-- lights off?" He had blown it and he knew he had blown it. He wanted to swallow his tongue.

That's how folk would feel as they'd reach for a hand on this young woman and a hand wasn't there. However, this woman would always take that awkward moment and say, matter of factly, "I was born with no arms. That's my challenge! What's yours?" She had power, not pity. She had power that is brought about by a pain predicament, a particular power that came only from the experience of her lifetime. She could not have gotten it any other way, and she lived in a spiritual palace rather than wallowing in a rundown shack of self-pity.

God intends for each of us to live in such a palace, but do you know what? Think back to the story of Joseph in the Book of Genesis, chapters 37, 39 and 40. Joseph had a special gift and his brothers didn't like either his prized possession or his privileged position. So they mistreated Joseph. They threw him in a pit. He ended up down in Africa the property of Potiphar, one of the king's officers who was the captain of the palace guard. Potiphar's wife had eyes for Joseph and she let it be known plain and simple, so Joseph would know exactly what was happening.

However Joseph had integrity and he wouldn't do what Potiphar's wife wanted him to do so she tricked him into the bedroom. When he found out what was happening, he started to get out. He didn't get out, though, before she grabbed the coat. Then she had proof that he had been in her bedroom. Then she told the lie about him that got him thrown into prison.

While Joseph was in prison, he interpreted a wine steward's dream, and asked the wine steward to remember him when he got out of prison and had his original position restored. Joseph, after all, was innocent. He was a kidnapped person and was now a framed prisoner, but do you know how chapter 40 ends?

It says that the wine steward never gave Joseph another thought when he was released from prison. He forgot all about Joseph! However, remember back to the time when God first gave Joseph the gift of dream interpretation. You see, God had a palace prepared for this patriarch. God had already fixed it so Joseph would be the number two man in the cabinet of all of North Africa. God had already fixed it so that Joseph would be the governor during Israel's grim days of famine and despair. God had already pre-ordained the combined position of Secretary of the Interior, Secretary of State and Secretary of Agriculture. He had that waiting for Joseph down in Chapter 41, and he had already prepared a palace to go along with the position.

**19**

God had a palace prepared for this patriarch just like He has a spiritual palace prepared for you. God intends for each of us to live in the same kind of palace in which this woman with no arms lived. However Joseph could have missed the palace if he had given up while he was in prison. Don't you miss the palace by giving up while you are in a pit, because someone has mistreated you. Draw from that power which comes from pain. Don't miss the palace and give up a Potiphar's house just because someone has lied on you. God has a palace waiting for you. Don't miss the palace giving up in prison, 'cause somebody has forgotten about you. God hasn't forgotten about you.

There is a valley that you must go through. The valley may be a pit. The valley may be in Potiphar's house. The valley may be prison. However, wherever the valley is--what did David say? "Yea, though I walk through the valley of the shadow of death, I will fear no evil for thou are with me" (Psalm 23). You don't go through that valley all by yourself. On the way to the palace, His power will sustain you. There is a particular power that comes from the predicament of pain and it is a power that only God gives.

Look at the way Paul puts it in his poignant prose. Paul was in pain. Not only was he in the physical pain he talks about in Second Corinthians in the twelfth chapter. He talks about a thorn in his flesh, but he was also in spiritual, mental and psychological pain. He was in the pastoral pain that comes about when relations between a shepherd and an undershepherd are strained, tense and tough. That's what's going on between Paul and the people in this congregation of Corinth, when Paul writes this letter that you and I call Second Corinthians.

Paul was in pain. Yet even in his pain, or perhaps because of his pain, he was able to write, "We have this treasure in earthen vessels," or "We who have this spiritual treasure are like common clay pots." Why? That the excellency of the power may be of God and not of us or in contemporary English, "In order to show that the Supreme power," I tell you there's a particular power that comes from the predicament of pain and it's a power that only God gives.

"In order to show," says Paul, "that the Supreme power belongs to God not to us." Then Paul takes off in two different ways, and, as teenagers would say, "Paul does it to death" in this chapter. First he resorts to some of his favorite language, language drawn from the world of sports and athletics. That was one of Paul's favorite pastimes, you know. He talks someplace else about seeing as how we are "compassed about", and he uses the word for spectators in a sports arena surrounding in an oval, the race track. He says that, seeing as to how we are compassed about, we should run this race with patience (athletics and sports language).

He talks about pressing toward the mark of the high calling which is in Christ Jesus like a good long-distance runner (again, athletics and sports language). He talks about, "I have fought the good fight" like a gladiator. "I have finished my course", like a track star. Now there's a laurel wreath, a "crown" for me like in the Olympics. Here Paul draws some exciting pictures.

First he says that we are often troubled. "We are troubled on every side" and the word he uses for trouble is thlibo and it has at its root the sport of wrestling. That means that it's close at home. The disturbance you are experiencing is no long-distance disturbance. It is something that is right up on you. It is close! It is like wrestling!

You can't wrestle unless you are close. There has got to be something that is touching you closely and when you are wrestling, you have to keep your concentration at all times. Otherwise you get thrown down on the mat. Paul is describing a pain that is caused by something close to home, something or someone with whom he's in close contact and a situation which causes him to concentrate. It is time-consuming and quite a bit of his time and energy are being spent. Again, he says that we are troubled (thlibo), on every side (wrestling).

Think about that which is causing you trouble. It isn't someone way off somewhere. It is someone or something that is close. If you're wrestling with it, it's up on you. You have constant contact with it. Paul says that is the first characteristic of that which causes him pain. Now, I'm not saying that your husband or your child is responsible for your particular pain predicament, but they are close. That's number one, says Paul.

Number two, Paul says we are perplexed. The Good News translates that as "in doubt" and you'll see why in a moment. The word Paul uses when he gets to perplexed is aporeo, and that has as its root a situation in the game of football. Now, in Paul's day it was soccer, but the football image means the same. The word means, number one, there is no clear vision of where you can run because of opposing obstacles. Every way you turn you can't see, because there's an obstacle. You are perplexed. The Greek word for this is aporeo. What makes bad matters worse is that you are being tackled by your own men. Now that will make you doubt!

Can you imagine going to a football game of the Washington Redskins, for instance, and upon arriving at the stadium, seeing Coach Joe Gibbs on crutches with both arms and both legs in casts, a neck brace and his jaw all wired up, and you're asking him, "Coach, was there an automobile accident? What terrible thing happened to you? Who did this?" Can you imagine him responding, "No, my own team did this to me." Can you imagine that?

In many churches and families, that is the very thing that happens! Before the team can take the field, the coach has been crippled by the deacons, wounded by his trustees, and knocked out by those close to him. His own team did it to him before the real action in life's arena ever started. These are examples of obstacles that block your view, and of being tackled by your own team. Paul says that brings a special type of pain.

The third point that Paul makes is that we are persecuted. The Good News Bible says that we are persecuted! The Good News Bible translates it to mean that "there are many enemies," and the Greek word that is used is dioko. Dioko means to pursue, to press toward, to follow after, to be chased or to be pursued. In other words, when you are dioko, someone is hot on your trail. They are right behind you for every step you take. You can hear their feet lock step with your feet and you can hear their breathing. You can almost feel it right down your neck. They are hot on your trail. Every time you vip, they vop. It's like white on rice. They are not trailing you because they like you. They are deadly enemies, intent on doing you serious bodily harm. You can't slow up one bit or you are a goner. You can't stop to catch your breath. You can't even miss a step or break stride or they have got you. What they will do to you isn't fit to print, if they can catch you. You are the grass and they are the lawnmower. You are the roadrunner, "Beep Beep" and they are the coyote. That's what dioko means, a deadly enemy, dead on your train like a heat-seeking missile tracking a supersonic jet, a pain that will not let up. "We are troubled on every side (thlibo)." "We are perplexed (aporeo)" and "we are persecuted (dioko)."

However, that's not all, says Paul. We are also "cast down". Here he uses a word from the sport of boxing. It is a word that means you are going down in a hurry. You've been stunned and caught out of the blue by a lightning punch--one you didn't see coming. It is one that you weren't prepared for, and one you couldn't block in time. It is one that you weren't expecting and it got you and it got you good. This boxing word, kataballo, and this perplexed word, dioko, are very similar, because it is often someone on your own team (or family) who catches you with a haymaker while you were looking the other way.

I was telling a couple this week about this boxing imagery and about how rich it is in all of its meanings. Dr. Patterson said that he told his wife three things when they got married some thirty years ago. He said, number one, as long as God gives me breath and strength, I will keep food on this table. Number two, as long as God keeps me healthy, I'll keep a roof over your head. You don't ever have to work to feed this family or keep it in shelter, but, then there is number three. When I come home after fighting out there in the ring of life...after fighting for my life in the ring, fighting for your life in the ring, fighting for Black people in the ring, fighting against racism in the ring, fighting folk who want to do me harm in the ring, fighting Satan who wants to tear up God's church in the ring, fighting centuries of ignorance and miseducation in the ring, fighting animals of greed and stupidity in the ring,...when I come dragging in out of that ring, cut up and bleeding, back into my corner, don't take the stool I'm supposed to sit on and go up aside my head with it. I don't want to fight in my own corner.

When I come back in my corner, I want to be massaged, made to feel good, made to understand that my fighting out there is not in vain, that it counts for something in here. Give me some pointers on what to do out there, but don't you attack me and beat me up in my own corner.

If you have to fight in your own corner, you can't last out there in the ring. If you get stung by your own folk, you can get knocked out before the next round starts, and when you get hit so that you are going down fast from a blow you weren't prepared for, in your own corner, Paul says, that's a pain which is at times indescribable. We have trouble, he writes, on every side--pain. We are perplexed--pain. We are persecuted--pain. We are knocked down--pain.

Yet there is a power that comes from pain. This Supreme power comes from and belongs to God and not to us. In order to demonstrate that, Paul employed one of God's special words. He uses the language from the world of athletics and sports. He also uses language that comes straight from the throne of Grace. We have a habit of assigning value to words by how big the words are and by how many syllables and letters the words have.

When I was a teenager, Gloria Lockerman (a little Black girl) won $16,000 on the "$64,000 Question" game show by spelling antidisestablishmentarianism. We think that is a big word. However, God has a little bitty word that's a whole lot bigger than that twenty-eight letter word! That word is "but". But has three letters. However, there is no more powerful word in God's Word than this little bitty word "but".

"But" is a divine conjunction and Paul just uses it like a master here in this passage. "But" is a heavenly stop sign used on the road through God's Word. Whenever you see the word "but," you better slow down. It means that God is somewhere around. "But" means that the hand of God is somewhere behind the scenes changing things. When you see "but," you had better put the brakes on because it means that the footprints of God are somewhere to be seen. "But" is a conjunction that links two separate phrases together. However, it changes the meaning of the second phrase and God likes to do that all throughout His Word.

"For God so loved the world that He gave His only begotten Son, that whosoever believeth on Him should not perish...but--they shall have everlasting life" (John 3:16). "He came unto His own and His own received Him not...but as many as received Him, to them gave he power to become the sons of God" (John 1:11-12). When Jesus heard that Lazarus was sick He said, "This sickness is not unto death, but for the glory of God" (John 11:4). When the disciples asked, Is it time now? Will you restore the kingdom to Israel now? Jesus answered, "It is not for you to know the times or the seasons which the Father has put in His own power. But ye shall receive power after the Holy Ghost is come upon you" (Acts 1:7-8).

"John truly baptized with water, but ye shall be baptized with the Holy Ghost" (Acts 1:5; 11:16). "Not by power, not by might, but by my spirit saith the Lord" (Zechariah 4:6). "I have planted, Apollos watered, but God gave the increase" (1 Corinthians 3:6). "Beloved, now are we the sons and daughters of God and it doth not yet appear what we shall be. But we know that when He shall appear, we shall be like Him" (1 John 3:2). "Behold, I show you a mystery. We shall not all sleep, but we shall all be changed" (1 Corinthians 15:51). Jeremiah said, "I will not make mention of Him nor speak any more in His name. But his word was in my heart as a burning fire shut up in my bones" (Jeremiah 20:9). David said, "Weeping may endure for a night, but joy, joy is coming in the morning" (Psalm 30:5).

Andre Crouch said, "I have had many tears and sorrows. I've had questions for tomorrow, sometimes I didn't know right from wrong, but in every situation, God gave this blessed consolation." Isaiah said what? "Even the youths shall faint and be weary and the young men shall utterly fall, but they that wait upon the Lord shall renew their strength. They shall mount up on wings like eagles. They shall run and not be weary. They shall walk and not faint" (Isaiah 40:30-31). This word "but", I tell you, is a divine conjunction. It is heaven's highway sign of a holy action taking place somewhere nearby. Paul said yes, there is pain, but there is also God's power.

Yes, we are troubled on every side, but we are not distressed. Yes, we are perplexed, but we are not in despair. Yes, there are many enemies. Yes, we're persecuted, but we are never without a friend. We are never forsaken, and yes, we are knocked down but we are never knocked out. We are stunned, but we are not stopped. We are damaged, but we are not destroyed. Why? Because this power that I'm talking about is God's power. "He gives power to the faint and to them that hath no might He increases strength."

My hope is not built on any power that man can generate. My hope is built on nothing less than Jesus' blood and righteousness. When it comes to His blood there is power, power that came from nails in His hand. Power came from the spear in His side. Power came from a crown of thorns on His brow. Power came from the pain of when they knocked Him down. They had not knocked Him out. He got up stronger than He was when He went down. Have you ever noticed that it was only after Jesus was knocked down on Calvary that He came up saying, "All power is in My hand?" It is "wonder-working power." When He calmed the sea, He didn't need all of His power. When He healed the sick, He didn't need all of His power.

When He raised the dead, He didn't need all of His power. Oh, but to save my soul, like Claypool's classmate saying, "Hi, I have no arms. That's my challenge. What's yours?" You know what I say? I say, "Hi, I'm a divorced parent and a divorced pastor. That's my challenge, what's yours?"

What can wash away my sin? Nothing but the blood of Jesus. There is wonder-working power. What can make me whole again? Nothing but the blood of Jesus! "Just as I am without one plea, but that Thy blood was shed for me!" There's power in the blood--I'm not what I ought to be, but I'm not what I used to be! There is power! Power! Wonder-working power in the blood of the Lamb!

# CHAPTER ONE

# ABANDONMENT

### Patricia Beason

*Mrs. Anderson could hear the children next door yelling and screaming. As usual, they were left home alone with 12-year-old Adam, their oldest brother. On this day, Adam could be seen leaving their house, heading for the grocery store, as usual, with money that his mother left for him to buy dinner. Hopefully, today he would return.*

*Mrs. Anderson had learned from her neighbor, Mrs. Smith, that Mrs. Lloyd, the children's mother, was rarely at home. Mrs. Smith said that the children's mother worked downtown at a department store. Nearly every morning, as early as 6:30 a.m., Mrs. Lloyd could be seen jumping out of some man's car and running into her house. A few minutes later, she would come out, jump into the man's car, and the two of them would drive away again.*

*Most of the time, the children were left alone. They had to get themselves ready for school without the help of their mother. When they returned in the evening, they had to make their own dinner and prepare themselves for bed.*

*Most of the responsibility for all of this was on Adam, the oldest child. However, Adam had begun to*

> *abandon these responsibilities. A few people had seen him hanging around with some members of the Viceroys, the gang that terrorized the neighborhood.*
>
> *Sarah, one of Adam's little sisters, told Mrs. Smith's little girl that Adam was not using the money his mother left to buy food for the children's dinner, but was taking it himself. He was often gone in the evenings. Sometimes he would get home just before his mother jumped out of her boyfriend's car in the morning. The children were afraid to tell their mother what was going on, because Adam might beat them up.*

Adam and his brothers and sisters are hurting as a result of feelings of abandonment. While their feelings may be similar to those experienced by most "latch-key" children, these children probably experience abandonment more intensely, because their mother, in addition to having to abandon them for employment, has also abandoned them for a boyfriend.

Abandonment is a feeling that is experienced by a variety of people in different situations. Feelings of abandonment can lead to counterproductive and self-destructive activities.

This chapter is about helping people who feel abandoned. It is for counselors, neighbors, friends and others who want to guide such people into productive lives.

## An Example of Abandonment from Scripture

There are many descriptions of people in the Bible who felt abandoned. One of the most vivid descriptions is of Jesus Christ. The theme of abandonment occurs throughout the story of His crucifixion. Beginning in the Garden of Gethsemane, Jesus is first abandoned by Judas who would betray Him. Then He is abandoned by Peter, James and John who slept when they should have been providing Jesus with support. Then all twelve of the disciples abandoned Him after He was arrested, while Peter abandoned Him a third time by telling people that he hadn't associated with Jesus at all. Pilate washed his hands of the matter and abandoned Jesus, claiming that he could not handle the situation. Finally, on the cross, Jesus cried out in His flesh, feeling that His heavenly Father also had abandoned Him. Later Jesus is abandoned and left in an empty tomb.

However, the tomb is not the end of the story for Jesus Christ. Jesus left an example for all people who feel abandoned when He broke forth out of the tomb, resurrected into a new life, and offered that same resurrection experience to anyone who wanted to receive it (Luke 24:1-7; Colossians 1:15-20; 3:1-4)! Counselors can use these passages in helping counselees set goals for "breaking out" of their dismal circumstances.

## from Scripture

**Matthew 26:14** Then one of the twelve, called Judas Iscariot, went unto the chief priests,

**15** And said unto them, What will ye give me, and I will deliver him unto you? And they covenanted with him for thirty pieces of silver.

**16** And from that day he sought opportunity to betray him.

**36** Then cometh Jesus with them unto a place called Gethsemane, and saith unto the disciples, Sit ye here, while I go and pray yonder.

**40** And he cometh unto the disciples, and findeth them asleep, and saith unto Peter, What, could ye not watch with me one hour?

**55** In that same hour said Jesus to the multitudes, Are ye come out as against a thief with swords and staves for to take me? I sat daily with you teaching in the temple, and ye laid no hold on me.

**56** But all this was done, that the scriptures of the prophets might be fulfilled. Then all the disciples forsook him, and fled.

**69** Now Peter sat without in the palace: and a damsel came unto him, saying, Thou also wast with Jesus of Galilee.

**70** But he denied before them all saying, I know not what thou sayest.

**27:24** When Pilate saw that he could prevail nothing, but that rather a tumult was made, he took water, and washed his hands before the multitude, saying, I am innocent of the blood of this just person: see ye to it.

**45** Now from the sixth hour there was darkness over all the land unto the ninth hour.

**46** And about the ninth hour Jesus cried with a loud voice, saying, Eli, Eli, lama sabachthani? that is to say, My God, my God, why hast thou forsaken me?

**59** And when Joseph had taken the body, he wrapped it in a clean linen cloth,

**60** And laid it in his own new tomb, which he had hewn out in the rock: and he rolled a great stone to the door of the sepulchre, and departed.

**28:1** In the end of the sabbath, as it began to dawn toward the first day of the week, came Mary Magdalene and the other Mary to see the sepulchre.

**5** And the angel answered and said unto the women, Fear not ye: for I know that ye seek Jesus, which was crucified.

**6** He is not here: for he is risen, as he said. Come, see the place where the Lord lay.

## What Is Abandonment?

According to the Second Collegiate Edition of the *American Heritage Dictionary*, abandonment is a noun form of the verb "abandon." Abandon is defined as: 1) to withdraw support or help from, especially in spite of a duty, allegiance, or responsibility; 2) to give up by leaving or ceasing to operate or inhabit, especially as a result of danger to another impending threat; 3) to surrender one's claim or right (to give up); 4) to desist from or cease trying to continue.

The feeling of abandonment has become common in America today, and in the Black community in particular. Sometimes a feeling of abandonment occurs when a parent or loved one dies or abandons his/her responsibility for his/her child. In other cases, people feel abandoned when any significant people in their lives leave or cease to operate on their behalf. Feelings of abandonment are not always directly tied to another person's intent to abandon. They may come as a response to a natural, unavoidable event of some kind.

Some of the most common situations leading to feelings of abandonment are divorce, broken love affairs, and the death of parent, sibling, friend, mentor or doctor. Feelings of abandonment can also occur within a parent when a child leaves home for kindergarten, college or marriage.

Such feelings can also be triggered by a child's entry into adolescence, and his/her increasing involvement in activities that cause the adolescent to become less dependent on the parent. One of the most common sources of the feeling of abandonment within children is when parents abandon them, because they are either unable or unwilling to care for the children.

**Abandonment by parents.** One of the by-products of the drug culture is abandoned children. In many families children watch parents change from being hardworking, productive citizens, to becoming heroin or cocaine addicts. While some parents with drug problems enroll in treatment programs, often their improvements are short-lived, and children witness their parents moving in and out of clean, sober lives and the "dirty" lives of the drug culture.

Such children may feel further abandoned when they learn that their parents are incapable of providing for them because they have lost their jobs due to drug abuse. Children often feel this failure by their parents as a loss. In addition to feeling abandoned, such children are often denied the chance to observe positive role models within their parents.

In some instances, parents move their families from one city to another, in attempts to free themselves of the influence of the drug culture, but they soon find themselves a part of the culture again, and thereby force their children into an endless cycle of uncertainty and despair. Such parents are usually not available to give their children the love, emotional support, care, and stability which they need. In many instances, one or the other parent will die as these cycles are taking place. In some instances, children may even witness such a parent's death.

The drug culture's cycle of despair often results in children not having food, clothing or shelter. Frequently the substance abusing parent will engage in such illegal activities as forcing the child to steal, and using public aid money to support drug addiction. Some drug addicts also sexually abuse their children.

Faced with the pain of their circumstances, children are often compelled to report the situation to police officers or school officials. When such situations are discovered by legal authorities, children are often taken away from the parents and made wards of the state. In many cases, the children of one family are separated from one another and placed in different foster homes.

If one were to interview such children, the feelings of abandonment often started when the parents first began using drugs and neglecting their children. Often the children were exposed to unsafe conditions. The counselor will find that children who have been abandoned in this way have many problems. First of all, they have poor self-images. They often blame themselves for things which happened in their families. Some feel that a parent who died as a result of drugs really died because the child was unable to rescue the parent. Often the abandoned children worry about siblings who are in foster homes, feeling that it is their fault they are there.

Often they feel that they were poorly treated by their parents because they were "bad." If sexual abuse became involved, the victims often blame themselves. Some also feel guilty about having reported their parents to the police, the pastor or a school official.

**34**

Feelings of abandonment are further aggravated when, in cases where the parents were drug addicts, the extended family members hesitate to become involved with the surviving children. When they reach out to relatives and are not taken in, their feelings of abandonment, guilt and worthlessness usually intensify.

Churches may encounter such children through their outreach ministries (such as Vacation Bible School or special ministries to detention centers, foster care centers and adoption agencies). However, many such children live in the neighborhoods of many of the people who belong to the local church.

**Death of a "significant other."** Another situation triggering a sense of abandonment is the death of a "significant other." The death of any significant person can bring with it feelings of anger, loss and confusion over what to do. However, it can also trigger feelings of abandonment. The surviving person can, on an emotional level, feel that the person who died has abandoned them. This feeling does not have to be in the immediate awareness of the survivor. However, on an emotional level, it is very real.

These feelings are particularly common among seniors who lose brothers and sisters, close friends, spouses and others through death. Feelings of abandonment can become very intense when a person experiences several such deaths within the same time frame.

The church comes into contact with such people within the church family, within the community surrounding the church, and within the extended families of members of the church.

**Divorces and broken love affairs.** Divorce, for some people, triggers feelings of abandonment that are similar to those experienced by one who is mourning the death of a loved one. To such people, the divorce is a death of sorts. It is the death of the idea of marriage. It is the death of the feeling of being affirmed that comes with marriage. It is also a death of the notion that marriage would be forever. Anger, guilt, confusion and loss of self-esteem often accompany divorce, along with feelings of being abandoned.

Broken love affairs can produce similar feelings of abandonment. While such feelings of abandonment are usually less intense than those experienced by the divorced, the broken love affair also raises questions of "Am I worthy?" Often the broken love affair is one of a series of such events, leading to questions of "I've been abandoned! How did I let this happen?"

People who are hurting from the feeling of abandonment following a broken love affair are often found among single people within the congregation, and among young adults who are seeking to establish marital relationships. In a culture with increased opportunities for women and changing sex roles, Black professional women and men often encounter difficulties establishing satisfying partnerships. Men might also occasionally experience feelings of abandonment due to the breakup of unsatisfactory relationships.

**Independence of children.** Many parents feel abandoned when their children make independent moves which result in their not needing as much nurturance from their parents as they did before. Probably the earliest instance of this is when the child leaves home for nursery school or kindergarten. The parent who was at home with the child can, on an emotional level, feel abandoned by the child.

Another instance of this is when the child reaches adolescence, and begins to take an interest in activities outside of the home. The child who was once available for most family activities is no longer as interested, and seeks instead to establish him/herself in his/her peer world. Such actions on the part of the child can be very threatening to the parent who consequently develops feelings of abandonment.

When children leave home for college similar feelings may occur in parents. These feelings are expressed through the parents' desire to continue making decisions and controlling the child's daily life. This may also occur when an adult child gets married. Conflicts develop as parents attempt to determine the details of the child's wedding, supervise the rearing of the grandchildren, and consequently become an "in-law" problem. Many of these behaviors occur as parents try to cope with feelings of no longer being needed, and of being abandoned.

Seniors can also feel the same sense of abandonment when their older children leave town to take on jobs in another city.

## How to Help People Who Feel Abandoned

Often people in our churches and in communities surrounding churches approach church members for help, even when they do not consciously recognize that what they are feeling is abandonment. There are a number of useful guidelines for helping such people. Some of the guidelines are tailored for the specific situations that triggered feelings of abandonment.

**Empathize.** Being empathetic means feeling with the other person. It means placing oneself in the other person's shoes, looking at life as the person sees it, and feeling that person's pain. Jesus, as the Great Counselor, was able to do this. Throughout His ministry, Jesus displayed empathy over and over again, as He walked among the hurting people of Galilee.

A woman approached Jesus, carrying her dead son and still hurting from the loss of her husband. This woman no doubt felt abandoned within the Jewish culture where women needed men to take care of them. Jesus looked upon this woman with compassion and then raised her son to life again (Luke 7:12-16; Hebrews 11:35). Upon seeing Lazarus lying in the grave, Jesus wept, and then raised him from the dead (John 10:32-44). Feeling a needy woman touch the hem of His garment, Jesus felt power go out of Him, and He healed the woman (Matthew 9:20-22; Mark 5:25-34; Luke 8:43-48).

It is important that counselors emulate Christ in the way He showed compassion for those who were hurting and those who were feeling abandoned (Joshua 1:5; Hebrews 13:5).

37

**Listen.** It is important to be attentive and supportive when the counselee comes for counseling. Being attentive and supportive involves being a good listener. It is important to allow counselees to talk through their situations, providing the supportive and affirming statements they need as they struggle with emotions related to feeling abandoned. We must be good listeners if we are going to gain the information about the person we need for that person to work through feelings of denial, guilt, and anger. Counselees must learn to talk about their feelings, whether they consider the feelings good or bad.

**Clarify.** The counselor must help the counselee clarify his/her emotions, and alter thought patterns that cause the counselee to have false guilt or to feel unworthy. It is important for counselees to develop more accurate and positive conceptions of themselves. Counselees must be encouraged to examine their strengths and weaknesses, and to achieve balance in the ways they see themselves and others.

**Teach new skills.** Counselees must learn ways of coping with the fact that a given person is no longer in their lives, for whatever reason. They must learn to avoid falsely blaming themselves and/or others, and instead to develop objectives and strategies that will help them achieve more satisfying lives. People who are feeling abandoned must learn to capitalize on their strengths, minimize their weaknesses, and pursue meaningful goals.

## Strategies for Coping with Specific Problems

Depending on the situation, there are some specific strategies for helping people deal with feelings of abandonment. The church family and the lay counselor can provide specific kinds of support to such persons. This can be done formally, through an expansion of existing ministries within the church, or it can be done informally, through the contacts of lay leaders and church members with persons within and outside of the local church membership.

**Coping with abandonment by a parent.** As mentioned above, many children lose parents due to the parents' involvement with drugs. In many cases, the drug use leads to a parent's death and may lead to the children being placed in foster homes. One of the first steps for the counselor, in dealing with such children, is to help the children work through the grieving process. The child must be helped to work through feelings of denial, guilt, and anger. In order for the child to do this, the child must be given support in his/her stand against the parent. The child needs to know that s/he is not to blame for the parent's actions. S/he needs to be encouraged not to feel guilty for what the parent has done to him or her.

The goal would be to encourage the child to understand that it is the parent who bears the responsibility for failure to perform his/her role as parent. Children need to be able to discriminate between what is and is not appropriate for them to expect of themselves as children and of their parents as parents. Further, the child who has reported a parent and who is called upon to testify in court must be shown that s/he has a right to protection when testifying against an abusive parent.

If a child has had to take a stand against a parent who tried to force the child to steal, and then has to seek protection from others, the child should be praised for doing this. Further, the child should be provided with help and with permission to live the life of a child or an adolescent. The child needs to know that s/he is not expected to become a caretaker for the other family members.

A child can only receive this type of assurance when given the opportunity to talk about his/her feelings, both good and bad. S/he will need help in examining strengths and weaknesses, in accepting things s/he cannot change, and in developing the courage to change the things s/he can.

Gradually, with this type of help, such children will feel better about themselves and will be less depressed and more hopeful. They will be able to put things in perspective, meet new people,

39

and trust others again. An understanding relationship with the counselor will breed trust and hope that things will be better one day. Feelings of abandonment will give way to feelings of acceptance and trust.

The local church can also come to the aid of the abandoned child. By offering after-school programs on weekdays, "latch-key" children might find an alternative to being at home alone until their parents come home from work. For example, Trinity United Church of Christ in Chicago has a full curriculum of such groups as Boy Scouts, Girl Scouts, Building Black Women, Building Black Men, the Young Adult Fellowship, and two youth choirs.

A church can also offer neighborhood Bible Clubs to reach out to children who are abandoned and left to roam the neighborhoods by themselves day and night. Such children can be reached for Christ, and in this way, perhaps leaders of the church can reach out to the child's family via follow-up.

**Coping with the death of a loved one.** In helping the counselee to cope with feelings of abandonment resulting from the death of a loved one or "significant other," the primary objective would be to locate new avenues whereby the counselee can "fill in the gap" which occurred with the death of the loved one. It is appropriate for the counselee to spend the appropriate amount of time grieving. During this period, it is useful for the counselee to express feelings of loss, anger, confusion and even guilt, if these feelings occur.

It is in helping people to cope with the loss of loved ones that the church is especially useful, with its many traditions and ceremonies surrounding the funeral and burial of the person. During this initial period of the grieving process, the church provides many supportive friends, making the grieving process much more bearable.

The church can also be useful during later stages of the grieving process, by providing support groups led by counselors. For example some support groups put widows and widowers in contact with others who have lost their spouses. The purpose of such groups would be to help such people lessen their feelings of abandonment and move into the mainstream of church life, finding new avenues for "filling in the gap" left by the deceased. In the event that the lost person is a mentor (as in a professional relationship) or personal physician, the counselor might help the person feel more independent. In doing so, the counselor will be assisting the counselee in identifying ways that s/he can use the help once gotten from the mentor or doctor to become a more independent person. The strategies that were taught to them by the mentor can be used to enhance their strengths and make them more independently successful. They can also be assisted in locating another doctor or mentor.

**Coping with divorce and broken love affairs.** In helping people cope with divorce, the counselor will discover that the person experiences a type of mourning that is similar to that experienced by a person who loses a spouse through death. The objectives for the counseling are basically the same. The counselor must lead the counselee into coping with the death of the idea that marriage would last forever and the resentment that the dream they once had for living "happily ever after" did not come true.

In dealing with divorce and broken love affairs, loss of self-esteem is a critical issue. The counselor must help the counselee to avoid falsely or completely blaming him/herself for the breakup. Again, the counselee must find new avenues for "filling in the gap" left by the loss of the spouse or potential spouse.

Divorce recovery support groups are useful in this respect, and churches can provide these support groups for members of the congregation. Singles' ministries can also develop such groups as a part of their ministry. "Rap sessions" are good places for people recovering from lost relationships to air their feelings and gain support from others who may be having similar feelings.

**Adjusting to independence in children.** As mentioned

**41**

above, some parents find it difficult to adjust to their children's growing independence. Usually the person who experiences these feelings most intensely is the mother, who usually has the primary caretaker role in relation to the children. In such cases, the counselor must help the counselee to recognize what is actually happening, and talk about feelings of abandonment when the child leaves for kindergarten, college, marriage, or a job out of town.

The counselor might assist the counselee in learning what is an appropriate parental role as a child moves from an absolute dependency stage into adulthood. The counselor will need to help the counselee in essentially restructuring his or her life. This may involve locating another caretaker role within the church or community where s/he can use caretaker gifts with other children and/or adults who need such a ministry.

Here the church can also be useful in providing support groups for women with young children, for men and women who are parents of adolescents and for people who are adjusting to the fact that their children are leaving for college or marriage. Such discussions can be built into the curriculum of many of the already existing church programs such as the adult Sunday School class, etc.

## Recognizing When to Refer a Person for Professional Help

In some cases, people who feel abandoned will not respond to the types of assistance described previously. In these cases, it is highly likely that the counselor should refer the counselee for professional help. There are agencies in the community which specialize in treating people who need more assistance than lay leaders, friends and family members are qualified to provide. This frequently occurs when the person has experienced more than one loss at a time.

One sign of the need for professional help is when the person who feels abandoned develops certain types of physical problems. These include: hypertension, ulcers, headaches, nervousness, rashes, hives, and general irritability. Other signs include: loss of sleep, eating problems, and unusual weight losses or gains. Other symptoms include constantly losing jobs and generally being dysfunctional for long periods of time.

The above signs are usually accompanied by depression in the person. This depression usually continues beyond the normal grieving period. In such cases, the counselor should encourage the counselee to seek professional help.

**Summary.** This chapter has focused on helping people who feel abandoned. It has provided guidelines for recognizing situations that lead to feelings of abandonment. These include the situation of a child being abandoned by parents, the death of a "significant other," divorce, broken love affairs and new independence in children. The importance of emphasizing, listening, helping the person clarify his/her feelings, and teaching the person new skills was emphasized. Special strategies were provided for helping abandoned children, widows and widowers, singles coping with broken love affairs, and parents of increasingly independent children.

Guidelines for determining when to refer a person for professional help were also presented. The following exercise provides the opportunity to apply the above principles to a case study abstracted from "real life."

## CASE STUDY

*INSTRUCTIONS: The exercise below allows you to apply principles presented in this chapter to a case study involving a person who feels abandoned. The first five exercises are "discovery" questions, followed by a summary question. The sixth exercise asks you to summarize and apply information you gained from the first five exercises. The seventh exercise asks you to make personal applications of the principles you learned in this chapter.*

## CHERYL

*The Women's Fellowship at St. Luke's Presbyterian Church had been visiting the Lewis Home for Girls for more than a year now. During that time two women from the group had adopted children from the home. However, Mrs. Watkins was having trouble with Cheryl, the girl she had selected.*

*She had enrolled Cheryl in the church tutorial program, for help with mathematics, but the tutor had reported that Cheryl was withdrawn and sometimes cried if she was "pushed too hard." Mrs. Watkins told the president of the Women's Fellowship that Cheryl had a long history of serious problems.*

*Cheryl was only 11 years old when she came to the Lewis Home for Girls. Her records showed that she was above average in intelligence. However, she was depressed, having been separated from her five brothers and sisters, and having lost contact with her parents and other members of her parents' families.*

*Cheryl's parents had once been hardworking and responsible but had become addicted to cocaine. They had spent all of their money on drugs. Both lost their jobs. The father died of an overdose in Cheryl's presence. After that, the mother abandoned the children altogether. A truancy officer from the public schools had discovered the situation and reported it to the police. The children were taken from the mother and placed in various homes.*

*Cheryl came into contact with Mrs. Watkins through the outreach program of the Women's Fellowship. The Women's Fellowship regularly sponsored social ac-*

*tivities for the girls at the Lewis Home and held Bible studies there. One day Cheryl's social worker told her that she had been selected to be Mrs. Watkins's adopted child. This is how Cheryl came to live at the Watkins home.*

*Mrs. Watkins decided to spend more time with Cheryl, encouraging the girl to talk about her problems and to determine whether Cheryl should be referred for professional help.*

## 1. What God thinks of children

Children who have been abandoned are often uncertain about whether they have a right to be a child. Many have been forced into adult roles before they were ready. Many are unsure whether they should feel guilty for not being able to handle adult roles.

a. In what manner did the Lord come to earth? (Isaiah 9:6; 11:6; Luke 2:10-14) What does this indicate God thinks about children?

b. What is evidence that the Lord loves children? (Matthew 11:1-6; 19:13-16)

c. What are some ways that the Lord expressed His love for children? (Matthew 15:21-28; Luke 7:1-15; John 4:46-54)

d. Who are some of the children of the Bible that the Lord loved? (Exodus 1:15-16; 2:1-10; Matthew 9:18-26; Mark 9:17-27)

e. In what ways has the Lord expressed His love for specific children like Cheryl today? (Psalm 139)

f. SUMMARY QUESTION: Considering your answers to questions a-e above, how should a foster parent, adoptive parent, or lay counselor help an abandoned child feel that it is all right to be a child?

## 2. God's family

Abandoned children are often confused about their relationships with their parents. Often they feel that they are responsible for their parents and that it is wrong for them to expect to be taken care of by their parents.

a. What is one thing that God expects from parents? (Proverbs 22:6)

b. What is another thing that God expects from parents? (Ephesians 6:4)

c. In whose family is every believer? (Ephesians 1:1-14)

d. What type of father is God? (1 John 3:1-3)

e. What type of mother is God? (Isaiah 66:13-14)

f. SUMMARY QUESTION: Considering your answers to questions a-e above, how should a foster parent, adoptive parent or lay counselor help an abandoned child to acquire a realistic idea about a child's relationship with his/her parents?

### 3. The presence of God

Abandoned children need to know that, if they turn their lives over to Christ, they will never be alone. What do the following Scriptures say about the presence of God?

a. Psalm 27:10

b. Psalm 37:25

c. Psalm 23

d. 2 Corinthians 4:7-9

e. Psalm 16:11; 140:13

f. SUMMARY QUESTION: How can the foster parent, adoptive parent, or lay counselor use the above Scriptures to lead an abandoned child into an intimate relationship with the Lord?

### 4. A new self-image

The Lord provides the basis of a new self-image for the abandoned child.

a. What can be one foundation of a child's self-image? (Proverbs 20:11)

b. What can be another foundation of a child's self-image? (Exodus 19:5-6; 1 Peter 2:5, 9)

c. What can be another foundation of a child's self-image? (Psalm 139:13-17)

d. What can be another foundation of a child's self-image? (Genesis 1:27)

e. What can be yet another foundation for the child's self-image? (1 Corinthians 12)

f. SUMMARY QUESTION: How can the foster parent, adoptive parent, or lay counselor use the above Scriptures to help an abandoned child develop a better self-image?

## 5. Learning new skills

The Lord provides the basis for the abandoned child to develop new skills to cope with life.

a. What is a fundamental way in which the child can become prepared for a successful adult life? (Psalm 16:8-11)

b. In addition to "a" above, what is another way that the child can become prepared for a successful adult life? (Psalm 119:11)

c. In addition to "a" and "b" above, what is another way in which the child can become prepared for a successful adult life? (2 Timothy 2:15)

d. In addition to "a," "b" and "c" above, what is yet another way that a child can become prepared for a successful adult life? (Hebrews 10:25)

e. What is yet another way that a child can become prepared for a successful adult life? (Matthew 25:14-30)

f. SUMMARY QUESTION: How can the foster parent, adoptive parent, or lay counselor use the above Scriptures to help an abandoned child prepare for a successful adult life?

## 6. SUMMARY EXERCISE

What are some ways in which the local church can help children who have been abandoned by their parents? Can current ministries establish new outreaches? Can new ministries be formed? Are there ways in which the church can cooperate with community agencies? Explain. List some specific ways in which the local church can help.

## 7. PERSONAL APPLICATION

Do you ever feel abandoned? If so, read some of the Scriptures contained in the above exercise. Then go to the Lord in prayer. If you feel it is necessary, seek counseling from a minister at your church.

# CHAPTER TWO

# ANGER

### Delores Holmes

*An interdenominational group of churches, along with the local Department of Social Services, organized a drop-in center for youth who live near the churches. Arts, crafts, tutoring, counseling and recreation were among the activities offered. Mrs. Young, director of the center, was very concerned about twelve-year-old Krishawn, one of the girls who had been coming to the center for more than two years.*

*Krishawn was from a family of five children. When Krishawn first came to the center, she was very outgoing. She had a beautiful voice and won the talent show competition for two years in a row. However, recently she had become very shy and withdrawn. One day Krishawn came to the drop-in center on a Saturday when it was closed. She told the janitor that she had been raped by her father.*

*When Mrs. Young received the report, she notified the authorities immediately. As a result her father was arrested and put in jail. The family was ordered into counseling. However, the mother didn't follow through, saying she didn't believe Krishawn was telling the truth.*

*Mrs. Young continued to see Krishawn. Krishawn*

*informed her that her older half-sister had also been raped by Krishawn's father (her older half-sister's stepfather). Krishawn's father called Krishawn's older sister a "rape baby," because their mother had been raped also. When Krishawn described her home, a picture of chaos emerged. She said that dirty clothes and papers were all over the floors and frequently the children were without regular meals. Her mother was "in and out." Krishawn didn't have a room of her own but had to share a room with five brothers and sisters.*

*One day she told Mrs. Young that she was really frightened because her father had been released from prison and was living with them again. She had been keeping one of her younger sisters with her at all times in order to reduce the possibility that her father would molest her again. She talked in a very low voice, and Mrs. Young could sense the smoldering anger that was beneath everything Krishawn was saying.*

The rage that Krishawn feels is not unique to Krishawn. Many people, caught in the web of very complex and difficult family problems, are angry. From outside, the Black family is often troubled by poverty related to unemployment. However, from within, frequently the Black family is also troubled. Such problems as domestic violence, child abuse, sexual abuse and incest are now exerting pressure within many Black families. Children in these and troubled families of other racial groups, who become either victims or witnesses of incest and sexual abuse, are often in a state of rage.

This rage can result in children growing up and abusing themselves or eventually creating environments in which their own children are also abused. Sometimes children in troubled families reach out to adults outside of the home, but often they do not.

This chapter is about helping children who are angry. It is

**50**

designed for people in local churches who desire to extend Christian love to the hurting, through counseling and appropriate social agency referrals.

## An Example of Anger from Scripture

Incest, rape and sexual abuse within families are not new to this age. Accounts of it date as far back as the Old Testament times. One example is found in the story of Absalom, son of King David the Psalmist. Absalom became aware that his sister Tamar had been raped by her half-brother Amnon, David's eldest son. Absalom, in his rage, became obsessed with avenging his sister's wrong. This rage drove him to kill Amnon and then flee to his grandfather's house.

## from Scripture

**2 Samuel 13:1** And it came to pass after this, that Absalom the son of David had a fair sister, whose name was Tamar; and Amnon the son of David loved her.

**10** And Amnon said unto Tamar, Bring the meat into the chamber, that I may eat of thine hand. And Tamar took the cakes which she had made, and brought them into the chamber to Amnon her brother.

**11** And when she had brought them unto him to eat, he took hold of her, and said unto her, Come lie with me, my sister.

**12** And she answered him, Nay, my brother, do not force me; for no such thing ought to be done in Israel: do not thou this folly.

**14** Howbeit he would not hearken unto her voice: but being stronger than she, forced her, and lay with her.

**19** And Tamar put ashes on her head, and rent her garment of divers colours that was on her, and laid her hand on her head, and went on crying.

**20** And Absalom her brother said unto her, Hath Amnon thy brother been with thee? but hold now thy peace, my sister: he is thy brother; regard not this thing. So Tamar remained desolate in her brother Absalom's house.

**22** And Absalom spake unto his brother Amnon neither good nor bad: for Absalom hated Amnon, because he had forced his sister Tamar.

**28** Now Absalom had commanded his servants, saying, Mark ye now when Amnon's heart is merry with wine, and when I say unto you, Smite Amnon; then kill him, fear not: have not I commanded you? be courageous, and be valiant.

**29** And the servants of Absalom did unto Amnon as Absalom had commanded. Then all the king's sons arose, and every man gat him up upon his mule, and fled.

**37** But Absalom fled, and went to Talmai, the son of Ammihud, king of Geshur. And David mourned for his son every day.

## What Is Anger?

Anger is an advanced stage of frustration. It is a feeling of being out of control and unable to cope. It is a deep-seated feeling of not being able to control others and/or one's environment. It is the feeling of not being able to set limits, of being victimized and/or in a state of rage.

For example, both Tamar and Absalom were so angry with Amnon that they were unable to cope. Tamar remained desolate at Absalom's home (2 Samuel 13:20), and Absalom became so angry that he could not speak to Amnon about what happened (v. 22).

There are many situations in families that are causing this same type of anger in children today. Among these are incest, lack of supervision by responsible adults, and children being forced to assume adult responsibilities before they are mature enough to handle them. The outcome is often the type of "acting out" that surfaces in gang violence, teenage pregnancy and various forms of juvenile delinquency.

**Incest.** Incest is becoming more and more widespread in the Black community today. In fact, in some communities, incest between fathers (or stepfathers) and daughters is running rampant. Early experiences with incest (or some other form of sexual abuse from an older male) often causes very young girls to become very precocious in the area of sex. These girls often become very forward with boys, and quite often become pregnant at very early ages. Often such girls feel that their only role in life is to be sexual objects.

As a result of their encounter with incest, they do not feel clean or whole. Notice that Tamar, after being molested by her brother, puts ashes on her head (a symbol of mourning and repentance), rends her garment of many colors (the symbol of virginity), lays her hand on her head and cries.

Today, victims of incest are often so young at the time of the encounter that it is easy for them to internalize the notion that they are meant to be mere sexual objects. This is why victims of incest often do not feel "right" unless they are in some compromising position with a man. Beneath their precocious behavior, however, is rage. They are not always able to articulate the rage or its source, but the counselor can notice the rage by the manner in which the victim talks or does not talk. Often such young people are very quiet and withdrawn.

Quite a large number of women who have entered the cycle of dependency on welfare and A.D.C. (Aid to Dependent Children) have had early childhood encounters with incest, and have subsequently become teenage parents.

**Lack of supervision by adults.** Children who are not adequately supervised, but left to "fend for themselves" are often in the advanced form of frustration known as anger. This angry rage results from being out of control and inadequately supervised. This often leads to absence from school. It also leads to encounters with the police. Often such children can be seen out late at night, wandering around or playing by themselves.

**53**

Many are left to take care of themselves and other younger brothers and sisters. They are not old enough or mature enough to take on such responsibilities. When they are given too much to handle, they often become frustrated and angry, not really knowing what to do.

Most are not mature enough to know what they need. As they grow slightly older, many join gangs or participate in other types of activities largely to "belong" to something that appears meaningful, and that provides some type of structure for their lives. More often than not, the activities in which they participate are not wholesome. Gang activities and activities related to selling or delivering drugs may lead to criminal records and lengthy stays at juvenile detention centers.

Children in these situations frequently experience anger. They are in a state of rage, but frequently are unable to express it or trace its source. Often they don't know what is controlling them, because they have not been exposed to any alternative life style other than the one to which they have been subjected. However, they express their rage through behavior that is subconsciously designed to "get back" at the adult world which has neglected them.

For example, Absalom's rage against his father and his brothers may have been related to his growing up in a situation that was somewhat out of control. He could have blamed his father David for this. David's life did not appear to provide the most structure for his sons. When he wasn't busy building the kingdom of Israel, he seems to have been preoccupied with women.

David had had numerous wives and concubines, and associated offspring (1 Samuel 27:3; 1 Chronicles 3:1-8; 14:4-7; 2 Samuel 3:2-5; 5:13-16; 15:16). By the time of Tamar's rape, David had also committed adultery (2 Samuel 11:2-5), and had murdered to cover up the adultery (11:14-17).

While today most adults are not involved in as many sexual relationships and liaisons as David might have been, many are so preoccupied with sexual relationships that they do not spend adequate time with their children. This disorganization and lack of supervision leaves many children feeling rage and engaging in behaviors designed to "get back" at the adults who create these situations for them. They are particularly outraged when an adult who has sexually abused them is considered more important to their mother or father than they are.

In all probability, an environment such as this did not provide the best type of supervision and guidance for children such as Tamar, Amnon and Absalom either. As is true in such situations today, often unsupervised, disorganized situations are the environments in which a young person encounters incest, rape or sexual abuse.

**"Acting out."** As mentioned earlier in this chapter, frequently the child who is angry finds a way to act out the anger by "getting back" at adults. For example, Absalom, after taking refuge in his grandfather's home for a few years, began to act out his frustrations by plotting to overthrow his father, David. He prepared himself an army (2 Samuel 15:1), parked outside a gate to the city (15:2) and conducted political activities that would get him support for the revolt that he would stage (15:3-6).

Finally he did succeed in getting David's attention by frightening David into fleeing from him (15:13-14). Absalom's forces were eventually defeated and he was killed (18:9-17). It is possible that all of this "acting out" was to "get back" at David for what Absalom perceived as neglect and lack of attention to his personal needs and the needs of his brothers and sisters.

Absalom's "acting out" was not so different from gang violence, teenage pregnancy, "doing drugs," stealing and other forms of modern anti-social behavior. These modern forms of "acting out" are also designed to get attention from adults, and/or "get back" at adults for their neglect.

## How to Help Angry Youth

Quite often the church and other related community organizations encounter angry children from disorganized families and neighborhoods, in Sunday School, Church School, Vacation Bible School, and various youth organizations. Community organizations may encounter these children participating in some of the activities for youth sponsored by community organizations. Some of these children become a part of the case loads of social workers and probation officers.

Wherever the angry child is encountered, it is important for the counselor to try to provide some of the elements that have been missing from the child's environment. These include: the opportunity to discover oneself, structure, meaningful communication with an adult, the chance to clarify values, and practice in decision making.

**Allowing for self-discovery.** Often the disorganized environments from which many angry children come, have caused them to be out of touch with themselves. They do not know who they are, and are usually not aware of the talents and gifts that the Lord has given them. Therefore, it is important for the counselor and directors of youth activities to design activities that lead to self-awareness.

Talent shows, opportunities for public speaking, role playing, videotaped role plays and skits, and allowing them to be in charge of certain activities are all ones which foster self-awareness. Asking children and teenagers to keep a journal is also a good way for them to get into touch with their feelings and ideas. After a given period of time, they can be encouraged to reread what they have written, reflect on their progress, and set goals for the future.

**Providing structure.** One of the elements missing from the life of children from disorganized environments, is structure. Part of the frustration they feel is associated with lacking a structure in which they can develop into healthy adults. Most such children are not accustomed to a schedule or regularity of any type, other than that which they may encounter in school, when they attend.

Through the church, and through activities sponsored by community groups, such children can experience structure and regularity. The youth leader, Sunday School teacher, director of a tutorial service, or director of a community center, can help such children by organizing the activities so that a regular, consistent pattern is established. For example, the Sunday School class could always begin with prayer, followed by a real life story, Scripture reading, discussion, real life application, and then culminate with prayer. While variety within each of these segments would occur, the student would learn to expect a certain pattern, and would gradually become comfortable within a structured environment.

At the community center or tutorial center, activities can also be structured. A calendar and a related schedule can be posted and children can be made aware of these.

It is also important that activities be designed so that children are not expected to do things which they are not prepared, developmentally, to do. Activities should be broken down so that a child can progress through them from simple to more complex tasks, and these can be arranged so that children can participate in them based on their developmental stages.

**Allowing for meaningful relationships with adults.** Often angry, neglected children have rarely, if ever, held meaningful conversations with adults. Often adults in such a child's environment believe that a child is to be "seen and not heard." Frequently the communication they have had with adults is one-way, taking the form of orders, directions concerning work to do, or reprimands (usually curses) when work is not done correctly. For the most part, such children have not been taken seriously by the adults around them, and have usually been ignored. Therefore, the most important truth which the counselor can communicate to such children is that their feelings and ideas are important, and that it is all right for them to talk.

The counselor needs to communicate to the child that every

person God made is important and unique (Ephesians 2:10). Every person has gifts, and every person is important to the Lord. God's love for children needs to be communicated to such a child.

The counselor can begin to do this by listening to the child and asking open-ended questions to which the child can respond. Questions such as "How do you feel about...", "What is your opinion about...", etc., are good questions for communicating to the child that his/her opinions are important. Following such questions with clarifying statements such as "Oh, you feel that...", etc. communicate to the child that the counselor is listening, and is concerned enough to want to be sure that his/her feelings are understood.

It is important for the counselor to be gentle, and not try to force the child to communicate before s/he is ready to do so. The counselor must be patient, and allow the child to develop confidence in the counselor, and the assurance that the counselor actually cares about him/her.

**Clarifying values.** It may be that, through interactions with the counselor, and with a more positive environment of the church or community organization, such a child may come into contact with alternative values and life styles for the first time. These children will need the opportunity to adopt values and life styles that are different from those taken by the child's parents. In order to take such an important and difficult step, the child needs the opportunity to clarify his/her values.

Learning to think independently from one's parents is very difficult, particularly for a child. It is even more difficult for such children to learn to think independently of most of the adults in their current world.

For example, a child may come from an environment in which most of the women over 16 years of age have already had children, are unemployed, are receiving public assistance, and have dropped out of high school. The only men that such a child may know are men who are without employment, who belong to gangs, or who are somehow involved with drugs. It may be rare, in this child's environment, for anyone to be seen doing homework, going to a library, attending school regularly, or going to church.

The idea of finishing high school, going to college, waiting until one is an adult to have a baby, avoiding gangs and drugs, learning about Black history and current Black achievers, may all be very new to children born in disorganized, neglectful environments. In some cases, such children may be "turned on" by these new options for their lives.

The counselor can provide the type of support necessary for the child to clarify and maintain the types of values that allow the child to take a different path in life than that taken by parents and other adults. Through "one-on-one" counseling, the counselor can allow the child to clarify his/her values. Through group discussions, films, books, field trips, and games, the counselor can provide support groups and reinforcement for such children.

In group counseling and in private "one-on-one" counseling, the counselor will want to guide the counselee with such questions as, "Am I betraying my mother, my household, etc., if I do something that is different than they have done?"

When, because of the child's new values, the child comes into conflict with parents and other adults, the counselor must be available to provide the verbal support the child needs in order to counter negativity which may come from other significant adults in the child's life.

**Practicing decision making.** In order to act consistently with new values that the child may develop (at the church or at the community center) the child may need to make strategic decisions. The counselor can develop an environment which prepares the child for decision making in general, and which enables the child to make the strategic decisions which will change his/her life.

To prepare the child for decision making, the counselor, youth leader or Sunday School may develop activities which allow the child to make decisions which affect the outcomes of certain group activities. For example, such a child might vote, along with other children, to select activities in which the group will be involved (field trips, class projects, parties), and/or the contributions which the group may make to a larger program (such as an Easter program, Black History Month program, or Christmas program).

Once the child receives reinforcement in this way, and once s/he sees that s/he can participate in decision making, then this new skill can be transferred into making decisions which affect the child's personal life. These decisions include whether to do homework or watch television, whether to attend school or skip school, whether to ask for help from one's teacher when help is needed, and so on. Once children learn to make decisions that are consistent with their newly found values, they can eventually make even more difficult decisions such as saying "no" to drugs, sex and other things that might serve as obstacles in their paths.

There are a number of books, currently on the market, which can be used to help children and teenagers learn to make decisions. *Choices and Challenges*, by Mindy Bingham, Judy Edmonds and Sandy Stryper, published by Advanced Press in Santa Barbara, California is one such book. *Play It Straight*, published by Goodwin-Geier Products in Tuscaloosa, Alabama is another.

**The role of Black professionals.** It is not always possible for children who need help to receive it through the traditional helping agencies. For one reason or another, services that are offered by professional community agencies do not always reach the children who need it. In other cases, the services provided by community agencies are for some reason inadequate. For example, while the public schools mean well, still thousands of Black children are dropping out and many who graduate are not receiving skills necessary to enter mainstream employment.

By volunteering through churches and other agencies, Black

professionals can help to meet needs which are not otherwise being met. By volunteering to tutor children, head a youth group (such as Boy Scouts, Girl Scouts, etc.), or participate in career education activities and health clinics, Black professionals can provide young people with much of the essential information that is not provided in their natural environments.

Black professionals can also help with networking. They can put such children in touch with people who may be able to give them part-time jobs and internships, and who may be able to connect them with the information needed to go to college and pursue careers.

**The role of the Black church.** The Black church has always been the hub of the Black community. It therefore has the potential to make a major impact on what is happening with children and teenagers in the Black community. However, recently, the church has not taken on its full responsibility of leadership in this area.

Unfortunately, a large percentage of church members, out of habit and family tradition, still confine most of their involvement with the church to Sunday morning worship service. Any involvement other than worship is usually limited to ushering and/or singing in the choir. Today there is a need for much more church and community involvement than this.

One way of becoming more actively involved would be for the church to form liaisons with community agencies who are servicing youth. In this way, the meager resources of the community agencies can be stretched and strengthened, and vice versa. Much of what has been mentioned in this chapter can be implemented through youth programming at the local church level.

**Summary.** This chapter has focused on helping angry children from disorganized family environments. It has presented some of the family problems that provoke anger and frustration in children. Principles for helping such children were also presented. These principles are: 1) allowing for self-discovery, 2) providing structure, 3) allowing for meaningful relationships with adults, 4) clarifying values, and 5) practicing decision making.

The following exercises provide the opportunity to apply these principles to a case study.

## CASE STUDY

*INSTRUCTIONS: Robert, in the following story, is experiencing anger that is in part due to conflicts within his family. The following exercises will lead you into an in-depth study of Robert's problem and will provide the opportunity to apply principles covered in this chapter to helping people with similar problems.*

*The first five exercises consist of a series of "discovery" questions, followed by a summary question. The sixth exercise asks you to summarize and apply information you gained from the first five exercises. The seventh exercise allows you to make personal applications.*

## ROBERT

*Brother Boyd of Bible Community Baptist Church and head of the prison ministry, took his small group of volunteers to the city jail. When Brother Boyd entered the chapel, he was met by a young man who was waiting for him and seemed to know who he was. At first Brother Boyd didn't recognize the young man. Then, as the young man told his story, Brother Boyd remembered.*

*The last time Brother Boyd saw Robert, he was eleven years old. He had caught Brother Boyd's attention when, with a cigarette in his mouth and a knife in his hand, he had terrorized the staff at the church youth drop-in center. At that time, he had threatened to blow up the entire church.*

*Today, at 19 years of age, the toughness that was once considered "cute" by the church staff had turned hard. However, Brother Boyd could see beneath the hardness to the tears that surfaced in Robert's eyes as he told Brother Boyd his story. Robert told Brother Boyd that he had watched as his father shot one of his brothers on their front porch. After that, all of his brothers had been in trouble with the police. He was the third one to be incarcerated. One brother had already been deported to Jamaica, his family's native country.*

*Robert went on to describe a family situation that was disorganized. He had grown up listening to his father and mother arguing over whether they should both become American citizens. Their mother really didn't seem to want to remain in this country. The brothers had learned to "play off" the mother against the father to get what they wanted. The mother would often lie for them, so that they could get their way.*

*Robert was in jail because he had broken into a neighborhood store and had been arrested. He was convicted of armed robbery.*

## 1. Self-discovery

It is important for young people who are angry to discover the potential they have in God, in spite of failures they may have experienced. It is also important for them to discover how important they are to God.

a. In whose image is everyone created? (Genesis 1:27, 31; 2:7)

b. What does God think of the human beings He created? (Psalm 139:13-17)

c. How important are young people to God? (Romans 8:39;

Psalm 139:1-12)

d. What is the highest potential that a young person can have? (Exodus 19:6; 1 Peter 2:9)

e. What does God think of young people? (Mark 9:35-7; Matthew 18:3-6; 19:13-14)

f. SUMMARY QUESTION: How can the information from questions a-e above be used to help young people, like Robert in the above case study, who are angry and confused?

## 2. Structure

Many angry young people come from chaotic backgrounds. When young people come from disorganized backgrounds, it is important that they experience the benefits of structure.

a. What evidence is there that order and structure are important to God? (Genesis 1:1-10; 1 Corinthians 14:33)

b. What are the arguments in favor of organized programs? (1 Corinthians 14:40; Ecclesiastes 12:9-10)

c. What Bible story illustrates the power of a program that is organized under God's direction? (Genesis 6:13--7:1; 7:18-21; 8:14-16)

d. What is another Bible story that illustrates the power of a program that is organized under God's direction? (Joshua 6:1-4, 15-21)

e. What is yet another Bible story that illustrates the power of a program that is organized under God's direction? (Judges 7:2-7, 19-21)

f. SUMMARY QUESTION: How can the information from questions a-e above form the rationale for organizing programs to help young people such as Robert in the above case study?

## 3. Meaningful relationships

Angry young people need to know that they, too, can have meaningful relationships with adults. However, many adults mistakenly believe that all young people should be "seen and not heard."

a. What is one Bible story that illustrates a positive relationship between an adult and a young person? (1 Samuel 1:11, 24-28; 2:11, 18, 19; 3:3-4, 16-20)

b. What is another Bible story that illustrates a positive relationship between a young person and adults? (Luke 2:22-41)

c. Symbolically speaking, what does the story of the widow's son being raised from the dead indicate about the role of adults in the healing of young people? (Luke 7:11-15)

d. Symbolically speaking, what does the story of the official's son being healed of a fever indicate about the role of adults in the healing of young people? (John 2:1-11)

e. Symbolically speaking, what does the story of the daughter of the Syrophenician woman indicate about the role of adults in the healing of young people? (Matthew 15:21-28; Mark 7:24-30)

f. SUMMARY QUESTION: Based on the information from questions a-e above, what are the arguments against young people merely being seen by adults and not heard?

## 4. Values

To become successful in life, angry young people from disorganized backgrounds may need to adopt a new set of values that is different from those of the adults and peers in their environments.

a. When a young person makes a decision to follow Christ, how should salvation ultimately affect the way he or she sees the world? (Romans 12:12)

b. What is the scriptural basis for seeing life differently than people in the world see it? (1 John 2:15)

c. What is the ultimate goal of the Christian? (1 Corinthians 13:12) What does this mean for the young person?

d. When a young person's values change, does this mean that s/he is allowed to show disrespect toward his/her parents? (Exodus 20:12; Deuteronomy 5:16; Matthew 15:4; 19:19; Ephesians 6:1-3)

e. Who becomes the young person's guide when the young person makes a decision to follow Christ? (Psalm 16:11; 23)

f. SUMMARY QUESTION: In what ways does the information presented in a-e above form the basis for supporting young people such as Robert, in the case study, in adopting new values for their lives?

## 5. Making decisions

In dealing with the sources of anger and frustration, critical decisions must be made. Young people as well as adults must make these decisions.

a. What is the most fundamental choice that any human being must make? (Joshua 24:15; John 14:6)

b. Why is it so important for young people to be willing to make decisions? (Matthew 7:14; James 1:6-8)

c. Is it enough to make an initial decision to follow Christ? (1 Timothy 6:12; 1 Corinthians 16:13; Ephesians 6:10-18)

d. How does a young person learn to make correct decisions? (Psalm 48:14; Jeremiah 3:4; Psalm 31:3)

e. How do adults help young people make correct decisions? (Deuteronomy 4:7-9; Proverbs 22:6; Titus 2:1-8; Ephesians 6:4)

f. SUMMARY QUESTION: How can the information from questions a-e above be used to help young people such as Robert learn to make correct decisions?

## 6. SUMMARY EXERCISE

Are there ways that your church can develop (or improve) programs to reach and support young people who are incarcerated in prisons and juvenile detention centers? How might the information from this chapter and from exercises 1-5 be used to form the foundation of the program?

## 7. PERSONAL APPLICATION

Do you have a family member who is hurting from anger? Are you hurting from anger? If so, use the contents of this chapter as a foundation for praying for this family member. Also use the information as a foundation for talking to the Lord about your personal anger.

# CHAPTER THREE

# ANXIETY

## Dr. Loretta Reid

*Mrs. Melton had signed up for pastoral counseling. She informed the counselor that she had been childless through two marriages. She was now thirty-seven years old and a widow. She was worried that she would never be able to have children and would never again find a man that she could really respect. Her decision to enter into counseling had emerged because she was concerned about how "down" she felt; she was brooding and insecure most of the time.*

*She began to cry as she told how she was worried that she might lose her job because her moods had caused her to be tardy and perform at a level that was lower than what was required. She felt her illness also affected her job; she had been experiencing pains near her heart. Her physician told her that these were actually simulated heart attacks. She said that these pains developed after the sudden death of her second husband.*

*She had an intense fear of death. Yet she could find no good reason to go on living. She had already seen a psychiatrist, and it had helped her, but she felt that the source of her problem was really spiritual. She felt that she needed to be released from her anxieties and find meaning in life.*

**69**

Mrs. Melton, like so many people who have experienced sudden, unanticipated losses, is experiencing anxiety. This chapter presents guidelines for helping people who are experiencing anxiety. It presents ways that such people can be guided into a more trusting relationship with the Lord.

## An Example of Anxiety from Scripture

Abraham was chosen by God to become the father of a new generation. He was promised divine favor, great posterity, and that he would become a blessing to all families of the earth. While Abraham is noted for his great faith, that faith did not develop overnight. Abraham was one of the Bible's greatest worriers.

## from Scripture

**Genesis 12:11** And it came to pass, when he was come near to enter into Egypt, that he said unto Sarai his wife, Behold now, I know that thou art a fair woman to look upon:

**12** Therefore it shall come to pass, when the Egyptians shall see thee, that they shall say, This is his wife: and they will kill me, but they will save thee alive.

**13:7** And there was a strife between the herdsmen of Abram's cattle and the herdsmen of Lot's cattle: and the Canaanite and the Perizzite dwelled then in the land.

**8** And Abram said unto Lot, Let there be no strife, I pray thee, between me and thee, and between my herdsmen and thy herdsmen: for we be brethren.

**15:2** And Abram said, Lord God, what wilt thou give me, seeing I go childless, and the steward of my house is this Eliezer of Damascus?

**3** And Abram said, Behold, to me thou hast given no seed: and, lo, one born in my house is mine heir.

**16:1** Now Sarai Abram's wife bare him no children: and she had an handmaid, an Egyptian, whose name was Hagar.

2 And Sarai said unto Abram, Behold now, the Lord hath restrained me from bearing: I pray thee, go in unto my maid; it may be that I may obtain children by her. And Abram hearkened to the voice of Sarai.

3 And Sarai Abram's wife took Hagar her maid the Egyptian, after Abram had dwelt ten years in the land of Canaan, and gave her to her husband Abram to be his wife.

4 And he went in unto Hagar, and she conceived: and when she saw that she had conceived, her mistress was despised in her eyes.

18:23 And Abraham drew near, and said, Wilt thou also destroy the righteous with the wicked?

24 Peradventure there be fifty righteous within the city: wilt thou also destroy and not spare the place for the fifty righteous that are therein?

25 That be far from thee to do after this manner, to slay the righteous with the wicked: and that the righteous should be as the wicked, that be far from thee: Shall not the Judge of all the earth do right?

## What Is Anxiety?

Anxiety is a state of uneasiness and distress about future uncertainties. Other words for it are apprehension and worry. When a person is experiencing an extreme form of anxiety, they are usually worried about future events that cannot be avoided. Then they become preoccupied with these events for a long time after the events have taken place.

People are not all alike in this respect. They vary in their reactions to life's pressures. What is stressful to one person is not to another. A person's background, neurological structure, and previous experience with pressure affect how s/he will respond. One person loses a job and is devastated. Another experiences the same type of loss but sees it as an opportunity to find a new position that might be more suitable.

Some people develop physical problems that are the result of anxiety. Studies show that nearly fifty percent of all people seeking medical attention today are suffering from ailments brought about by such emotions as prolonged worry, anxiety, or fear. Emotional tensions often play a major role in certain types of heart and circulatory disorders. High blood pressure, peptic ulcers, colitis, headaches, joint pains, muscular pains, skin disorders, and some allergies are all examples.

## Dealing With Anxiety

While we may not easily change many of life's stressful situations, we can improve the way we adapt. The Bible presents principles for adapting to life's pressures. To discover some of these principles, let's look at one of the biblical characters listed in the Hebrews' "Hall of Faith"--Abraham (Hebrews 11:8-10).

God told Abram (later called "Abraham") to leave his country and go to a land that He would show him. Abraham obeyed God's command even though he did not then know where God wished him to live. Abraham left his home in Haran, taking with him his wife Sarai (Sarah), his nephew Lot, his servants and all of his riches (Genesis 12:1-3).

Although Abraham was rich and had been promised that all the land would be his, he was not without trouble. The people of the country where he settled, the Canaanites, were fierce and unfriendly. Then there came a famine, so that Abraham could not get enough food for himself and those who were with him. He knew that Egypt was a rich and fertile country, and he made up his mind to go there and take with him his wife and family (Genesis 12:10). (God did not tell him to do that!)

On the way to Egypt he said to his wife Sarah, "You are a very fine-looking woman, and I fear that the Pharaoh of Egypt may want to take you from me. He might even kill me so that you will be a widow and he can marry you. So when we meet any of Pharaoh's people, tell them that you are my sister, instead of my wife" (12:11-13).

As mentioned previously Abraham was one of the Bible's greatest worriers. From his introduction in Genesis 11 to his death in Genesis 25 are ten recorded occasions when Abraham worried excessively. Surely many day-to-day instances were left out of the biblical record. The major ingredient in Abraham's anxiety was his tendency to make absolutes out of possibilities. Even though, based on his history of success, his speculations were unlikely to occur, Abraham always believed that danger was inevitable.

For example, in addition to worrying that foreign kings would covet his beautiful wife and kill him to get her (Genesis 12:11-13; 20:11), he worried that the loss of one water well would spell the destruction of all his herds (21:25). He worried about shortages of grazing land for his animals (13:6-8), about retaliation (15:1), about a lack of an heir (15:2-3), about God's possible inability to honor His covenant (16:1-4), and about God's intent to destroy Sodom and Gomorrah (18:23-33).

In spite of God's promises, Abraham worried that he and Sarah were too old to bear children. After the birth of Isaac, Abraham worried that God wouldn't know which of his two sons to use in fulfilling the promise of many descendants (21:11).

Abraham grew from his experiences, but he was not always a heroic symbol of faith. However, God saw in Abraham the potential for greatness. Because of Abraham's obedience, he was eventually able to achieve what God planned for him.

A brief study of some of the incidents from Abraham's life reveals many basic truths that can be used by counselors to help people who are experiencing anxiety. Following is a discussion of some of these truths.

**God is with us during stressful times.** Abraham had to learn that God could be with him in anxiety-provoking situations. The

Lord assures us in Isaiah 43:2 that: "When you pass through the waters I will be with you; and through the rivers, they shall not overflow you; when you walk through the fire you shall not be burned, and the fire shall not consume you."

People experiencing anxiety must be assured that, while they are not promised a life free of difficult situations, they do have the promise that they are not alone when problems occur. Tension did not originate in the 20th century. However, like Abraham, who lived centuries before Christ, we too can arrive at such a high stress level that seemingly the only way out is sin.

We also come to those times when we think we've "got it together." But then, one by one, things begin to pile up. The stress begins to build to such a point that we see no way out. There is nowhere to turn and we are quickly running out of resources and ideas. We can turn our thoughts to negativism and despair; or we can work at changing the beliefs, assumptions, and negative ways of thinking that can cause us to become victims of stress.

Our perceptions and evaluations of the world around us can actually cause stress. Changing our attitudes may be difficult, but it may also be the best way to reduce stress, tension, and anxiety. Meditating on Isaiah 43:2 is a good exercise for beginning to see difficult situations in an entirely different light than we might have seen them before. When counseling an anxious person, this is an appropriate Scripture to discuss.

**God will be faithful to us in all situations.** Abraham had to learn that God is faithful. God is not a "sometimey" God. Continuing with Abraham's story, we see that things happened just as Abraham predicted. Pharaoh saw Sarah and took her into his house. For her sake he treated Abraham (whom he thought was her brother) very well.

However, the Lord was angry with Abraham for telling a falsehood and with Pharaoh for taking Sarah away. Therefore the Lord sent plagues into the house of the king. The king, at length, learned the truth, and he was glad to give Sarah back to

Abraham. Pharaoh then scolded Abraham. "Why did you do such a thing?" he demanded. "You very nearly caused me to commit the sin of taking another man's lawful wife, and making her my wife" (Genesis 12:17-20).

Abraham, Sarah, Lot, and Abraham's cattle all returned to Bethel safely. There, they built an altar and gave thanks to the Lord for their escape from Pharaoh's anger (13:1-4). The natural consequences of Abraham's acts could have been disastrous, but God prevented that disaster. Even when Abraham failed, God's purpose for him did not fail. This is an illustration of God's mighty faithfulness. It shines as a great shaft of light from the days of Abraham, to our times.

Abraham had to learn that the situations which he thought were peculiar to himself were merely ones in which his faith was being tested. This is also true of us today. When helping someone who is anxiety-ridden, it is important to explain this to the person and show that difficulties are settings in which God can show us His faithfulness. They are settings in which we can learn to relax and trust!

We are sometimes tempted to believe that our trials and perplexities are peculiar to us and that they constitute complications unfamiliar to anyone else. Such is not the case. They are familiar to God. He says that no temptation can overtake you or lay hold on you that is not common to humanity.

God is faithful and He can be trusted not to let you be tempted and tried beyond your ability to endure. With the temptation He always provides a way out (1 Corinthians 10:13).

**There is no limit to God's power.** Abraham had to learn more about the awesome power of God. In the 14th chapter of Genesis we find Abraham taking a small army of his servants and pursuing the armies of four kings. The purpose of the battle was to rescue Abraham's nephew Lot, who had been taken captive. God allowed Abraham to be successful in this battle.

God's power is able to overcome any imaginable stress. A

counselor can encourage a person who is dealing with anxiety to believe in God's unlimited power. This is very important in dealing with tensions. While we cannot avoid difficulties in life, we do not have to be broken or beaten by them. We can rise above them and surmount their assaults with God's power.

The Bible assures us that: "Greater is he that is in you, than he that is in the world" (1 John 4:4). Jesus said: "In this world you will have trouble. But be of good cheer! I have overcome the world" (John 16:33). So can we!

**God's grace is sufficient for our weaknesses.** When a person is experiencing anxiety, a counselor can point to Scriptures such as 2 Corinthians 12:9: "...My grace is sufficient for thee: for my strength is made perfect in weakness. Most gladly therefore will I rather glory in my infirmities, that the power of Christ may rest upon me."

With all of Abraham's riches and power, he was not happy. He had no children, and he thought when he died his chief servant would take his place. However, the Lord spoke to Abraham in a vision and reminded him that He had taken care of him before and had given him all the things that were good for him. Then God promised to reward him again.

Abraham wondered how he could be rewarded. He already had great worldly wealth. All he wanted was a son who could take his place when he died (Genesis 15:2-3). Still Abraham worried. He and his wife Sarah were old, and it did not seem to him that they would ever have any children. Abraham was not the first or last person to experience these emotions. Anxiety and worry have always had the potential to hang over us like the darkness that came over Abraham (15:12). Anxiety can be terrifying.

However, counselors must constantly reassure people who are feeling anxious that God promised to be with them and care for them. When we come to God out of a sense of need, we can turn this need into prayer. Then we develop self-confidence (not self-sufficiency), and a dependency on God. We learn to depend on

**76**

God only when we recognize His awesome power, and how His power can work in our individual lives. We learn this when we see how God works in a situation that was too much for us to handle by ourselves. God's strength is made perfect in our weakness.

**We must wait on God.** Abraham was nearly one hundred years old when God repeated His promise that Abraham would be the father of a great nation. Abraham showed no indication of believing what God had said (15:4). Abraham, the worrier and Sarah, his wife, decided to help God along by means of a "surrogate mother" (16:1, 2). A son, Ishmael, was born to Hagar, the "surrogate mother" and Abraham. Thirteen years after Ishmael was born, the Lord again appeared to Abraham and told him that Sarah would bear his son, and that her son would become the founder of a great nation of people. However, again, Abraham did not believe God. Abraham thought God meant that Ishmael would be the one to father the great nation. Abraham asked God if this was what He had intended. However, God again told him that it would be Sarah who would conceive a son (17:1-17).

It is difficult for anxiety-ridden people to believe that God will intervene in situations that seem impossible to overcome. It is important for a counselor to point out to such a person that our thoughts are not God's thoughts. God is more powerful that we can even imagine (Isaiah 55:8, 9). The anxious persons must be encouraged that, even if they do not understand, they should wait on God.

**God comes on time.** There's an old song that says, "He may not come when you want Him, but He's right on time." People who are anxious can be reminded of this old song. They can also be told about Abraham's bouts with anxiety. Abraham did not believe the promise God repeatedly made to him. It seemed too strange to him that Sarah and he would have children when they were so old. But God did fulfill His promise and gave them a son, even though Sarah was ninety and Abraham was one hundred when Isaac was born (Genesis 21:1-3).

We can hardly blame Abraham for being a little discouraged and impatient. It had been about twenty-four years since he had first been informed of God's plan. Few people want to wait that long! However, our human vision is very limited. We cannot see all that God sees. Therefore, when we pray, we should avoid trying to instruct God what to do. Instead, we should wait for His direction. We should submit to Him. We should avoid praying as if we are saying: "Lord, I've got to straighten You out." We should not presume we know best. It is the very act of taking on the task of knowing everything that brings on tensions.

A symptom of anxiety is a faint heart, or heart trouble. The Psalmist has a cure: "Wait on the Lord: be of good courage, and he shall strengthen thine heart: wait, I say, on the Lord" (Psalm 27:14). When we do that the Lord will strengthen our hearts. He is really the great heart specialist. And He's always right on time!

**Anxiety can lead to victory.** Throughout all his trials and tribulations, Abraham (from the "Faith Hall of Fame") grew and he finally learned, through his constant bouts with anxiety, that his struggles could actually lead to victory, and to a reduction of his anxiety! Spiritual growth is an important factor in overcoming anxiety.

As we walk in close fellowship with Christ, we become increasingly aware of the security and peace which we can have in Him. The realization that God is interested in each one of us gives us added confidence which helps us overcome feelings of apprehension. Such spiritual concepts, however, are not gained automatically.

Instead, they are usually developed over a period of time, as a troubled person identifies himself closely with a dedicated believer (often a counselor) and as he discusses his problems and their origins. A gradual understanding of biblical teachings will eventually take root in the heart and mind of the one suffering from anxiety and will help to permanently dispel apprehensions.

The counselor can assure the anxious person that: "...we glory in tribulations also: knowing that tribulation worketh patience; And patience, experience; and experience, hope: And hope maketh not ashamed..." (Romans 5:3-5). In explaining this to a client, we can use Abraham's life as an example. Abraham was always a stranger and a pilgrim in the land that God had promised to him. Abraham was always in the spiritual growth process. So are we.

Our own faith will have its ups and downs, trials and tribulations just as did Abraham's. However, we have the choice of depending only on our own understanding and resources for solving life's frustrations, or of trusting the Lord God of Abraham. We also have the chance to learn from our experiences. Abraham did.

At the end of Genesis, we see him at the refining point of his growth process. God tested Abraham. He said to him, "Abraham...take your son, your only son Isaac, whom you love, and go to the region of Moriah. Sacrifice him there as a burnt offering" (Genesis 22:1, 2).

Based on our knowledge of Abraham's past experiences we might expect Abraham to have a heart attack! But at this point Abraham's faith was strong and optimistic. He had learned the lesson of Proverbs 3:5-6: "Trust in the Lord with all your heart and lean not on your own understanding; in all your ways acknowledge him, and he will make your paths straight."

When Isaac asked about the sacrificial lamb, Abraham could say with confidence, "God himself will provide the lamb" (Genesis 22:8). The ultimate test came as Isaac was bound to the altar and Abraham prepared to slay his son in whom lay the destiny of God's covenant. At that moment, God intervened and said to Abraham, "Now I know that you fear God" (22:12). He had passed the test! There was no hint of anxiety! He didn't try to bargain with God! Abraham knew God would provide and he responded according to that belief.

The story of Abraham is an excellent source of Scriptures for working with people who are chronic worriers. It is also an excellent scriptural source for personal devotions, while we, personally, also struggle.

At times, counselors will encounter people who are beyond the point where simple edification, studying the Scriptures and praying through difficult situations seems sufficient. Such people are experiencing an advanced stage of anxiety and should be referred to professional counselors, social workers or psychologists who are trained to help such people.

## When to Refer the Anxious Person to a Professional Agency

While sensitive and trained laypersons and pastors can do a high percentage of the counseling within the church, they can't do it all! Some people have problems that require professional help. In determining when a person requires professional help, consider these factors:

1. **Intensity of their feelings.** How strongly is the counselee experiencing anxiety (or grief, anger, jealousy, guilt, tension, etc.)? Is it overwhelming the person and thus prohibiting him/or her from functioning in a normal way? Is it a concern the person is struggling with while still being able to continue functioning?

2. **Depth of the disturbance.** Is the person's behavior within the realm of normalcy, or is it becoming clearly abnormal? Has the problem arisen recently, or is it a long-term pattern?

3. **The person's sense of reality.** A psychosis is a clear break with reality. The counselor should ask if the person has the ability to communicate and hear accurately.

4. **The nature of the behavior.** Is the person's behavior producing pain or stress for him/herself or others to the point where it cannot be tolerated?

If the counselee has serious problems with any of these four factors, the person should be referred to professional counseling or therapy. If the above four factors are not involved, then a minister or layperson with some training would probably be able to help that person.

Remember, the medical community refers people frequently. Just because a doctor cannot see you does not mean the doctor is not a good physician. It just means your disease is not in the area of his or her expertise. The same is true in the counseling area. No counselor can deal with every person or every problem. As a counselor, be honest with yourself and recognize your strengths and limitations. It is in the best interests of the people God has called you to serve.

**Summary.** This chapter has dealt with the subject of helping people who are experiencing anxiety. It presented six spiritual truths, taken from the life of Abraham, that can be presented to people who are experiencing anxiety:

a) God is with us in stressful situations. b) God will be faithful to us in all situations. c) There is no limit to God's power. d) God's grace is sufficient for our weaknesses. e) We must wait on God. f) God comes on time. g) Anxiety can lead to victory.

Counselors can remind anxiety-ridden people of these spiritual truths in order to help them reduce their anxiety.


## CASE STUDY

*INSTRUCTIONS: Mrs. Ellis, in the following story, is experiencing anxiety. The following exercises will lead you into an in-depth study of Mrs. Ellis' problem, based on the principles that were introduced in this chapter.*

*The first five exercises consist of a series of "discovery" questions, followed by a summary question. The sixth exercise asks you to summarize and apply information you gained from the first five exercises.*

**81**

*The seventh exercise asks you to make personal applications of the information you have received.*

## MOTHER ELLIS

*Deacon Jemison, as usual, was administering communion to the sick and shut-in of Olivet Baptist Church. It was the first Sunday morning. When he got to Mother Ellis' home, he noticed something was wrong. Although it was 10:30 a.m., she had the Venetian blinds closed throughout the house. She invited him in and sat in her rocking chair, with a blanket covering her feet.*

*She told Deacon Jemison she was afraid that someone would break in. She also said she was convinced that she had a serious heart condition, even though the doctors said they didn't find a problem. She said she was experiencing difficulty in breathing and her chest felt heavy.*

*During the following weeks, Deacon Jemison continued to visit Mother Ellis on his usual sick visitation rounds. During his visits, he got to know Mother Ellis outside of the usual environment of the church. Mother Ellis told him that she had been forced to move in with her sister, because she could no longer pay the mortgage on her home. Her husband had died last year. She had recently been forced to retire from a job she had held for twenty years, cleaning office buildings, because she had reached the age of 65. However, the job didn't provide retirement benefits.*

*She was finding it difficult to "make ends meet" on the combination of food stamps and Social Security benefits that she was receiving. Her relationship with her sister with whom she shared the apartment had never been harmonious, and there were a number of old family conflicts that had never been resolved. However, she had been keeping all these troubles to herself. She was worried that one day her sister and she would have an argument and she would be put out in the street.*

*She hadn't been coming to church because she was worried people would notice that her clothes were no longer in fashion.*

## 1. God's faithfulness

Deacon Jemison can remind Mother Ellis that God is faithful and will be with her in this stressful situation.

a. How can Philippians 4:6, 7 help reduce Mother Ellis' anxiety? What does this Scripture indicate about God's faithfulness?

b. How can 1 Peter 5:7 quiet Mother Ellis' anxiety? What does this Scripture indicate about God's faithfulness?

c. How can John 14:27 quiet Mother Ellis' anxiety? What does this Scripture indicate about God's faithfulness?

d. How can Psalm 37:25 bring calm to Mother Ellis? What does this Scripture indicate about God's faithfulness?

e. For what can Mother Ellis be thankful? (Psalm 43:5)

f. SUMMARY QUESTION: If you were a member of the sick visitation team at your church, and you were visiting Mother Ellis, how would you make use of the information from exercises a-e above?

## 2. God's power

Deacon Jemison can remind Mother Ellis of God's awesome power.

a. What does Psalm 27:3 say about God's power to work in Mother Ellis' situation?

b. What does Matthew 28:18 say about God's power to work

in Mother Ellis' situation?

c. How does Genesis 1 reflect the power of God? How does this passage relate to Mother Ellis' situation?

d. What can Mother Ellis learn from the life of Abraham about the awesome power of God? How does this apply to Mother Ellis' current situation?

e. What does Psalm 23 say about God's power to work in Mother Ellis' situation?

f. SUMMARY QUESTION: If you were on the sick visitation team, visiting Mother Ellis, how would you make use of information from exercises a-e above?

### 3. God in times of weakness

Deacon Jemison can remind Mother Ellis that God can "come through" in a time of weakness.

a. What does Matthew 6:31, 32 say about God's willingness to act on behalf of the weak? How does this passage relate to Mother Ellis' situation?

b. What does Philippians 4:19 say about God's willingness to act on behalf of the weak? How does this passage relate to Mother Ellis' situation?

c. What does Proverbs 3:26 say about God's willingness to act on behalf of the weak? How does this passage relate to Mother Ellis' situation?

d. What does Philippians 4:13 say about God's willingness to act on behalf of the weak? How does this passage relate to Mother Ellis' situation?

e. What does 2 Corinthians 12:9 say about God's willingness to act on behalf of the weak? How does this passage relate to Mother Ellis' situation?

f. SUMMARY QUESTION: If you were on the sick visitation team, visiting Mother Ellis, how would you make use of the information from exercises a-e above?

## 4. We must wait on God

Deacon Jemison can remind Mother Ellis that we must wait on God.

a. How does Isaiah 30:15 relate to Mother Ellis' situation? What does it say about waiting on God?

b. How does Job 14:14 relate to Mother Ellis' situation? What does it say about waiting on God?

c. How does Isaiah 40:31 relate to Mother Ellis' situation? What does it say about waiting on God?

d. How does Habbakuk 2:3 relate to Mother Ellis' situation? What does it say about waiting on God?

e. What do the lives of Abraham and Sarah say about waiting on the Lord? How does this apply to Mother Ellis' situation?

f. SUMMARY QUESTION: If you were on the sick visitation team, visiting Mother Ellis, how would you make use of information from exercises a-e above?

## 5. God will come on time

a. How does Proverbs 14:26 relate to Mother Ellis' life? What does it say about God coming on time?

b. How does Exodus 16:14-35 relate to Mother Ellis' life? What does it say about God coming on time?

c. How does Exodus 17:5-7 relate to Mother Ellis' life? What does it say about God coming on time?

d. How does Luke 11:5-10 relate to Mother Ellis' life? What does it say about God coming on time?

e. How do Matthew 18:12-14 and Luke 15:4-7 relate to Mother Ellis' life? What do they say about God coming on time?

f. SUMMARY QUESTION: If you were on the sick visitation team, visiting Mother Ellis, how would you make use of information from exercises a-e above?

## 6. SUMMARY EXERCISE

Do people with problems similar to those of Mother Ellis attend your church? In what ways might your church help Mother Ellis reduce her anxiety by developing (or improving) ministries that offer people such as Mother Ellis help in the following areas:

a. food

b. finances

c. counseling

d. referrals for professional counseling

e. housing

f. fellowship with other seniors

g. part-time employment

## 7. PERSONAL APPLICATION

Are you anxious? Do you anticipate future events with trepidation and fear? Meditate on some of the Scriptures listed in Exercises 1-5 above, during your personal devotions. Then be open to learning to trust God for His protection of your future.

CHAPTER FOUR

# DEPRESSION

### Dr. Pauline Reeder

*It had been six months since Rose of Sharon Church buried Jeffrey. Jeffrey was the third young person at Rose of Sharon, in a period of two years, to be killed in a gang shootout. This time, the young man who was killed was the only son of Brother and Sister Hampton, members of the Sanctuary Choir. Brother Wright, president of the choir, had noticed that Brother Hampton hadn't been to church for the past five months and had been missing choir rehearsals. He asked Sister Hampton about him when he dropped her off after choir rehearsal last night.*

*In the car, Sister Hampton broke down crying and told Brother Wright that Brother Hampton had completely changed since the death of their son. He had become very violent, cursing and screaming at her unpredictably. He had been complaining about headaches, and he was having back pains.*

*Sister Hampton asked Brother Wright if he would drop by and visit Brother Hampton sometime and see if he could help him. A week later, Brother Hampton dropped by the Hamptons' home.*

*It was about 7:00 p.m. when Brother Wright arrived, but Brother Hampton was still wearing a robe*

87

*and slippers. He was sitting in a chair, staring out the window. On a nearby table were pictures of his deceased son. Before long, Brother Hampton informed Brother Wright that he had been staying home from his job as an insurance agent, and he was having financial trouble because of it. However, he found that he could not concentrate at work and didn't have any enthusiasm for carrying out his job.*

*This had been going on since the death of his son.*

*He told Brother Hampton about his back pains, and about how the doctors didn't find anything wrong with him. He was quite upset, because he had already seen three doctors.*

*He went on to say that he thought about his son every day, and could not figure out why something like that had happened to him. He had not found the energy to resume any of his former activities and had been spending most of his time at home.*

Brother Hampton, in the above story, is suffering from depression. Depression is a growing problem in today's society. Many people who are suffering from depression do not seek professional help because they fear the stigma of mental illness. However, some may reach out to lay counselors, friends, ministers and others from their churches. Lay persons need some knowledge about how to deal with some of these situations as they arise within their families, churches and among their friends.

This chapter focuses on how to help people who are suffering from depression. It is for lay counselors, friends, ministers, or other persons who want to provide support to such people.

## An Example of Depression from Scripture

Depression is an ancient illness that can be found occurring in

Scripture long before the time of Christ. Job, Moses, Jonah, Jeremiah, Elijah, David and others all suffered from depression. David, suffering from depression, cried out in Psalm 42, talking to himself to keep alive his hope in the Lord.

## from Scripture

**Psalm 42:1** As the hart panteth after the water brooks, so panteth my soul after thee, O God.

**2** My soul thirsteth for God, for the living God: when shall I come and appear before God?

**3** My tears have been my meat day and night, while they continually say unto me, Where is thy God?

**4** When I remember these things, I pour out my soul in me: for I had gone with the multitude, I went with them to the house of God, with the voice of joy and praise, with a multitude that kept holyday.

**5** Why art thou cast down, O my soul? and why art thou disquieted in me? hope thou in God: for I shall yet praise him for the help of his countenance.

**6** O my God, my soul is cast down within me: therefore will I remember thee from the land of Jordan, and of the Hermonites, from the hill Mizar.

**7** Deep calleth unto deep at the noise of thy waterspouts: all thy waves and thy billows are gone over me.

**8** Yet the Lord will command his loving kindness in the daytime, and in the night his song shall be with me, and my prayer unto the God of my life.

**9** I will say unto God my rock, Why hast thou forgotten me? why go I mourning because of the oppression of the enemy?

**10** As with a sword in my bones, mine enemies reproach me; while they say daily unto me, Where is thy God?

**11** Why art thou cast down, O my soul? and why art thou disquieted within me? hope thou in God: for I shall yet praise him, who is the health of my countenance, and my God.

## What Is Depression?

Depression is an illness that takes a great deal of time and energy out of a person's life. The effects of the illness become more intensive as the depression deepens. The more depressed the person becomes, the more withdrawn s/he becomes. The more withdrawn s/he becomes, the more difficult it is for others to communicate with the person. As the person gets deeper into depression, the person becomes more unhappy and more inefficient. Eventually, the person can lose the desire to face reality altogether. Up to verse 11 of Psalm 42, David can be seen going through these various stages of depression.

**Types of depression.** There are different types of depression. Exogenous or reactive depression comes as a reaction to a traumatic event in a person's life. The event may be real or imaginary. People sometimes think something has been said or done to harm them which is not factual and they brood themselves into depression. Endogenous depression is believed to arise within the person. The inability to attain certain goals may touch off this feeling. It is also very prevalent among the elderly.

Then there is psychotic depression. Persons with psychotic depression may have alternating levels of anxiety but they are not usually self-destructive. Chronic depression is of lengthy duration, while acute depression lasts for shorter periods with differing levels of intensity.

**Signs of depression.** Hopelessness is a sign of depression. Other signs are: lack of self-esteem, guilt, shame, insomnia, loss of interest in sex, loss of interest in other activities, a lack of ability to enjoy normal pleasurable activities, and a constant desire to be alone.

People often try to hide these symptoms to avoid being thought mentally ill. Sometimes the depressed hide their illness behind physical problems and emotions such as anger, aggression, and lashing out at friends and family members. They complain about physical illnesses such as: headaches, stomach pains, and fatigue. They may become prone to accidents. Sometimes they hurt themselves rather than others. In some cases, they may engage in excessive drinking, gambling, and sexual promiscuity. Frequent temper outbursts and arguments are some of the effects of depression.

Family members and others often misinterpret these symptoms. Often they take the depressed person to a medical doctor for some of the physical symptoms, only to be told by the doctor that there is no physical illness. The depressed person will insist that there is a physical problem and will become even more angry as he is taken for a second opinion.

The second or third doctor will finally begin to suspect that the problem is emotional and begin to treat the patient for it. At this point, some depressed persons will even stop going to the doctor. Once it is mentioned that the real problem is depression, the depressed person may withdraw even more and will communicate with close family members and others even less.

As a depressed person goes deeper into depression, the threat of suicide is a reality. Therefore, the person must be watched. The person may attempt suicide by taking too many drugs or by drinking along with the drugs, even when the drug is a prescriptive medication. One sign of suicidal tendencies is when the person begins to take reckless chances that can result in a fatal accident. In some cases, the depressed person may resort to living on the streets.

## Situations That Can Trigger Depression

There are a number of situations that can trigger depression in persons of almost any age. The counselor can identify persons who are suffering from depression by recognizing the symptoms discussed previously, and by recognizing situations that gave rise to these symptoms.

**91**

**Loneliness.** People who are left alone, without human contact for long periods of time, can become depressed. That is because people are social beings and require other human contact. For example, infants who are left alone and only given the fundamental needs to exist can become depressed; while infants who are given love and attention are happy and thrive.

**Parent/child conflicts.** There are a variety of parent/child conflicts which lead to depression. Conflicts between parents and children can be triggered by the birth of a new brother or sister. Older siblings in this situation can become depressed when all love and affection are given to the new infant. Wise parents know this and make an effort to spend time with the older children.

Many depressed young people, facing this or other conflicts with parents, run away from home and live on the streets. Many children have become street children simply because they have become extremely unhappy at home and cannot work through their problems with family members. They join gangs for the same reasons.

On the other hand, parents of adult children can be quite unhappy when they do not get the affection they feel they need from their children. For them, these problems add to all the other stressful influences in today's society. This is particularly difficult for them when their adult children abuse them. Adult children abuse their parents for a number of reasons, two of which are: resentment for having to care for them, and the desire to obtain a living space for themselves. Most of these abusers need counseling.

**Loss of a loved one.** The loss of a spouse, child or parent can trigger depression. The loss of one's spouse can be like losing a part of oneself. The longer the duration of the relationship, the longer it seems to take for the surviving spouse to overcome the grief. When the spouse is lost through death the anguish seems unbearable. A spouse who has been nursing the loved one may wonder whether he/she did everything possible to keep the

92

spouse alive, and for a while may feel some guilt.

This same type of guilt, mixed with depression, can also follow the loss of a loved one through divorce, especially a bitter one. The person who is left alone must be helped to sort out his/her feelings about the situation and face them in order to go on living a comfortable life. Unless the person can learn to forgive, the bitterness will keep going and may worsen the depression.

Losing a child through kidnapping or death can also trigger depression. This causes some parents to become depressed to the point that they spend all their time brooding about the child. They cannot be around other children without becoming terribly upset. Some parents have taken other children to try to replace their own child. This kind of depression requires professional help and may not be quickly cured.

The parents of kidnapped children also suffer deep depression, but many of them find self-help groups who have suffered the same loss and aid each other in many ways.

The loss of a parent can be extremely difficult. This is particularly true when parents and adult children are extremely close. The parent's death can be unusually difficult for the child. In my own case my mother was ill for a long time but was not bedridden. When her death became imminent she talked with me daily about plans for our lives after her death. She was always able to soothe me with her soft, encouraging manner by saying to me, "Remember the prayer Jesus prayed in the Garden of Gethsemane, 'Father, not my will, but thy will be done.'"

When grief goes beyond the normal range of time, the loss of a parent can lead to depression, coupled with guilt. The adult child often suffers from guilt of having not done enough for the parent. The parent may have been placed in a home and the child may feel badly about not having been able to keep the parent at home. Others, who cannot make enough money to take care of both themselves and their families, fall into depression when they lose a parent who shared their financial burden. Most who

face this situation do not know where to turn for help.
Losing a close friend or other relative can be a cause of
depression. I recently had a client who lost a very close friend
upon whom she depended too much. The friend had helped her
make many decisions and she had come to rely on her friend's
advice. When she lost the friend she was so upset she could not
function for a while. She spent much of her time crying and asking why it had to happen to her friend when there were so
many bad people in the world.

**Rape.** One reaction to rape can be depression. Many kinds of
rape are happening today. Males rape females and males as well
as children. Females join some males in raping other women.
Groups rape a person. Older teens rape younger teens. Rape is a
cause of depression which is often very long lasting; sometimes
even into the marriage of the abused.

**Domestic violence.** Domestic violence often results in depression. It is growing at an alarming rate. Spousal, child, and parental abuse are serious problems for many people today. The most
difficult part of the problem is the fear of the family secret being
exposed to the public. People suffer quietly in fear and depression. Most murder victims knew the person who murdered them,
that is because most murders are the result of severe domestic
conflicts.

Family members as well as friends and acquaintances may become murderers. Sometimes the person who commits the act
goes into depression. The family of the murdered needs counseling to cope with the terrible loss and the way it happened. The
loss of a job may cause family abuse when the unemployed person takes out his/her frustrations on family members. Jobless-
ness is a great problem in our society. Wives become abusive in
many of these cases and verbally abuse their husbands or physically abuse their children.

**Homelessness.** The growing problem of homelessness often
triggers depression. People who live on the streets become
depressed and lose hope of rejoining the normal life of our

society. Sometimes they form their own groups and resist help from mainstream agencies. Frequently, they may not accept the fact that they need help in lifting themselves to their former status. In many cases, they affirm that they would rather be on the street. In some cases, when they are forced to accept medical treatment they become depressed and need counseling. However, the longer they remain homeless the more likely it is that they become depressed. They find it increasingly difficult to regain their former status. Much of the difficulty involves inadequate services and other resources they need to obtain employment, medical treatment, drug or alcohol abuse counseling, and of course low cost housing.

**Extreme fatigue**. Extreme fatigue can trigger depression. People with stressful jobs and long working days without breaks or vacations often suffer depression. This frequently happens to working students in medical, law and other graduate schools. They have full credit schedules, longer working hours than they should work and no time for relaxing and enjoying some of their favorite activities.

People who work two jobs have the same problems. Trying to handle two jobs while married and while trying to care for one's family is extremely difficult. The fatigue that results can lead to depression. Usually this type of depression can be cured with some time off for rest and play. Many ministers who carry a very heavy schedule either recognize the need to take a break or they get the feeling of being burned out or depressed. Most of the time they take the appropriate steps and soon return to normal. However, occasionally people suffering from fatigue and depression turn to drugs or alcohol, another problem that usually requires counseling.

## Setting the Tone

Counseling the depressed person can require varying lengths of time commitments. In some cases, helping the depressed person may require more than one or two counseling sessions. It may take time for the person to sort through the feelings that are at the core of the problem and develop the strategies needed to overcome the depression. Following are general guidelines for lay counselors for helping people deal with depression. These guidelines can be formalized as part of a church-based counseling ministry, or they can be used by anyone who is called upon to provide crisis intervention for people with whom they come in contact.

**Recognize personal limitations**. The first step in helping a depressed person is for the counselor, friend, or minister to deal with him/herself. One must first be honest and recognize personal limitations. The counselee will require much from the counselor. It is essential that the counselor recognize when to recommend professional help, and when short-term counseling by a lay counselor may suffice.

In recommending professional help, the counselor must be tactful but firm. In no case should s/he recommend drugs to the counselee; this is always to be done by medical doctors. The counselee must understand that most forms of serious depression need to be treated as any other illness, without the client feeling ashamed of it.

The counselor must always remember personal limitations. Never hesitate to ask other professionals for help if this is necessary. The counselee may need the services of an employment counselor if unemployment has triggered the depression. In other cases, the counselee may need a psychologist. This is particularly true if rape is involved. Rape and unemployment are only two of the many types of situations which trigger depression and which may require the assistance of specialists other than the lay counselor.

The counselor must lead the counselee toward whatever help s/he needs as soon as s/he sees the problem is beyond his or her range of counseling skills. A counselor who feels s/he must do the complete job of counseling, without any help from some more trained professional, is not facing reality and may do more harm to the counselee than good.

Medical doctors often refer their patients to other doctors with specializations outside of their particular range of skills. For example, general practitioners often recommend patients to psychologists, psychiatrists, gynecologists and others for examinations, evaluations and treatment. They do this when they are unable to locate the physical causes or cures for particular patient complaints. Ministers and lay counselors must do the same.

**Maintain professionalism**. Professionalism must always be maintained in counseling the depressed. Depressed people are very emotionally dependent and sometimes misunderstand acts of kindness for deeper feelings than intended. The counselor must not let feelings of empathy for the counselee overrule good judgment. The counselor must never allow the counselee to become too emotionally attached or dependent.

Never touch the counselee unless it is absolutely necessary. A handshake when the person arrives is enough. A warm smile or an understanding nod at the appropriate time is sufficient to let the counselee know that you are listening and you care enough to want to aid the person. When the counselee begins to cry or show other emotions, simply hand the person a tissue which you keep available in your office and wait for him/her to calm down.

Make every effort to see the counselee in your office. Avoid public places and the counselee's home unless other family members are someplace in the home. Luncheon and dinner dates are not proper times for counseling the depressed; again your motives might be misunderstood.

Many counselors, attorneys and doctors have been sued by patients or clients who claim that the professional person has misled or misused them. Many of these cases have been won at great loss to the professional. This is especially risky in the minister's life because depressed persons look up to the minister for love and sympathy and simultaneously will want to respect the minister even when they reach out to him physically.

The minister has to always be alert as to when he can respond to the counselee without risking his ministry and personal family life. Many counselees have publicly relayed things said by the minister which are taken out of the context in which they were said.

When the counselor is aware that the counselee is continuously making advances, he or she should make the counselee aware that the counselee's feelings are misguided and lead the counselee to understanding a personal need for friendship. Suggest ways in which the counselee can find satisfactory relations which need not be sexual. There can be excellent platonic relationships if people work at them honestly.

**Maintain confidentiality.** All counselors should be strongly ethical and confidential. The depressed person needs more than many other counselees. One betrayal of a small bit of information can throw the person into deeper depression and mistrust of people in general.

**Exhibit morality.** The counselor must be warm, gentle, patient and intensely desirous of helping people. The counselor might not be connected to any religious body but must be a moral and wise person. A counselee will hardly respect a counselor who says one thing and does another. For example, the counselor cannot help the counselee with temper tantrums when he is constantly yelling at his secretary in the next room while the counselee listens.

The counselor cannot be hypocritical in counseling or in private life. His/her feelings and actions must be genuine if s/he is to deal with the depressed. The depressed person needs to see the counselor in a very positive manner because s/he needs someone who can exemplify a healthy life-style.

**Remain impartial.** The counselor must be impartial at all times and be careful not to place blame. No matter who the counselee, blames for his or her predicament the counselor can never join with the counselee even as the person vehemently claims the problem is caused by others. However, the counselee needs to see him/herself in the problem without the feeling of being criticized by the counselor. This requires a great deal of diplomacy on the counselor's part.

**Be understanding**. The counselor who seeks the most effective cure for the counselee will try to understand the person as well as the problem. The counselor must understand that the personality of the depressed changes during the period of depression. The introvert acts like an extrovert. During depression, the introvert may become the life of the party to the point of acting completely out of his/her normal character.

Extroverts, on the other hand, may become quiet and sullen or sad. They are simply trying to hide behind a mask so that their real feelings of despair and low self-esteem are not revealed. Persons who do not easily cry may cry at the least incident while those who are thought to be sensitive may become cold and sullen. The counselor has to see beyond these feelings to the real problem.

**Be patient**. The counselor may use one or more approaches with the counselee but in each case caution must be used. Do not be too forceful in getting the counselee to talk or reveal more than he or she is willing to reveal. Do not probe or question if the person is hesitant about an item that seems important to you as counselor. It will probably come out later in behavior, if not verbally.

The counselor must be patient for the information that brings out the whole problem. It probably did not happen suddenly and will take more than one session to solve; unless it is an acute depression, such as some sports players have when they are on a losing streak, or such as that experienced by a young boy and girl when s/he suddenly breaks up an ego-deflating relationship. This kind of acute depression is usually self-corrective in a short period. Chronic depression is quite a different story. Following are additional guidelines for dealing with the chronically depressed person.

## Exploring the Problem

Counselors can use various techniques to help counselees through the process of sorting through and understanding the problems which triggered the depression. Clarifying the problems should be done prior to actually developing objectives and strategies for overcoming the depression.

**Encourage the counselee to talk**. Help the counselee to talk about his/her feelings and thereby relate at least some of the problem. This is often the most difficult part of the counselor's work. However, s/he must gently work at this if the counselee is to feel better and think through the problem. Begin by assuring the person that all information is safe, and make sure this is a fact.

Then tactfully lead the person to talk comfortably about him/herself, explaining how s/he thinks the problem began and where s/he thinks s/he can find solutions. When the counselee pauses, do not push him/her to continue. Rather, give the person time to collect his/her thoughts.

**Allow expressions of emotion**. Do not be embarrassed by the show of emotions by the depressed person. Instead, quietly wait for the person to become composed. This is particularly true when it is a male client. Counselors should be aware that we often do not allow men to cry. Therefore, as a culture, we often deny men the right to cry publicly. However, this must not be conveyed to the counselee during the counseling session. Instead, the counselor should convey that it is all right for anyone to cry. Men are just as capable of deep feelings and tears as women are. The counselor should allow the counselee to be free in emotional expression.

The counselor must be in touch with his or her personal feelings, particularly when the counselee is "thinking out loud" to the counselor. The counselor must be sure not to indicate horror, indignance or any other judgment. The counselor is available only to help the counselee and must continue to show genuine love and concern. Any negative feelings or related actions by the counselor could seriously damage the counselee. **Help the counselee to clarify the problem.** Once the counselee feels safe within the counseling environment, it is appropriate to begin exploring the nature and scope of the problem. First help the counselee to think through the problem. This will require remembering as much as possible of what the counselee is saying as his or her thought processes are being explored.

During this clarification phase, ask questions about the causes of the feelings and when the feelings began. Ask him or her to describe what was actually happening when s/he began to have the depressed feelings. Help the counselee to identify such feelings as guilt, anger, vengefulness and violence. Ask such questions as whether the counselee feels that s/he can go on living.

Watch for suicidal words and phrases such as "Life is no longer worth it," or "People would be better off without me around to make problems." When these thoughts are expressed, ask why the counselee has such negative thoughts and low self-esteem. Help them to evaluate each feeling in a positive manner. Then ask whether there is a need to forgive others or to forgive him/herself.

## Solving the Problem

This phase of the counseling will include talking, thinking, evaluating and setting new goals and objectives for the life of the counselee. This can all happen in one session only if the depression is acute and of very short duration as with the sports player. However, usually it takes more than one session to bring the counselee to this final stage. This stage itself may require even more time, seeing that it requires the counselee to work on new objectives for happiness and serenity.

**Develop realistic expectations.** During the problem-solving phase, the counselee should be encouraged not to expect too

**101**

much of him/herself or of others. This is particularly true when the depressed person has set unrealistic goals and is depressed about being unable to attain them.

**Seek the Lord's help**. During the problem-solving phase, presenting alternative models for dealing with depression is helpful. Scripture contains such models, and is often useful in providing such support. For example Psalm 51, in which David asks the Lord to forgive him and restore his joy, can serve as a model for how the counselee can begin to cope with depression. Scriptures of comfort and hope, such as those found in the Psalms and in the New Testament promises of Jesus, can also be used. Psalm 23, "The Lord's Prayer," and intercessory prayers (such as John 17) can be very useful with counselees who are Christians.

Both the counselor and the counselee can benefit from studying Jesus, the Counselor. Jesus was always warm, loving, gentle and wise. He reached out to the person who needed someone to understand or help him pick himself up from where he lay. The man at the pool knew Jesus was concerned when He told him to "take up thy bed and walk." The man must have been depressed after thirty-eight years of being impotent, but he heard love and authority in the voice of Jesus.

The counselor must gain a voice of authority from the voice of Jesus. This voice of authority can lead the depressed to take charge of his/her own life, to pick himself or herself up and to live again. The counselor will want to always reach out and help the depressed in love and warmth, teaching him/her how to cope with problems and live the abundant life about which Jesus spoke in the Bible.

Prayer is also useful in counseling. The counselor may help the person to converse through prayer. This can allow the person to talk about the problem indirectly, giving the counselor some insight into how s/he can further give help.

However, the counselor must be mindful of the fact that religion is often used as an escape from reality. The counselor

**102**

must detect whether the counselee is using the worship experience as the answer rather than the means of gaining hope and courage to deal with the problem of depression, and help the counselee make better use of the worship experience.

**Develop strategies and identify resources.** The counselor will find that a variety of situations can trigger depression. Accordingly, the counselor will need to use different resources with different counselees, depending upon the types of situations that triggered the depression. For example, the counselor may need to help the unemployed direct his/her skills in another direction in order to find new employment. Such a person may need to develop self-confidence again, after perhaps being laid off from a job of long duration.

Adult children of parents who die after very long and serious illnesses may need yet a different type of help. Such adult children often feel guilty because they feel relieved of the burden of their parent's lengthy illness, which drained them personally, physically and emotionally. In helping such counselees deal with depression, the counselor must help them to recognize that they did their best. Through talk therapy, the person can be encouraged not to feel guilty, and to recognize that the death itself was not their fault.

Depressed senior citizens can require special resources. The aged need attention in their declining years. When they can no longer function on their own they become quite depressed. The church, as a body, can provide some support for senior citizens. For example, our church and another church in our area run a senior center. Through the center, we get a chance to talk with many senior citizens. Seniors with less serious depression respond well to attention from the attendants and their families. We get many friendly responses from them each time we visit. They look forward to someone coming to see them and showing them affection. When they do not get this type of attention, they go back into their "shells."

Seniors who withdraw in this way can sink into psychotic

depressed states where they physically assume child-like positions for long periods of time. Such seniors need medical and
psychological counseling. In many cases, professional
psychological counseling may be needed.

Family members who have become victims of abuse and the
abusers who have abused them may also require professional
psychological counseling. The abuser, in this situation, may have
a need to feel power and to achieve this by making his/her family afraid of the abuser. This type of person usually requires
professional psychological counseling. Psychological counseling
may also be needed for victimized members of the abuser's
family.

For substance abusers, still other types of resources and
strategies are needed. Some counselees use drugs or alcohol as a
means of escape from the problem of depression. Such substance
abusers need to see that these escape mechanisms really do not
solve the problem. Substance abusers must first be helped to
build the self-confidence necessary to take on personal responsibility for their problems.

Then they need to see that these substances do not get to the
root of the problem. The goal would be for the counselees to locate more constructive ways of working through difficult times
of depression. To help such counselees, the counselor can direct
substance abusers to Alcoholics Anonymous and other such
groups in the counselee's neighborhood.

Helping rapists and their victims will also require referring
them for professional counseling. The rapist usually needs long-
term professional counseling. S/he does not respond to a jail sentence without counseling. S/he has to be taught to see himself or
herself differently than other people do, and s/he must learn to
channel anger and frustration in non-destructive ways. The victim of the rapist needs to regain self-confidence and a sense of
control over the bitterness s/he may feel from having such a
drastic act performed upon his/her body. A limited amount of
help can be provided through talk therapy. However, the coun-

selor will need to refer such counselees to professional counseling.
**Summary.** This chapter has dealt with helping persons who are hurting from depression. It explained what depression is, listing signs of depression and situations which often trigger depression. The chapter stressed the importance of the counselor recognizing his/her own personal limitations, and stressed the importance of professionalism, confidentiality, morality, impartiality, understanding and patience. Strategies for encouraging the counselee to talk, express and clarify emotions were also presented. The importance of referring certain types of depressed persons for professional help was also underscored.

## CASE STUDY

*INSTRUCTIONS: The exercises below involve developing guidelines for establishing a counseling ministry in a local church. The guidelines would be used by lay counselors who service depressed people.*

*The first five exercises are "discovery" questions, followed by a summary question. The sixth exercise asks you to summarize and apply information you gained from the first five exercises. The seventh exercise asks you to make personal applications of the principles you learned in this chapter.*

## MRS. HAMILTON

*It was Mrs. Hamilton's first counseling session with Mrs. Fleming of the Counseling Ministry at Beacon Street Baptist Church. Mrs. Fleming noticed that this first meeting was very difficult for Mrs. Hamilton. She was extremely nervous and wept frequently. Once Mrs. Fleming was able to calm her down, she began describing very difficult and painful experiences.*

**105**

*For the past two years, she had been living with Bill, her live-in lover. She had met him through a friend. Bill had been kind to her five children as well as to her before he lost his job. Then his behavior changed. She soon learned that Bill had never kept a job for more than two years. According to his sister, he had always been irresponsible. His sister had thought that he was so attracted to this new family that he might become more stable, but he had not.*

*It wasn't long after Bill lost his job that his behavior changed. Bill expressed resentment over Mrs. Hamilton's attending church as frequently as she had begun to do, and he began questioning her as to whether she was really going to church. Although she urged him to come to church with her, he refused. Therefore she had started attending church less frequently, and had become very depressed.*

*She said that her relationship with this man was almost as bad as the one she had with her former husband. She had always been a great conversationalist and had many friends. However, her former husband had also become jealous of her friendships outside of the home. She talked about how much her relationship with her ex-husband depressed her.*

*Considering the fact that this was her second major relationship with a man, and it was almost as bad as her relationship with her former husband, she had low self-esteem. She spent most of her time wondering what was wrong with her. She had set a goal of having a marriage that was as happy as that of her maternal grandparents. She had even tried to select men who were similar to her grandfather, and had asked the men to do things she had observed her mother asking her grandfather to do. She could not understand why she had "failed" in two relationships.*

## 1. Understanding

Jesus showed understanding of the woman who was about to be stoned for adultery (John 8:1-11).

a. What attitudes did Pharisees and others have toward people with problems? (Luke 15:21; 18:11-12)

b. How were "harlots" usually treated? (Genesis 38:24-25; Leviticus 21:9)

c. What was fundamentally missing from the Mosaic Law regarding adultery? (John 8:5)

d. What is one way that Jesus showed understanding of the woman caught in adultery? (8:7-9)

e. What is another way that Jesus showed understanding of the woman caught in adultery? (8:9-11)

f. SUMMARY QUESTION: How can the story of Jesus' treatment of the woman caught in adultery serve as a model for counselors counseling depressed people?

## 2. Being patient

Jesus patiently counseled His disciples and the sisters of Lazarus, even though their immature grasp of spiritual truth grieved Him (John 11:1-46).

a. What evidence is there that the disciples did not fully understand who Jesus was? (John 11:7-13, 16) What was Jesus' reaction? (11:14-17)

b. What evidence is there that Mary did not fully understand the truths that Jesus was presenting to her? (11:20-24) What was Jesus' reaction? (11:25-26)

c. What evidence is there that Martha did not fully understand the truths that Jesus was presenting? (11:32-33) What was Jesus' reaction? (11:33-34)

d. What evidence is there that some of the Jews also did not understand the truths that Jesus had been teaching? (11:37) What was Jesus' reaction? (11:38-43)

e. What was the outcome of Jesus' patience and persistence with the spiritually immature people surrounding Him? (11:44-46)

f. SUMMARY QUESTION: How did Jesus help the woman at the well to clarify her problem? What techniques did He use? What traits did He exhibit? How can this story be used as a model for helping counselees clarify problems?

## 3. Clarifying the problem

The story of the woman of Samaria at the well illustrates how Jesus helped a counselee to clarify a problem.

a. What relationship existed between the Jews and the Samaritans? (John 4:9)

b. What was one source of the woman's confusion? (4:11, 13-15)

c. What was another source of the woman's confusion? (4:10, 12)

d. What was the woman's basic problem? (4:16-24)

e. What was the outcome of Jesus' counseling session with the woman at the well? (4:28-30)

f. SUMMARY QUESTION: How did Jesus help the woman at the well to clarify her problem? What techniques did He use? What traits did He exhibit? How can this story be used as a model for helping counselees clarify problems?

## 4. Allowing the counselee to show emotion

Jesus didn't condemn a weeping woman He met for expressing her emotions (Luke 7:36-50).

a. Why was this woman so upset about being considered a sinner? (7:37; 15:21; 18:11-12; Genesis 38:24-25; Leviticus 21:9)

b. What emotion was being expressed when the woman fell at Jesus' feet? (1 Samuel 25:23-24; 2 Kings 4:36-37; Esther

8:3)

c. What emotion was being expressed when the woman kissed Jesus' feet? (Isaiah 49:22-3; 1 Kings 19:18)

d. What did Jesus see beneath the woman's emotions? What was Jesus' reaction to her? (Luke 7:40-50)

e. What was the outcome of Jesus allowing this counselee to express emotion? (7:49-50)

f. SUMMARY QUESTION: How can the story of the weeping woman be used as a model for those who counsel depressed persons?

## 5. The Lord's help

The Lord has resources for the depressed. Examine each of the following Scriptures, and identify the promises that the Lord makes to the depressed person.

a. John 8:12

b. John 4:13-14

c. Matthew 21:22

d. Luke 11:9-13

e. James 1:17; John 14:15-21

f. SUMMARY QUESTION: What hope do the above Scriptures provide for the counselor and counselee?

## 6. SUMMARY EXERCISE

How might the counselor help a woman or man with problems similar to those of Mrs. Hamilton locate a "place" in the Community of Faith? How might women such as Mrs. Hamilton learn to more creatively deal with single life? How might such a person be encouraged to develop his/her potential through education and acquisition of skills?

## 7. PERSONAL APPLICATION

Are you depressed? If so, re-read some of the Scriptures in the above exercises. Then reach out to your pastor or someone at your church as a first step toward overcoming the problem.

# CHAPTER FIVE

# FEAR

### Bertha Swindall

*Mrs. Baker, the Primary Sunday School teacher, was planning her usual follow-up visits to parents whose children had been absent for more than three weeks. Today she telephoned Mrs. Allen, mother of eight-year-old Shirley, and Mrs. Allen seemed more than eager to talk to her. As soon as Mrs. Baker arrived at the Allen home, Mrs. Allen quickly invited her to sit at the dining room table and began a long story about the previous three months.*

*The problems centered around Mrs. Allen's desire that Shirley do some of the housework and take care of the younger children for her. Mrs. Allen complained that Shirley would not do these things correctly. She had punished Shirley several times, but her behavior didn't get any better. For example, when her daughter was washing the dinner dishes, she broke two glasses. Mrs. Allen whipped her with the ironing cord for this, but that didn't make Shirley improve her ways.*

*When Shirley made up the beds she didn't tuck in the corners of the sheets correctly. She was again whipped, but that, too, didn't do any good. Then, while Mrs. Allen rested Shirley tried to make some spaghetti for dinner. However, she put too much cheese in the spaghetti. She was again whipped. "It just looks like I can't teach her anything and she won't mind me," she said.*

*Shirley had begun to stay in her room by herself. One day, as Mrs. Allen was checking to see if Shirley had cleaned her room correctly, she found a brand-new rag doll, similar to one that Shirley had when she was younger. She knew that Shirley did not have enough money to pay for the doll. When she asked Shirley about it, her daughter said she borrowed the doll from a friend. Mrs. Allen told her to return the doll.*

*When Mrs. Allen checked on this, Shirley said she had returned the doll; but in the week following, Mrs. Allen found the same doll hidden under Shirley's bed. Along with it were several other new items. Mrs. Allen now believes that Shirley is stealing.*

*Mrs. Allen asked Mrs. Baker, Shirley's Sunday School teacher, what she should do. Right now, she was keeping Shirley "grounded," and would not allow her to go to Sunday School until her behavior improved. She said that she has been whipping Shirley, but that Shirley just won't "mind."*

The situation which Mrs. Baker found at the Allens' home reveals two troubled persons. Both Shirley and her mother are hurting. They are troubled and hurting from fear. Shirley's mother is afraid Shirley's behavior will never change. That will make Mrs. Allen a failure as a mother and as a parent. Mrs. Allen also seems to think that obedience and respect are gotten through fear of punishment. She feels that when Shirley does not do her chores or is disobedient it is because she does not respect her mother. Therefore Mrs. Allen believes Shirley must be beaten into respecting (fearing) her. She also has an additional fear that Shirley has become a thief.

Shirley, on the other hand, is just as fearful as her mother. Shirley also feels rejected because she cannot do adult chores in an adult fashion, even though she is still a child. This may not "make any sense" to Shirley. Therefore, she fears that her mother will reject and beat her for whatever she does, even when she does her very best. It is possible that she is stealing in order to "get back at" her mother (and therefore other adults). Subconsciously Shirley is trying to get something from adults other than blame. However, now that she really is doing something that she knows is wrong, she is unable to open up to her mother, out of fear of an unsympathetic punishment that will be even more harsh.

This chapter is about helping people such as Shirley and Mrs. Allen, who are hurting from fear. It provides guidelines for counselors, friends and others who want to lead such persons into a more trusting relationship with the Lord, and thereby with each other.

## A Biblical Example of Fear

Joseph, whose brothers sold him into slavery for no reason that was apparent to him, also exhibited fear. He also exhibited a fearful hesitancy when his brothers returned to Egypt many years later. With the childhood memory of his abandonment in mind, even though Joseph had been exalted to ruler of Pharaoh's house, he did not readily reveal himself to his brothers.

## from Scripture

**Genesis 37:3** Now Israel loved Joseph more than all his children, because he was the son of his old age: and he made him a coat of many colours.

**4** And when his brethren saw that their father loved him more than all his brethren, they hated him, and could not speak peaceably unto him.

**5** And Joseph dreamed a dream, and he told it his brethren:

113

and they hated him yet the more.

**23** And it came to pass, when Joseph was come unto his brethren, that they stripped Joseph out of his coat, his coat of many colours that was on him;

**24** And they took him, and cast him into a pit: and the pit was empty, there was no water in it.

**26** And Judah said unto his brethren, What profit is it if we slay our brother, and conceal his blood?

**27** Come, and let us sell him to the Ishmeelites, and let not our hand be upon him; for he is our brother and our flesh. And his brethren were content.

**28** Then there passed by Midianites merchantmen; and they drew and lifted up Joseph out of the pit, and sold Joseph to the Ishmeelites for twenty pieces of silver: and they brought Joseph into Egypt.

**42:3** And Joseph's ten brethren went down to buy corn in Egypt.

**6** And Joseph was the governor over the land, and he it was that sold to all the people of the land: and Joseph's brethren came, and bowed down themselves before him with their faces to the earth.

**7** And Joseph saw his brethren, and he knew them, but made himself strange unto them, and spake roughly unto them; and he said unto them, Whence come ye? And they said, From the land of Canaan to buy food.

**14** And Joseph said unto them, That is it that I spake unto you, saying, Ye are spies:

**16** Send one of you, and let him fetch your brother, and ye shall be kept in prison, that your words may be proved, whether there be any truth in you: or else by the life of Pharaoh surely ye are spies.

**17** And he put them all together into ward three days.

**18** And Joseph said unto them the third day, This do, and live;

for I fear God:

## What Is Fear?

In our language today, fear is a disabling, negative emotion. In Shirley, we see fear as fright, tension, and also disabling. In our language we have separated fear and respect. Many people have trouble admitting they are actually afraid. By the time the average person reaches adulthood, s/he has so lost the direct connection with fear that s/he rarely recognizes fear. In fact, most adults prefer to call fear by other names, such as: nervousness, anxiety, depression, and shyness. However, all of these are the many faces of fear.

**The nature of fear.** Fear is a phenomenon of which there are two components, biological and emotional. When we are afraid our bodies get ready to protect us by fighting, running, or hiding. One type arouses a biological defense against a perceived physical danger. The other is not as clearly so, but on the surface is primarily based on an emotionally perceived danger. Native, biological fear is fear of death. This type of fear is native to everyone. It is there in order to preserve the life of the human being.

Biologically-based fear is a normal feeling. It is a physical state of tension in the presence of a perceived or suspected danger to the body. This type of fear involves the total physical, biological, sociological, psychological, mental, and spiritual self. Sudden fear of death can invade one's total being and is there to ready a person to take action directed towards eliminating the source of the fear. The person responds to native, biologically-based symbols of death--pain and apprehension.

An example of biologically-based fear is fear of falling, which seems to be the only fear present at birth. It can therefore be assumed that all other fears are learned within the context of the environment.

Emotionally-based fears, on the other hand, are either directly or indirectly related to this basic fear of death. For example, Joseph's fear, upon meeting his brothers again, was directly related to the fear of death (Genesis 42:18). In his mind, his brothers' rejection of him was at one time directly paired with the threat of death, as they pushed him into a ditch and considered killing him (37:19-24). Certainly he would not reveal himself to them too quickly when they returned to Egypt many years later, begging for food.

Shirley, in the opening case study, is another example. She is afraid to tell her mother that she has been stealing toys. However, underlying this fear is the fear of punishment and her mother's rejection. In Shirley's memory, her mother's rejection is usually paired with whippings. Fear of the rejection is really fear of the whippings, and fear of the whippings is really fear of death, which could accidentally result from the whippings.

Mrs. Allen's fears can also be traced to the native fear of death. However, the connection is a little less obvious. Mrs. Allen's obsession with Shirley's being able to do everything perfectly is, on a very deep level, associated with Mrs. Allen's desire to cheat death. It is the desire to continue, in some form, beyond death itself, and to absolve oneself of any guilt for personal imperfections. Subconsciously, Mrs. Allen probably believes that both perfection and continuity can be achieved through her child. Her fears are related to her knowledge, at a very deep level, of the Hebrew concept that continuity is through the seed, one's children.

Therefore the child is not its own entity but is an extension of the parent. The child is a part of the parent. If the child does something that is wrong, the action disgraces the mother or father. This sense of not separating the child from the self heightens feelings of parental anger, resulting in attack and distress.

In this scheme of thinking, the child must be like the mother, but better. The child's perfection subconsciously is seen as a cleansing agent for the mother. On a subconscious level, the

**116**

mother believes that her child must achieve a level of perfection the mother never attained, because it is through the child's perfection that, somehow, the mother will be admitted to heaven and also will continue on earth, through the "seed" (the perfect child).

Through possessiveness, the parents attempt to satisfy their obsession with keeping their children pure. If children cannot be kept pure, then the parents fear being doubly punished. The parent must be a good parent because that will redeem both the parent and the child. Redemption of the child comes by preventing the child from any wrongdoing. That is what a "good" parent does.

Fear can present itself in many forms. It may come through feelings of worthlessness. It may appear as an exaltation over others. People who exalt themselves over others often become paranoid, feeling that they are perfect and therefore others are "out to get" them.

**Fears within families.** Our basic patterns of living and thinking evolve from experiences within our famiilies. This is unavoidable because we learn from family members. From birth onward we do not change these patterns; they are learned from experiences as we grow from childhood to adulthood. Family values and organizational structures are imposed upon children, whether the children want them or not. Most fears, anger and habits in general, come from within the family.

**Fears rooted in parent/child relationships.** In American culture parents are in control of children. American culture still honors the idea that husbands are in control of their wives, and employers are in control of their employees. When control is not based on trust between the persons involved, it is customary to establish rules, regulations, and punishments to effect control.

The persons in "controlling" positions can avoid instilling fear in the person they "control" by practicing what Fred S. Buschmeyer calls the "art of relinquishment." The art of relinquishment lies in recognizing that the life process will require all

**117**

of us to "lose" or "give up" many of our capacities or skills. Eventually the ruler must make place for the ruled as time brings changes in the relative positions of both. Every person must be allowed the opportunities needed to "be" and to "self-actualize" without fear of punishment and without resentment of the "controller."

Other situations in the parent/child system can produce tensions that can lead to fear. When parents cannot provide basic needs for food, shelter and protection of their children, the children often become fearful in their relationship to the parent. When the parent consistently denigrates and criticizes the child unfairly, this also evokes fear in the child.

When the parent punishes the child for things that do not require punishment (such as not knowing how to do something, due to their age level), this also leads to fear of the parent. Parents need to be wary of confusing fear with respect.

When parents fear that they are unable to control a child they often feel it is necessary to beat the children into an attitude of what they see as respect; this attitude may really be fear on the part of the parent. In trying to deal with fear of the parent, a child will often exhibit behaviors which develop from fearfulness. For example, the child may seem uncertain about the future; or may be uncertain about decision making; or may exhibit a constant sense of concern about some impending trouble, danger, or disaster.

Such a child can grow into an adult who experiences extreme nervousness about evaluations from supervisors and others and may constantly fear losing his/her job or money. A fear of the future is often present. As the same child ages, s/he may exhibit a constant sense of anxiety about health, marriage, his/her own children, the aging process, and threats of impending injuries from another person.

**Signs of a fearful person.** A person who is experiencing fear displays certain signs. The person may talk about his/her failures to live the Christian life, about personal sinfulness before God ("all I am is a filthy rag"), and may exhibit a general lack of trust in God. There may be fear about the loss of salvation or doubt about God's promises. S/he may be uncertain about personal spiritual status or worth.

The person often talks about the threat of poverty, lack of love, personal intimacy, sexual gratification, and success. The fearful person may also talk about difficulties in relationships with spouses, children, friends, or fellow employees. Often the fearful person expresses an inability to protect him/herself from abuse from others, and an inability to confront those who injure via drugs, physical abuse, alcoholism, sexual abuse and neglect. In some cases, the person may already have been deserted by a loved one.

**Crippling fear.** Fear can sometimes cripple the fearful child or adult so that s/he can't carry out daily functions. Physical pain, nervousness, "shaky" feelings, and some illnesses can result from this type of actively crippling fear. The actual status of the hurting person's fear may not be known to the sufferer. It may have to be ferreted out and identified.

When fear becomes so intense that it cripples, the fearful person's motives focus on protection of the self. Perceived failures in this area increase the fear and add dread. This cycle can result in complicated emotional disabilities. Fear, in this sense, is an alarm system that warns the person of such an impending danger.

People living under such tensions want to get rid of them. They are weary of the discomfort in their lives. They would like to have some personal peace, social pleasure, and better interpersonal relations.

## Helping the Fearful Person

In dealing with fear, the most important task for the fearful person is to place the fear in realistic perspective, in order to reduce the anxiety associated with it. What appears as irrational fear can be diminished or erased by applying the test of reality to it. In order to carry the fearful person through this process, the counselor must be sympathetic and able to see the fear as it is probably seen by the counselee.

It is important for the counselor to give supportive, friendly directions. S/he must be careful to comment but not criticize. S/he must share insights but avoid being judgmental. It is also important not to exert pressure but to explore attitudes and support them.

**Responding to fear.** There are three types of strategies for eliminating or reducing disabilities from fear. These are:

1) fight (attacking, destroying or understanding the source of fear)

2) flight (running away from fear)

3) compromise (adjusting oneself to the threat while in the environment with it).

In combatting fear, an individual employs whichever of these possibilities that are available. However, in a given situation, the way a person chooses to use these strategies may not be functional and may not result in greater comfort. In fact, the ineffective use of these strategies may result in an increase of danger rather than an elimination of it. In some instances, the improper use of these strategies in one area of life may cripple the person in some other area. This may occur even when the person temporarily succeeds in avoiding the danger that originally evoked the fear.

The counselor can help the counselee examine those strategies s/he is using and whether that strategy is helpful.

**Clarifying thoughts about fear.** As mentioned earlier in this chapter, most people have difficulties admitting they are fearful. However, in order to deal with fear, the person must admit it is there. This is made easier for the counselor and counselee if the counselor begins by examining his/her own attitudes about fear.

The counselor must avoid categorizing emotions as good or

bad. All emotions serve a purpose. It is extremely important to come to grips with and learn this fact. Emotions have not come into existence in order to torment people. They're given by God for protection. Emotional problems develop when the reaction to the threat of some incident, accident, or circumstance interferes with daily life. In these instances, emotions such as anger, hatred, and fear are often distorted, misused and abused. In short, it is not the emotions that are bad or negative, but the use of the emotions that is dysfunctional or negative.

All organs are good when they function properly. It is when they do not function properly that we must try to rescue and restore the organ to health. The mind is a good organ. However, when it becomes dysfunctional, the issue becomes why the mind is dysfunctional. As with the diseased organ, we must make every effort to restore the diseased, distorted, misplaced emotion to its healthy state. We cannot work to eliminate an emotion, for that would cripple total life functions.

One must be able to discern when an emotion is functional or dysfunctional. In adjusting one's attitude toward fear in this way, one is much closer to being able to deal with dysfunctional fear.

Without a toleration of the conglomeration of people--experiencing a variety of emotions such as fear, anger, hatred, vanity, envy, grief, guilt, loneliness, impatience, a sense of superiority, a sense of inferiority, worry, pride, defensiveness, depression and other feelings--the capacity to live in a community would be seriously damaged, and the community itself would be much less rich. No, it is not possible to eliminate these emotions, but it is possible to learn (and teach others) to manage them so that they are useful to oneself and to the community in which one lives.

**Exploring fear.** Jesus provides us with many examples in the New Testament of His willingness to allow His counselees to explore their own feelings and reach their own conclusions. While He was Divine, and knew all things, He usually provided His subjects with the opportunity to first state what was bothering

**121**

them, and then to explore it. For example, He didn't just walk up to the woman at the well and start preaching to her. He let her talk and asked her strategic questions.

To help the counselee get a "handle" on fear, and to move toward its management, the counselor can use Jesus' counseling techniques as a model. The counselee must first understand fear. In beginning to understand it, it is important for the person to first determine whether fear has any basis in reality. The counselor might ask the counselee if what he or she fears will happen has any chance of occurring.

The counselor might also ask the counselee to recall a time when s/he was actually feeling the fear. Then ask the person to hold the memory for a few moments. Ask for a description of the level of discomfort felt. Listen for such words as terrified, frozen, alarmed, frightened, apprehensive, anxious, etc. Labeling the emotion helps the counselee to begin the move towards managing it. This procedure is effective with both children and adults.

**Avoiding fatalistic thinking.** Many Americans who are Black live in a world that they experience as divided into "Black" vs. "white." This often causes people to adopt a fatalistic attitude about emotional problems, feeling that they have them because they are Black. However, it is important for the counselor to encourage the counselee not to engage in this type of fatalistic thinking. All human beings have the attributes outlined in this chapter in exactly the same way, regardless of their color.

Everyone experiences fear. Things happen to all people all over the world. Most of these things are common human experiences. Americans who are Black must learn to think of themselves as being part of the world community and the family of humanity. They must avoid allowing themselves to think of themselves as different simply because they live in a society where many people have negative attitudes based on skin color.

The counselor needs to encourage the counselee to be realistic about separating personal feelings and identifying: 1) those that

**122**

are brought on by negative reactions to skin color, and 2) those which most human beings experience to some degree or another. The counselee needs to be aware that life must be lived in a very complex world, and he or she must learn to relate to him/herself, to other minorities and to non-minorities in a way that does not lead to anyone being stigmatized.

**Helping parents who fear.** As mentioned earlier, parents often exhibit a variety of fears regarding their children. They are frequently petrified that the child will not graduate from high school. Often they fear the child's sexuality. They fear the child's entry into kindergarten and later fear the child's entry into adulthood. They fear that the child cannot exist apart from the parent.

On a more subconscious level, this fear is the fear of the loss of the child. This fear is related to other, more self-centered fears such as the fear of personal loneliness (resulting from the child leaving home), and fear of loss of love.

As mentioned earlier, the Hebrew notion of continuity through the seed also becomes involved, with the parent subconsciously hoping that the child can be an extension of the parent and thereby continue his/her image on earth. The counselor can help the fearful parent apply the test of reality. The parent needs to learn to relinquish what is unrealistic about the fear.

For example, in the event that the underlying fear is the fear of loss of love, the counselor can guide the fearful parent into a better image of him/herself. Often such parents have isolated themselves, or have been isolated from other human beings. Isolated parents are most aware of lack of love from other adults. This causes them to rely on the only secure source of love they have (the love of their child). They feel that they can rely on this love because the child has no recourse other than to love.

Such parents have such low self-esteem that they rely too heavily on their child's love as possibly the only real source of love that the parents can experience. In this case, the parent can be guided into a better appreciation of him/herself. Such a parent needs to distinguish between self-love and self-centeredness.

Such parents need to be guided into feeling that they are worthy and good, and other people can appreciate the goodness that is within them. They need to be shown they have something to give that does not necessarily relate directly to their children.

In the case where the underlying fear is of the daughter's or son's sexuality, the parent first of all needs to be guided through questions of whether the fears have any true basis in reality, and whether the reaction to the fears is appropriate. Then the entire concept of the need for a perfect son or daughter should be explored, and what that need has to do with personal needs for cleansing through the daughter or son.

Thirdly, the concept of sexuality as carnality needs to be explored. God made us sexual beings. Why is the expression of sexuality in itself carnal or sinful? Is the issue sexuality itself or is the issue appropriate expressions of sexuality, given specific circumstances. The parent needs to identify which signals s/he is sending to the child, and be sure that s/he is sending the correct ones.

Poor sex education is one source of developing fears within the child. Threats of punishment for natural sexuality can be very damaging; they can communicate to the child superstitions and false notions. Providing a child with the same type of sex education that one received as a child is not necessarily good. Related to this is the notion that the parent's experience with sex is not necessarily always the best source for teaching the child. It is necessary to remember that a generation separates parental experiences from those of children.

When an experience is automatically transferred from one situation to another, without careful thinking, it is not always the best application of the experience. In fact, some experiences may be the very worst teachers. The parent must be sure the lesson learned is the one that needs to be taught. Because the parent learned to do something a particular way does not mean he/she should teach the same thing to the children. Sometimes time dictates certain changes.

Placing unrealistic expectations on the child can only create conflict and fear; children can't do the impossible. For example, it may be impossible for the daughter not to be a sexual being and not have sexual feelings. However, it is possible for the daughter or son to make an appropriate decision about the circumstances under which s/he will have sex and with whom. S/he can be provided with guidelines for discerning between young men and young women who can help him/her keep a commitment to God in this area and those who, on the contrary, will only make indecent proposals.

Parents also need to avoid punishing children for things that do not require punishment, thus evoking fear in their children. Blaming the child for something that is not within the child's control is in this category. Recall that Joseph's brothers inappropriately blamed Joseph because he was his father's favorite child. This soon triggered confusion and fear in Joseph. He could not understand why his brothers were cruel to him.

This also led to fear in Joseph's brothers. They feared Joseph's influence with their father, and this fear caused them to rationalize their attempted murder.

Another example of blaming a person for something over which they have little control is when Mrs. Allen, in the introductory case study, blames Shirley for not performing as an adult. There is no need to punish children for having difficulty doing things they must first learn to do. For example, making a bed correctly is something a child must first learn to do. Whipping a child for not automatically knowing how to do this accomplishes no purpose. Almost all early tasks such as this do not require whipping, but require training and practice.

If training is done consistently, children will not need to be punished but will always seek to be trained. The Lord, in His relationship with His people, is a good example of this. He provides His people with a guide (the Bible). As one learns to follow this guide, one does not experience pain that would have been experienced without the guide.

Often children who become victims of parental beating engage in behaviors designed to "get back at" the parents and other adult figures. Frequently such children begin to steal either from the parent or from stores, as an act of solace or aggression. In these instances, children feel that they diminish the adults from whom they are stealing by taking something from them.

**Distinguishing between fear and respect.** In translations of the Hebrew language, "fear" was used to mean "respect." When Joseph says he fears God (Genesis 37:18), he uses fear as "respect." A worshipful attitude toward God differs from a fearful attitude laden with anxiety and distressful feelings. In the Old Testament, reverence leads to feelings of joy, not despair. Fear, in the Old Testament, is not the negative, dysfunctional fear that people often equate with respect. Jeremiah the prophet wrote that reverence would cause us never to depart from God (Jeremiah 32:40).

It is reverence that causes one to rejoice and anticipate good (rather than evil) things that the Lord will do for His people (v. 41).

In the New Testament, further clarification is given about the distinction between fear and respect. Respect for God has rewards. Salvation itself brings about a relationship with God that is based on reverence without fear (1 John 4:18). The counselee needs to know that Jesus Christ can bring us into a relationship with God that is not fearful. The believer does not need to stand in dread of God's terror. Instead, s/he must aspire to live in His love.

This same model of the relationship between the believer and God is to be followed in the relationship between a parent and child (Ephesians 6:4). The Bible says that parents should not provoke their children to wrath. Children learn to respect parents who love them. That respect is not the same as fear. True respect cannot be evoked from the child through beatings, whippings and other forms of physical punishment which cause pain. Good

**126**

trainers train with rewards, not with infliction of pain through blows to an animal's body.

Physical beatings followed by hugs and kisses only create confusion. Hugs and kisses after a whipping can leave the child with the question of which is true, the pain inflicted by the whipping, or the affection demonstrated afterwards? Children who are victims of such treatment grow up never really knowing whether their parents loved or hated them. They often grow up and beat their children in turn; thus we all observe an increase in violence in the community, much of which occurs behind the closed doors of the family home.

Physical attack does not give any direction or teaching. It merely shows the child who is bigger and stronger. When children are raised by fear, they can have only one objective: escape the parent who is the source of the fear.

**Experiencing God's protection.** Often fearful people are driven by both guilt and fear. However the most important concept for the fearful person is learning and being thankful for the grace of God. S/he needs to know that God accepts him/her just as s/he is. Grace cannot be earned. It doesn't come through anything else. It is a gift of God. If a person learns to trust in it, then the person experiences direction being given.

The fearful person must be reminded of the fact that God is love and God operates through love. Loving God with all one's heart and loving one's neighbors is our basic requirement from God. Therefore, there is no need to constantly dread some impending punishment that will be sent from God.

Trusting in the grace of God ushers a person into a sheltering, protective and empowering relationship with Him, and this relationship can affect all the persons in one's life.

**The role of the church.** Once Jesus was visiting Simon Peter's home, some of His disciples approached and told Him that His mother and other relatives were outside, and they wanted to see Him. Jesus told them He was among His relatives, the disciples (Mark 3:31-35). In telling them this, He informed them that the spiritual bond was more important than the biological bond. In other words, He spoke against the old Hebrew notion that primary human relationships exist only in the "seed."

He implied that a new family was being created between believers and it was bonded by the Spirit. The sins of the fathers would no longer be visited upon the children (Hebrews 12:9; Romans 6:23). That is, people would no longer be bound by bad family relationships. They can now enter new relationships within the Christian family.

The local church can be the center where these new relationships are formed. It is within the local church where nurturing, supportive relationships that lead to management and elimination of fear can take place. The counselor in the local church can use the church's resources to provide the counselee with the types of new family experiences they need in order to be healed.

**Summary.** This chapter has focused on helping fearful people. The difference between native biological and emotional fears was presented. Situations that evoke fear, along with signs of a fearful person, were also presented. Guidelines for helping fearful people were presented. These guidelines include:

1) helping the counselee to identify the best strategies for coping with fear;
2) clarifying both the counselee's and the counselor's attitudes regarding fear;
3) helping the counselee explore his/her particular fears;
4) encouraging the counselee to avoid fatalistic thinking.

Specific guidelines for helping parents who fear were presented. The chapter also emphasized the importance of the counselee's experiencing God's personal protection, and the role of the local church in the healing process.

Next the chapter provides the opportunity to apply some of these principles to a case study.

## CASE STUDY

*INSTRUCTIONS: The exercise below allows you to apply principles presented in this chapter to a case study involving a person who is hurting from fear. The first five exercises are "discovery" questions, followed by a summary question. The sixth exercise asks you to summarize and apply information you gained from the first five exercises. The seventh exercise asks you to make personal applications of the principles you learned in this chapter.*

### ALICE'S MOTHER

*Sixteen-year-old Alice came to the Oak Street Baptist's shelter, seeking a meal and a place to rest. She had run away from home but didn't have a job. She found life on the streets too foreign to her, and she didn't feel that she could cope any longer. She told Mrs. Carey, the woman on duty, that she wanted to return to her parents, but she felt that she needed an adult to go home with her.*

*The following day, Mrs. Carey and Alice left the shelter and went to Alice's home. Alice's mother seemed grateful to see her again and embraced her tearfully. However, one week later, Alice's mother came to the shelter and asked for counseling from Mrs. Carey on what to do with her daughter. She was afraid her daughter might leave again.*

*Alice's mother told Mrs. Carey that Alice was rebelling because she no longer wanted to obey house rules. Alice had asked many times if she could go to after-school activities at her school and church, but her mother had said she could not. Alice's mother was afraid that, if she allowed Alice to interact with other teenagers, she would sooner or later become preg-*

*nant, just as her mother had. As a single parent with very few friends, Alice's mother was very careful about who came to her home. She insisted that Alice spend her time with family members only, and that she use any extra time she had either studying or doing housework.*

*She was sending her to church so that she could get some Bible training from the people there. However, Alice's mother was surprised one day when Alice asked her if she could go to a basketball game with a boy from her church. This led to an argument over when Alice would be old enough to date.*

*Alice wanted to begin dating because she had reached her 16th birthday. However, her mother set the dating age at 21, when she felt that Alice would be accountable for all her own actions. Alice tried to explain how she felt about the boy at church, but her mother slapped her, feeling that she was being disrespectful and unattentive. She was particularly angry because Alice did not fear her enough to keep her feelings to herself.*

*This year, when school began and it was time to buy Alice's clothes for school, Alice told her mother she wanted to select her own clothing. This led to another argument. Shortly after that incident, Alice failed to come home from school one day and hadn't been seen since.*

*While she was back home now, none of the original issues that led to Alice's leaving home had been resolved. Spring was coming, and Alice's mother was afraid that as soon as the weather was warm enough Alice would return to the streets again.*

## 1. Facing Fear

One of the first steps Alice's mother must take in dealing with her situation is to recognize the degree to which fear is controlling her life.

a. What types of thoughts might have led to unfounded fears that would cause a parent such as Alice's mother (who has a child born outside of marriage) to hesitate to come to church? (Matthew 21:28-32)

b. What types of thoughts might lead to the unfounded fears that would cause a parent such as Alice's mother to believe she can't be loved by anyone other than her child? (John 8:1-12; Romans 3:23; 5:12; Ephesians 2:8)

c. Is the child merely an extension of the parent? How might misunderstandings in this area lead to unfounded fears in a parent's relationship with the Lord and with his/her child? (Psalm 139:13-17)

d. If a child sins, does this mean that his/her parents are also counted as having sinned, and vice versa? (Ezekiel 18:2-4, 19-24, 30-31)

e. Is there any hope for the fear-ridden person? (1 John 4:7-10, 15-16, 18; 2 Corinthians 12:9)

f. SUMMARY QUESTION: How might information from questions a-e above be used by the counselor to help overly fearful parents?

## 2. Recognizing "dysfunctional" fear

Alice's mother may need to deal with some of the false ideas that are leading to the fears damaging her relationship with her daughter.

a. Is there any basis for a parent thinking that s/he can relive (and cleanse) the past by forcing his/her child to be perfect? (1 John 4:11-13, 17-18)

b. Can rules and domination in themselves prevent a daughter or son from becoming a parent too soon? (Zechariah 4:6)

c. What is the best way for a parent to prepare a young person for life outside of the home? (Proverbs 22:6; Leviticus 26:3-4, 6-8)

d. To whom has God given the primary responsibility for providing spiritual guidance for a child, the parents or the church? (Ephesians 6:4)

e. What is the best attitude for Alice and her mother to develop about Alice's mother's pregnancy outside of marriage? (2 Chronicles 7:14; Ezekiel 18:4, 19-24, 30-31)

f. SUMMARY QUESTION: How can a counselor use the information presented in exercises a-e above to help a parent who has beliefs that lead to dysfunctional fear?

## 3. Fear of loss of love

Alice's mother has few friends of her own and seems to hesitate to become involved with the church to which she sends Alice. She also fears losing her relationship with her daughter to other people.

a. When Alice grows up and leaves home, will Alice's mother be without someone to love her? (John 14:18; Joshua 1:5; Ephesians 1:3-7)

b. In what ways can the Community of Faith become Alice's and Alice's mother's family? (Matthew 12:46-50; Ephesians 2:8-22; 1 Corinthians 12:13)

c. Does Alice's mother have a place set aside for her in the body of Christ? (1 Corinthians 12:12-18; Ephesians 2:6-10)

d. How does Alice's mother become a part of the Community of Faith? (Acts 16:31; 12:13; Hebrews 11:1--12:2)

e. Does God intend for the members of the Community of Faith to love and care for Alice's mother, a single parent? (Leviticus 19:18, 34; 1 John 4:8, 21; Romans 13:9)

f. SUMMARY QUESTION: How can a counselor use the information presented in exercises a-e above to help a parent who fears losing her child's love?

## 4. Distinguishing between fear and respect

Alice's mother feels that Alice is disrespectful because she shared her real feelings without fear. She wanted to slap "the fear of God" into her.

a. Does "fear," as the term is used in the Bible, mean being afraid of harm from God, or anticipation of good from God? (Jeremiah 32:40-41)

b. Does one accept Christ because one is afraid of God or because one loves God? (1 John 4:18-19)

c. Do parents gain respect by beating it into children? (Ephesians 6:4)

d. Is it better to beat a child into submission or train a child? (Proverbs 22:6)

e. Should a parent ever listen to a child, or should the parent always do all of the talking and make the child listen? (Ephesians 5:19-21; 6:4)

f. SUMMARY QUESTION: How can a counselor use the information from questions a-e above to help a parent who feels that s/he gains respect from his or her children by making them afraid and using corporal punishment?

## 5. Trusting God and His people for love and protection

Alice's mother needs to learn how to trust God for love and for the protection of both herself and her daughter.

a. What role will Alice's mother's personal relationship with God play in both Alice's and her mother's protection? (Job 11:13-20)

b. What hidden lesson about parenting can be found in the story of Jesus' healing of Tabitha, the daughter of the ruler of the synagogue? (Mark 5:35-42)

c. What role does faith in God play in the parent/child relationship? (Hebrews 11:1-3, 32-35; Luke 7:11-15)

d. Does a parent need to keep a teenager under his/her eye within the house in order for the teenager to be healed and/or protected by God? (John 5:46-54)

e. What argument is there in Scripture for single parents to come to the Community of Faith with their children? (Matthew 12:46-50)

f. SUMMARY QUESTION: How can a counselor use the information from questions a-e above to guide a single parent into a closer relationship with the Lord?

## 6. SUMMARY EXERCISE

In what ways can the church more effectively minister to parents of teenagers? What kinds of supports can be developed? Are there any new ministries or activities that can be formed? Compile a list of these ministries.

## 7. PERSONAL APPLICATION

Is fear controlling your life in some way? If so, read some of the Scriptures presented in the above exercises, and pray for deliverance from your fears. Also consider locating professional help from a trained counselor.

# CHAPTER SIX

# FRUSTRATION

### Rev. Paul Sadler

*It was Friday night. Jacqueline was eating alone in a restaurant because her husband Jim was out of town. Suddenly she noticed the waitress seating a woman directly across the room from her. She recognized the woman immediately because she had accepted Christ several months ago, had joined Jacqueline's church and had been attending the Singles Ministry with which Jacqueline and her husband were working.*

*When Jacqueline noticed that the woman was alone, she decided to invite the woman to join her at her table. As they talked, Jacqueline learned that Beverly had just completed a master's degree in business administration from the local university, and was a pianist. Before long, Beverly was in tears. She said that seeing Jacqueline had reminded her of the fact that she had been running from the Lord.*

*She began to talk about how frustrated she was. She wanted to get married but couldn't find a suitable mate. Beverly said that she had been engaged to a man who didn't have as much education as she did. He was very traditional and insisted that, when they married, she should not pursue her career but should plan on having more children than his father had. His father had 12 children. He didn't understand the Black civic organizations she had joined, and had said that she was too involved with "that Black stuff." After the novelty of being engaged wore off, Beverly began to resent the fact that her former fiance rarely listened to her and really knew very little about her.*

*She soon realized that she didn't really love this man but got involved with him because of social pressure. Since she ended the engagement, she had been very lonely. She mentioned the "Black male shortage" and how "spoiled" the educated Black men she knew seemed to be, because of it. She said that most such men claimed that they were in "demand." Therefore, according to these men, Black women should be willing to give up their bodies on demand. Otherwise Black men would seek white women whom they imagined would give up their bodies more easily. The men warned that if this happened they said it would make life even worse for educated Black women.*

*Facing this line of argument, and the grim statistics that seemed to support it, Beverly had grown weak and frustrated. She was afraid to continue her Christian life. Wouldn't being a Christian mean that she couldn't have sex outside of marriage? None of the men she knew would put up with that from her. She hadn't been to church for the past two weeks because she had been spending Saturday night with a man she called an arrogant "peacock." Tonight, he had abandoned her for his other woman, saying that she couldn't expect any man to have only one woman. She was frustrated with this man, but felt she had to hold onto him. At least he had a degree and a job, she said. She felt that she might be able to change him. Then maybe he would marry her one day.*

*As Jacqueline sat listening, she silently prayed that she would be able to help Beverly decide to follow*

*through on her original commitment to live a new life
in Christ.*

Beverly is hurting from frustration. She finds herself in one of
the many types of situations currently causing frustration in the
Black community. Frustration is being experienced by people
both within and outside of church families. Frustration threatens
to draw many away from the body of Christ to lifestyles that are
different from those to which God has called them. The circumstances causing this may seem, on the surface, to be insur-
mountable. However, it is the purpose of this chapter to point the
way from frustration to Christ. The chapter highlights some of
the options that God has for frustrated people. Hopefully the
contents will help ministers, counselors, lay leaders and friends
who want to help such people find new fulfillment in Christ.

## An Example of a Frustrated Person in Scripture

Jonah was a frustrated man. God had pointed him in one
direction, but he wanted to go in a different direction. In spite of
heroic efforts, Jonah found himself unable to take the direction
that he had charted for himself. In his frustration, he found himself in the dark and dangerous belly of a whale. However, due to
circumstances beyond his control, he ultimately found himself in
the place where God wanted him to be.

## from Scripture

**Jonah 1:1** Now the word of the Lord came unto Jonah the son
of Amittai, saying,

**2** Arise, go to Nineveh, that great city, and cry against it; for
their wickedness is come up before me.

**3** But Jonah rose up to flee unto Tarshish from the presence of
the Lord, and went down to Joppa; and he found a ship going to
Tarshish: so he paid the fare thereof, and went down into it, to
go with them unto Tarshish from the presence of the Lord.

**4** But the Lord sent out a great wind into the sea, and there was a mighty tempest in the sea, so that the ship was like to be broken.

**5** Then the mariners were afraid, and cried every man unto his god, and cast forth the wares that were in the ship into the sea, to lighten it of them. But Jonah was gone down into the sides of the ship; and he lay, and was fast asleep.

**6** So the shipmaster came to him, and said unto him, What meanest thou, O sleeper? arise, call upon thy God, if so be that God will think upon us, that we perish not.

**7** And they said every one to his fellow, Come, and let us cast lots, that we may know for whose cause this evil is upon us. So they cast lots, and the lot fell upon Jonah.

**8** Then said they unto him, Tell us, we pray thee, for whose cause this evil is upon us; What is thine occupation? and whence comest thou? what is thy country? and of what people art thou?

**9** and he said unto them, I am an Hebrew; and I fear the Lord, the God of heaven, which hath made the sea and the dry land.

**10** Then were the men exceedingly afraid, and said unto him, Why hast thou done this? For the men knew that he fled from the presence of the Lord, because he had told them.

**15** So they took Jonah, and cast him forth into the sea: and the sea ceased from her raging.

**17** Now the Lord had prepared a great fish to swallow up Jonah. And Jonah was in the belly of the fish three days and three nights.

**2:1** Then Jonah prayed unto the Lord his God out of the fish's belly.

**2** And said, I cried by reason of mine affliction unto the Lord, and he heard me; out of the belly of hell cried I, and thou heardest my voice.

**4** Then I said, I am cast out of thy sight; yet I will look again toward thy holy temple.

**9** But I will sacrifice unto thee with the voice of thanksgiving; I will pay that that I have vowed. Salvation is of the Lord.

**10** and the Lord spake unto the fish, and it vomited out Jonah upon the dry land.

**3:1** And the word of the Lord came unto Jonah the second time, saying,

**2** Arise, go unto Nineveh, that great city, and preach unto it the preaching that I bid thee.

**3** So Jonah arose, and went unto Nineveh, according to the word of the Lord. Now Nineveh was an exceeding great city of three days' journey.

**4** And Jonah began to enter into the city a day's journey, and he cried, and said, Yet forty days, and Nineveh shall be overthrown.

**5** So the people of Nineveh believed God, and proclaimed a fast, and put on sackcloth, from the greatest of them even to the least of them.

**10** And God saw their works, that they turned from their evil way; and God repented of the evil, that he had said that he would do unto them; and he did it not.

## What Is Frustration?

According to *Webster's Dictionary*, frustration is "a deep chronic sense or state of insecurity and dissatisfaction arising from unresolved problems or unfulfilled needs." Frustration is the feeling that something is missing from one's life. It is the awareness that the joy once experienced in one's Christian life is gone. Frustration is felt when a person comes to church Sunday after Sunday and goes away feeling empty and void. It is the feeling one has when one has not found fulfillment in work and when one has not found happiness at play.

Many circumstances can trigger frustration. It can result from unfulfilled human relationships. These are the frustrations everyone feels from time to time. Other frustrations result from the racial, economic, and political oppression which impact on the Black community and which affect nearly every African American to some extent or another. In these cases, frustration can result from anxiety over unachieved goals and unfulfilled desires. Other circumstances triggering frustration can evolve when a person tries to achieve some legitimate goal of happiness in a way that is not directed or sanctioned by the Lord.

**Frustration in human relationships.** Sometimes frustration comes from being unable to develop fulfilling human relationships. Often these unfulfilling relationships develop because a person is not happy with him/herself. Because the person is unhappy with him/herself, s/he does not believe that s/he can be happy with anyone else.

People who are frustrated in human relationships often complain that something is missing in their lives. They may complain that their husband or wife does not understand them or is insensitive to them. They may also complain that they are unable to relate within their families, to brothers, sisters, or parents. Parents of teenagers who are unable to master appropriate parenting skills often experience this type of frustration.

Frustration in human relationships can result when one is trying to adjust to retirement and feels that s/he can never replace the fulfillment once received from working within one's chosen vocation. Older parents may complain about the children having grown up and the sound of emptiness that is now in their homes. Frustrations experienced during a divorce are also in this category.

The gradual disintegration of the Black family is also causing frustration of this type. In middle income as well as lower income Black families, there has been a gradual breakdown in communication between parents and children and between the children themselves. Sometimes the parents are so busy trying to "make ends meet" that they rarely have time for their children or for each other. Role conflicts between husband and wife result, and conflicts with children result because people within the same

**140**

family do not really know one another.

Frustrations in human relationships do not occur solely within family units, however. Single people experience frustrations in communicating with one another. On one level, Beverly, in the introductory vignette is suffering from this type of frustration. Unable to locate a man with whom she feels compatible enough to marry, she is frustrated. Jonah experienced frustration when he was unable to gain sympathy from his crew members. He experienced it again, in Nineveh, when he was unable to control the fact that the people repented of their sins, and God decided not to destroy them (Jonah 1:8-11; 4:1-3).

**Frustration over unachieved goals.** A person can seek to fulfill a basic human goal but can find that the goal seems elusive. This type of frustration results from such problems as not being able to locate employment to support one's family. Frequently this problem results when factories move overseas and department stores close, plunging many honest, hardworking people into poverty.

Not being able to gain access to training and higher education can also trigger frustration. This problem has become more common following the cutbacks in supports for higher education by a conservative national administration, and the cancellation of such programs as the Basic Educational Opportunity Grants and others. Not being able to locate finances that can overcome these obstacles leads to frustration. A resulting general lack of mobility within the society also leads to frustration. Frustration can become intense when a person feels powerless over the circumstances that are thwarting his/her progress.

As mentioned earlier, many of the circumstances leading to this type of frustration are the results of racial, economic, and political oppression that impact the Black community as a whole, and individuals within the Black community in particular. Losing one's job due to racism, becoming homeless and not being able to break out of its cycle of despair, and dealing with a social service agency such as welfare which seems un-

**141**

responsive to a person's needs are all examples of situations that lead to this type of frustration.

When people become frustrated, they often blame themselves for not achieving certain goals. As the person starts blaming him/herself, s/he may also develop a negative self-image. Then it becomes difficult for them to accept themselves as God made them.

When a person is suffering from these types of problems, the person may seriously question various aspects of him/herself. On a sometimes subconscious level, the person might ask him or herself why God made the person the way he/she is. They might question the very motivation for their creation. They may wonder why they look the way they do, act the way they act, or think the way they think. In fact, the frustrated person may, on a deep subconscious level, believe that either through an accident of the environment, or through heredity, they are now irreversibly who they are. They may resent the fact that they had no control over it and may really want no part of it now.

This type of frustration can lead to unyielding passion, unbridled desire, uncontrollable anger or unexplicable hatred, unwarranted insecurity and unwanted impulsiveness.

Some frustrated people may even desire to change the color of their hair, skin or eyes, in order to feel more accepted in their own eyesight. All of these actions are expressions of a need for love and affirmation. Frustration often triggers a sense of needing to belong. However, in some cases it triggers a need to be alone, in order to exclude others from one's world.

On one level, Beverly, in the introductory case study, is experiencing this type of frustration. Due to circumstances beyond her control, Black women outnumber Black men. The circumstances leading to the mortality rates among Black men were not manufactured by Beverly. Beverly does not control the type of psychological problems that some Black men may develop because of the advantage they perceive themselves to have over Black women in the "dating game."

Beverly is also not in control of the relative numbers of Black men who have educational backgrounds and political orientations that would cause them to be incompatible with a woman with Beverly's interests. It would be quite easy for Beverly to blame herself for these situations, and attempt to change herself from the person God made and saved, to fit some other image that she feels makes her more acceptable to others and perhaps more acceptable to herself.

Similar types of problems are encountered by Black men. For the most part, they do not control many of the factors that lead to their unemployment, and they are not in control of the factors that cause such large numbers of them to be unable to experience mobility within society.

**Frustration from trying to avoid God.** When faced with some of the situations outlined above, many Christians, in a desperate attempt to solve the problems they face, are tempted to try solutions that are not sanctioned by God. Many even leave the church, running from God, attempting to solve their problems without Him. Some have once heard the voice of the Lord taking them in one direction, but initially they are not attracted to that direction, lacking faith in God's ability to provide.

Jonah is a classic example of this type of struggle with God. Jonah did not want to go to Nineveh. Nineveh had a bad reputation. It was a carefree, sin capitol (Jonah 3:3). It had the types of problems that disgusted Jonah (Nahum 2:1--3:19; Zephaniah 2:13-15; Jonah 1:2; 3:3-4). To Jonah, Tarshish must have been much more glamorous, and he thought he could be much happier there. Therefore, he decided to ignore God's voice and take a path that was not sanctioned by God. That is how he eventually found himself in the dark belly of a whale.

In a manner of speaking, Beverly, in the introductory vignette, also finds herself in the "dark belly of a whale." In her attempt to take a path not sanctioned by God, she encounters the same frustration Jonah did as he hid in the basement of the ship. While taking this path, Beverly finds herself in a relationship that could destroy her emotionally and spiritually.

Another example of this type of frustration occurs when Christian young people get caught in the cycle of having babies too soon and depending on welfare and A.D.C. Another example is either "doing" and/or selling drugs, etc., in order to cope with serious financial problems.

## Helping People Who Are Frustrated

There are a number of basic guidelines that a counselor can use in helping people who are frustrated. Frustration, to a large extent is a spiritual problem or dilemma, particularly for the Christian. Therefore, at the most fundamental level, it must be addressed from a spiritual vantage point. Spiritually speaking, frustrated counselees need to learn to appreciate themselves as God has created them. The counselee also needs a deeper faith in God. The counselee needs to be encouraged to hold on to his/her Christian beliefs and s/he needs to learn to rejoice in the midst of difficult circumstances. To make a long story short, the frustrated person needs a fresh touch from God.

However, an effective counselor will attempt to go beyond strictly spiritual counseling, and try to help the counselee address some of the problems triggering the frustration. The effective counselor will also attempt to assist the frustrated counselee in finding alternative goals, and in locating an avenue of freedom from the problem.

**Learning to appreciate oneself as God's creation.** As mentioned earlier, when people become frustrated, they often blame themselves for not achieving certain goals. It was also mentioned that this may lead to intense emotional feelings such as uncontrollable anger, hatred, insecurity, and unwarranted aggressiveness. The frustrated person, looking at the thwarted goal and undesirable behaviors which his/her frustration provokes, often begins to reject him/herself.

In helping a counselee who is suffering from this problem, it is important for the counselor to help the person separate him/herself from the situation that is causing the frustration. The person can be shown that most situations now causing frustration in the Black community can be traced directly or indirectly to the entire history of slavery of Black people and to current forms of racial oppression. Quite a few of these situations may be outside the control of the counselee.

In helping the counselee develop a healthy respect for him/herself in spite of these situations, it may be useful to discuss with the counselee the story of the Ethiopian Eunuch (Acts 8:26-39). The Ethiopian Eunuch, in many ways, was affected by circumstances outside his control. He was an Ethiopian, one of the sun-kissed children of mother Africa. However, he was a eunuch and as such had been surgically castrated. Thirdly, he was a convert to Judaism. All of these factors, in themselves, were ones he either inherited or was compelled to assume.

However, in spite of all of these obstacles, including the fact that he could not achieve the natural goals of loving a wife and being a father, this man had set other goals for himself. He had become in charge of the finances of Ethiopia. He had become a certified public accountant of his day.

However, this regal, noble, unapologetically Jewish and unashamedly Black man did something else, of even more significance. He discovered a new identity for himself. We see him in Scripture, sitting in the back of his chauffeur-drawn chariot, reading the Word of God. The Lord used His Word to show this man who he was in God's eyesight. The Lord, through His Word, showed the Eunuch that there was something very special about what he and the Lord had in common. The Lord shared with the eunuch the experience of being oppressed by the society in which He lived. The passage he was reading (Isaiah 53) told the eunuch that Jesus Himself had been led as a sheep to the slaughter and as a shearer was silent and did not open His mouth. In His humiliation, He was deprived of justice, and who could speak of His descendants, for His life was taken from the earth.

Acts 8:30-39 tells us that, once Philip explained to the eunuch who Jesus was, the eunuch was baptized and then went back to Ethiopia rejoicing in the Lord, with a new identity as a Christian. It is important to point out to the counselee that this man, although frustrated in such goals as sexual intimacy and fatherhood, did not allow this to shape his identity. He looked beyond these circumstances to discover who he really was. He developed a healthy appreciation for himself and for his Creator. One of the outcomes was that he went back to Ethiopia and (either directly or indirectly), was responsible for establishing the first extensively organized Christian church in the world, the Coptic church.

This story is loaded with implications for a person such as Beverly in the introductory case study of this chapter. Beverly can be shown that her primary identity does not have to be connected with whether she is in a sexually intimate relationship with a man, or whether she bears children. Her identity as a woman is beyond the biological functions of her body. She must look beyond the society which seeks to castrate her and look to Jesus who is ready to provide her with an entirely new identity that He, rather than the world system defines. She must learn to see herself as God's creation, with a purpose in life that He can give her. Similar parallels can be drawn with counselees experiencing frustration from other sources.

**Developing deeper faith in God.** There is a cure for frustration. It is not a new cure. It has been around as long as the disease. It is not an expensive cure. It doesn't really cost a cent. It is available to anyone who asks for it. The name of the cure is faith. That is what Matthew 17 is about: faith. Faith can move mountains. Faith can right relationships. Faith can transform individuals and reform institutions.

The words of the song sung by Vanessa Belle Armstrong are certainly true. One must have faith to remove the unmovable, to see the invisible and to fight the unbeatable. Faith can conquer anything. Matthew 17 tells us that a man had an epileptic son, and he took him to the disciples but they could not heal him. So they took him to Jesus. Many of us are like this man.

We've taken our problems to everyone else to no avail, and finally we bring them to Jesus. If we would only listen to the words of the following old hymn, we would know where we should take our problems: "What a friend we have in Jesus! All our sins and grieves to bear. What a privilege to carry everything to God in prayer."

Many of us are also like the disciples who took the epileptic man to Jesus. They did not realize it was not who they were that would enable them to do great things, but that it was whose they were! It was not their goodness that would bring about healing and other miracles. It was their faith in Jesus!

Once the counselor has diagnosed that the counselee's problem has to do with faith, the counselor is in a position to give the counselee a prescription. Tell the counselee to take some heaping doses of prayer each day and to be sure to let the counselor know when faith begins to do its healing work. A little bit of faith goes a long way. Jesus told His disciples that if they had faith the size of a mustard seed they could tell a mountain to move and it would move.

The counselee doesn't have to have faith as strong as Abraham or Isaac. All he has to have is a little faith, about as much as Paul had, in order to look at the decaying ghetto around him/her and see a thriving community coming into being. A little faith can cause a person to look at a vacant lot and see a new building rising on it. A little faith can cause a counselor to look at the discouragement and disillusion of a counselee and see dedication and faithfulness coming into being. With a little faith, a preacher can look around at empty pews and see people standing against the walls and lined up outside the church to get in to hear what thus saith the Lord! A little faith goes a long way! However, be sure to tell the frustrated counselee that faith is not faith until s/he puts it to work. If the person has enough faith,

**147**

God will change the problem, and he will the change the person, too! Faith can be a cure for frustration!

**Encouraging the counselee to hold on.** When frustration grips a person's life, rational thinking sometimes departs. When a person is overcome by the reality of what appears to present endless dangers, s/he often forgets the ever presence of God. Frustration can be disarming and paralyzing. Frustration can control a person. Frustration can destroy a person.

This is why it is so important for the counselor to encourage the person over and over, to hold on to his/her Christian faith, and not abandon it for non-Christian solutions to problems. The story of the disciples, in the boat, amidst a life-threatening storm (Luke 8:22-25) is a good one for illustrating the need to hold on to our faith.

The disciples did not anticipate that the storm would arise. Neither did they expect Jesus to go to sleep, undisturbed, during the storm. Often frustration can intensify when a person feels that God has "gone to sleep" on them in the midst of despair. In frustration, a person can think that God does not hear the person's cries. This was certainly the case with the disciples when the storm of wind came down on the lake and the boat was filling with water.

When they went to Jesus and said, "Master, Master, we are perishing", their very words indicated they were unaware of the person with whom they were sailing. So many times a frustrated person will abandon hope and lose faith because the person has forgotten who is the Captain of the ship of life. However, it is important for the Christian not to get entrapped by the threat of failure and be overcome by waves of desperation. It is important to "hold on" and watch the Lord bring calm into the situation.

Problems may seem greater than resources. Winds of trouble may seem raging out of control. However, the counselee must be encouraged to slip his/her hand into the wheel of trust when his/her boat is rocking on the sea of confusion. Tell them, "Don't jump ship!" Counselees must be encouraged not to put faith in

**148**

the vessel in which they are traveling, but to place faith in God. The counselee must be encouraged not to put faith in the rudder of riches, in the oar of ability or in the motor of one's mind. Otherwise, when all of those things fail, the frustrated person will find him/herself floundering hopelessly in the midst of the storm.

Frustrated people must realize that God didn't bring them this far to abandon them. God has already brought them over many mountains and through many valleys. Encourage them to "hold on" because the Lord may be using their storm to prepare them for a special work that He has for them to do. Doing a great work for the Lord requires faith. Faith must be tested and tried in a storm. Then it becomes faith that is built on nothing less than Jesus' blood and righteousness.

The counselee must learn to "hold on" because help is always at hand. The lifeline is not just sitting there, disconnected, it is extending from the counselee's little boat into the sky. The counselee may not be able to see where the lifeline is going, but s/he can know that it is going upward. It will not be long before the storm clears and the great ocean line appears. However, the counselee must hold on!

**Rejoicing in the midst of difficult circumstances.** One of the spiritual principles the frustrated person needs to practice is rejoicing in the midst of difficult circumstances. A good model to use, in illustrating how this works, is the Apostle Paul. When Paul says, in Philippians 4:4, to always rejoice in the Lord, he is writing with a historic vision of a sinful past.

His own past was wrought with hot-headed fanaticism and insensitivity to beliefs. However, Paul is also writing with a harsh reality of a painful present. Paul is in prison. He writes from the anguishing setting of a Roman jail cell. There is no executive desk or cushioned chair, but the empty barrenness of a first century penitentiary.

When Paul writes to the Philippians and to us today, from this setting, he is not speaking with the glee that emanates from one who is experiencing no suffering and feeling no pain. He is not referring to the empty happiness that is temporary. The type of rejoicing about which Paul speaks is a kind that is unconcerned about specific situations or circumstances. This type of rejoicing can be sustained through fire and flood. It can be experienced both in season and out of season.

This type of rejoicing is not dictated by feeling, but will give a person a feeling. It is not based on sentimentality, but it can make a person sentimental. This type of rejoicing is different from what a person does at a football game or at a graduation or carnival. It is different because it is not predicated on any present external circumstances, but is the result of a historical theological occurrence. It is the result of internal spiritual activity.

We rejoice in the Lord because of what Jesus did on Calvary and because of what the Holy Spirit is doing in the person's heart at the moment. A rejoicing Christian has a particular character. S/he is gentle (Galatians 5:22), and s/he avoids gossiping and "tattle telling." The rejoicing Christian is difficult to anger over trifling things. S/he doesn't "sweat the small stuff," but reserves anger in order to utilize it to right injustice and correct inequality.

Paul also says, in Philippians 4:6, that the rejoicing Christian will be "anxious for nothing", knowing that the Lord is at hand. This attitude will naturally lead to confidence in heavenly providence, not in confidence in human protection. It will lead to confidence in divine intervention. This is not confidence in who one's friends are, but confidence in whom your faith is in. The latter type of confidence is sustaining. That type of confidence can uplift and cause the Christian to rejoice. It is not confidence in what one sees, but confidence in the fact that "his eye is on the sparrow, and I know he watches me!"

Another characteristic of the rejoicing Christian is prayerfulness. In Philippians 4, Paul says that the rejoicing Christian should, by prayer and supplication, let his/her requests be made known unto God. This doesn't mean the Christian should be prayerful on Sundays only, but all during the week. A prayerful person knows that God hears and God answers prayer. S/he does not take blessings for granted, but thanks God!

If the Christian practices what Paul presents in Philippians 4, then s/he will experience peace. Verse 7 says that "the peace of God, which surpasses all understanding, will guard your hearts and minds through Christ Jesus." Prayer is another cure for frustration!

**Getting a "fresh touch" from God.** God wants to give the frustrated person a fresh touch. From the beginning of time, the touch of the hand has had power. We touch in greeting, we touch in parting, we touch in loving, we touch in scolding, we touch in fighting, and we touch in teaching. We touch in healing, we touch in building, we touch in comforting, and we touch in rejoicing. In every significant act of life, we touch. The touch of the hand has power and import.

In the early church, laying on of hands by the apostles signified the imparting of the Spirit of God. We lay on hands in blessing, baptism, confirmation and ordination. In Psalm 80, we find the Children of Israel asking God to lay His hand upon them, His chosen people. Even the people of God need a fresh touch sometimes. You see, the Children of Israel had turned from the Lord and in their meandering had found the emptiness that results from a life without God.

Every morning, when we wake up, we need to fall on our knees and, after thanking God, we need to ask the Lord for a fresh touch. We need to say, "Father, I stretch my hand to Thee. No other help I know. If Thou withdraw Thyself from me, whither shall I go?"

This past week, I worked hard giving my best to the Master. I had some successes and I had some failures. I had some "ups" and I had some "downs." I did some good and I did some wrong. However, I made my way to the throne of God this morning. I came not just wanting, not just expecting, not just desiring, but needing a fresh touch from my Father's hand.

**151**

What the Psalmist is saying, in Psalm 80, is, "With Your hand on my shoulder, Lord, we can't turn back anymore. Revive us and we'll sing Your praises. Revive us and we'll preach the Gospel. Revive us and we'll teach Your Word. Revive us and we'll serve Your people. Revive us and we'll feed the hungry, clothe the naked and house the homeless. Revive us and we'll call on Your name!" No more meaningless messages, no more spiritless singing, no more pitiful praying, no more dead worship. A touch of the Lord will make a difference!

If your religion doesn't make you feel good, then something is still missing in your life and you need a fresh touch from God. A fresh touch from the Lord is another cure for frustration.

**Setting alternative goals.** As mentioned earlier, the effective counselor will, in addition to providing spiritual counseling, attempt to help the counselee deal with the sources of the frustration. One of the ways of doing this is to help the counselee establish alternative goals. Sometimes we have goals that are not God's goals for us, and this is the source of our frustration.

Jonah wanted to go to Tarshish. He wanted to avoid Nineveh. However, God wanted to use Jonah's life in Nineveh. Beverly, in the introductory case study, wants a husband. However, God has called Beverly into the Community of Faith to serve Him there. Beverly wants to flee God to pursue a goal that may not be God's goal for her, particularly not for the moment.

A counselor can help a person such as Beverly to discover gifts and strengths of which she is not aware. Then s/he can guide Beverly into using these gifts and strengths in the church and in the community. In this way, Beverly becomes an instrument whereby human lives are healed and broken spirits are repaired. In Beverly's case, she is a trained musician. Certainly this gift is needed in the church. She also has business administration skills. Perhaps there is a place for her in the music ministry, on the trustee board, or in some other ministry in the church. This is a far cry from the destructive role that she had been carving for herself in the cold and rejecting "dating game"

**152**

of the current evil world system. This path would lead to self-destruction. However, God's path would lead to renewal of life.

As Beverly sees the power of God working through her to help others, she can more easily ask God to help her find fulfillment in His service, that she would not be able to find married to an unsaved man. Aligning one's goals with God's goals for one's life is another cure for frustration!

It is so important that African Americans and other minorities who are frustrated by this world's oppressive and racist system, develop alternative goals for their lives. It is a mistake to set one's goals according to soap operas and the "silver screen" of Hollywood. It is much more satisfying to set one's goals according to the Word of God.

The Black church needs the talents and skills of all its members. It is through focusing on God's program, rejoicing in the Lord, and seeking the Lord for personal needs, that a frustrated person begins to experience real relief from the frustrations of this world.

The Black church has always had this role in the Black community. As a community of faith, we need to continue this healing ministry on into the 21st century.

**Finding an avenue of freedom from the problem.** The counselor and the church can also help frustrated persons find an avenue of relief from their problem. There are many church and community resources that the church can use to relate to the whole person (body, mind and spirit). Often people who need these resources do not have the information to access them. This is where the church can play an important role.

Counselors might develop a file of community and church resources to which a person can be referred for meeting specific needs. For example, if a person doesn't have a job, the church can sometimes find a means of employing the person. The community of faith can certainly create job ladders within the church itself. The church can employ more people for lower wages, and the employment itself can provide skills and "on-the-job training".

The church can also be instrumental in helping single people (of all ages) who are frustrated by loneliness. Many churches have formed singles' ministries which provide fellowship and community service projects for singles of their congregation. There is no reason that networks of such singles' groups could not be formed between churches. Some might even take the form of interdenominational groups. This would allow single people to meet one another and find fulfilling relationships with other people, regardless of whether such relationships result in marriage partnerships.

It is also possible to refer people to agencies outside of the church for help in achieving goals such as locating a job, gaining access to higher education, accessing health care (both physical and emotional), and accessing shelter (if homeless). The church can direct people to food pantries or can establish soup kitchens so that hungry people can be fed. Some churches have collected used clothing and distributed free clothing to people who need it. Other churches have established tutorials to help people obtain G.E.D. (General Educational Development) certificates. All of these actions are part of helping the person find the means of being freed from problems that are frustrating him/her.

**Summary.** This chapter has focused on helping frustrated people. It has presented spiritual principles for helping the person deal with frustration. These include: a) learning to appreciate oneself as God's creation; b) developing deeper faith in God; c) holding on to one's faith; d) rejoicing in the midst of difficult circumstances; and e) getting a fresh touch from God. The chapter has also presented several other ways of dealing with the sources of frustration. These include setting alternative goals and finding a means of freeing oneself from the problem causing the frustration.

# CASE STUDY

*INSTRUCTIONS: The exercise below allows you to apply principles presented in this chapter to a case study involving a person who is hurting from frustration. The first five exercises are "discovery" questions, followed by a summary question. The sixth exercise asks you to summarize and apply information you gained in the first five exercises. The seventh exercise asks you to make a personal application of the principles you learned in this chapter.*

## SCOTT

*Brother Daniels was driving along Payne Street near his church when he noticed Scott standing on the corner with some other young men. All of them seemed to be aimlessly staring into space. Brother Daniels pulled over to the curb, let his window down and called Scott to the car. He hadn't seen Scott for over a year, and he wondered why the young man had stopped coming to Youth Meeting.*

*When Scott came over to the car, Brother Daniels opened the door and invited him to get in so that they could talk. It was then that Scott told him what had happened to him. Scott had just been released from jail a few months ago, where he had spent six months. Scott was very depressed, because he had spent time in jail for something that he hadn't done.*

*Apparently he was working at a sales job in a department store when the incident that led to his jail sentence took place. On that day, his cousin, who was visiting him from out of town, pushed Scott into a white woman who was standing near his work area. The woman thought she was being attacked, so she started defending herself. Scott was arrested, and his cousin ran away, refusing to come to Scott's defense. By the time of his trial, Scott's cousin had left town.*

*Since Scott had been out of jail, he had been unable to find a job. He didn't have any money, and spent most of his time "hanging out" with friends on the corner. He was beginning to feel like a bum. He had worked very hard to finish high school and at one time had aspirations to go to college. One of the things he never wanted to happen was to have a prison record.*

*Recently, he had tried to enroll in school at a local college, but he could not locate any scholarships or a job that would pay the expenses. He mentioned that he was becoming desperate. Several of his friends had decided to sell or deliver drugs in order to "make ends meet." As a Christian, he really didn't want to get involved with this, but he didn't know how long he could hold out.*

## 1. Holding on

The frustrated person should not abandon his/her Christian principles in order to solve the problems causing the frustration.

a. What is one reason for holding on to one's faith in spite of difficulties of the moment? (Philippians 1:27-28)

b. What is another reason for maintaining one's faith in spite of difficulties? (Hebrews 3:12-13)

c. What evidence is there that Jesus understands how frustrated people feel when they are tempted to turn away from a life-style to which God has called them? (Hebrews 4:14-15; Matthew 26:36-39)

d. Will everyone's behavior remain consistent with Christian beliefs in spite of persecution? (1 Timothy 4:1-2)

e. As a community of believers, how can we help one another to hold on to our faith in spite of difficulties? (Hebrews

**156**

10:23-39; 11:1-3)

f. SUMMARY QUESTION: How can the information from questions a-e above be used to help frustrated people such as Scott in the above case study?

## 2. Faith

One of the cures for frustration is looking beyond current circumstances and exercising faith in God.

a. Describe one person who exercised faith and obeyed God in spite of what could have been frustrating circumstances. (Hebrews 11:7; Genesis 6:1-9; 9:1-17)

b. Describe another person who exercised faith and obeyed God in spite of what could have been a frustrating circumstance. (Luke 1:1-24)

c. Describe yet another person who exercised faith in God in spite of what could have been a frustrating circumstance. (Hebrews 11:35; Luke 13:11-13)

d. Describe yet another person who exercised faith in God in spite of what could have been a frustrating circumstance. (John 21:1-14)

e. What is faith, and what is the basis of it? (Hebrews 11:1-3; 12:1-4)

f. SUMMARY QUESTION: How can the information from questions a-e above be used to help frustrated people such as Scott in the above case study?

## 3. Appreciating oneself

Often circumstances of this world send out messages to African Americans that are different from the messages that God sends.

a. What does God think of His people? (Ephesians 1:3-10)

b. What evidence is there, in the Word of God, that each person God created is a work of art? (Psalm 139:14-17)

c. What evidence is there that African Americans have just as much potential as other people? (12:1-14)

d. If a person comes upon hard times, is it because s/he is a bad person? (Job 1:1-22)

e. What evidence is there that God will not allow His people to perish? (John 3:16; Luke 15:11-32)

f. SUMMARY QUESTION: How can the information from questions a-e above be used to help frustrated people such as Scott in the above case study?

## 4. Rejoicing in the midst of difficulties

a. What is the proper response to have when we become frustrated by injustice? (Ephesians 4:26-28)

b. What evidence is there that God does not intend for His people to remain in oppressive and frustrating circumstances? (Luke 4:16-21)

c. What evidence is there that God will deliver those who are frustrated by financial problems? (Luke 12:22-32)

d. Why should the Christian rejoice in the midst of difficulties? (Hebrews 12:1-3; Romans 8:29)

f. SUMMARY QUESTION: How can the information from questions a-e above be used to help frustrated people such as Scott in the above case study?

## 5. Locating alternative goals

God often has goals for us that are different from the goals we have for ourselves.

a. How were God's goals for Paul different from Paul's goals for himself? (Acts 8:3; 22:4; 26:11; 9:3-9)

b. How were God's goals for John different from John's goals for himself? (Mark 1:20; 3:17; John 1:35-43; 19:26, 27; Revelation 22:20)

c. How were God's goals for Peter different from Peter's

goals for himself? (Matthew 4:18-22; Mark 1:16; Luke 5:10)

d. How were God's goals for Matthew different from Matthew's goals for himself? (Matthew 9:9-10; Mark 2:14-15; Luke 5:27-29)

e. How were God's goals for Mary Magdalene different from those that she and society may have had for her? (Luke 8:2; 23:49; Mark 16:1, 19; John 20:11-18)

f. SUMMARY QUESTION: How can the information from questions a-e above be used to help frustrated people such as Scott in the above case study?

## 6. SUMMARY EXERCISE

What are some specific ways in which the Community of Faith can develop employment opportunities for people such as Scott? Are there other ways that the Community of Faith can help people such as Scott to discover and develop their gifts and talents? As a group, compile a list of these possibilities.

## 7. PERSONAL APPLICATION

Are you frustrated? If so, use the principles and scriptural references in this chapter as a starting point for setting new goals and approaching life differently.

# CHAPTER SEVEN

# GRIEF

### Rev. William Butler

*It had been three weeks since Keith had first con-tacted the New Hope Counseling Center. He had al-ready canceled two appointments. Brother Jones, head of the counseling ministry, sat wondering whether Keith would keep this third appointment, when Keith walked through the door.*

*It was obvious that Keith was uncomfortable. Brother Jones could hear bitterness and anger in his voice, and it was difficult for him to get started. How-ever, with Brother Jones's help, he slowly described the event that led him into counseling.*

*It happened one cold, Friday afternoon, at his job, where he was foreman. In the sub-zero weather, he stood on the ramp at the back door of the small plant, watching two workers load paint onto a truck when suddenly the edge of the truck and ground below turned orange as the can of paint first fell to the ground and then rolled down the alley toward the street.*

*"I lost my temper," he said. "All I remember now is kicking the side of the truck over and over again, yell-ing and cursing. I was totally out of control."*

*Later that day, the plant manager called him into his office and told him that he was in danger of losing his job. The manager had received several complaints from the men Keith supervised and from other foremen. The complaints were about Keith's violent temper. The manager strongly advised Keith to seek counseling. Otherwise, he would be dismissed.*

*In the counseling sessions that followed, Keith described a very difficult childhood and a marriage that was now ending in divorce. At five years of age, his father had left him with his grandmother. His natural mother was ill at the time and his father thought his grandmother could care for him while his father sought more secure employment. Keith remembered feeling abandoned at the time.*

*Keith quickly became the center of his grandmother's attention. She was very warm and nurturant. However, when he reached 12 years of age, his grandmother died, leaving him feeling abandoned again. His parents returned for him at that time, and he went to live with them again. However, he never achieved the type of closeness with them that he felt with his grandmother, or that he had felt with his parents before they abandoned him.*

*When he became 19, he married, but soon problems in the marriage developed which never really improved. He complained that his wife was too dependent, except when raising the children was involved. He wanted the children to be independent, but she wanted them to be dependent. Therefore, he felt that she did not respect his authority. During the 15 years of the marriage, he had five affairs with other women. Sometimes he felt guilty about his behavior.*

*He had seen several counselors but never continued beyond the first few visits. When Brother Jones asked*

**162**

*Keith about his relationship with the Lord, Keith expressed distrust and fear that God would not forgive him for the affairs he had while he was married.*

Where are You, God? Why did You allow this to happen? If You had been there, my loved one would not have left me. These are some of the questions and thoughts that enter the minds of those who grieve. These questions and thoughts are not always on a conscious level. Sometimes they are buried beneath a sense of pain that is often masked by the person's attempts to lead a normal life. The grieving person is often unaware of the effects of the unattended grief on his/her life. However, unattended grief leads to unanticipated crises.

Keith, in the above story, is experiencing unattended grief. The losses of his natural mother, his natural father, his grandmother and his marriage are all sources of grief for Keith. He is unaware of the relationship between his unattended grief and the temper tantrums which have produced the crisis he is experiencing at work.

This chapter focuses on grief and how the Community of Faith and the lay counselor can support people as they travel through the grieving process. It presents information on how to attend to grief in productive ways, and how counselors can help people to avoid the type of pathology that can come from unattended grief.

## A Biblical Example of a Grieving Person

Job suffered losses in almost every area of his life. He experienced grief in response to each of these losses.

## from Scripture

**Job 1:1** There was a man in the land of Uz whose name was Job; and that man was perfect and upright, and one that feared God, and eschewed evil.

**2** And there were born unto him seven sons and three daughters.

**3** His substance also was seven thousand sheep, and three thousand camels, and five hundred yoke of oxen, and five hundred she asses, and a very great household; so that this man was the greatest of all the men of the east.

**13** And there was a day when his sons and his daughters were eating and drinking wine in their eldest brother's house:

**14** And there came a messenger unto Job, and said, The oxen were plowing, and the asses feeding beside them:

**15** And the Sabeans fell upon them, and took them away; yea, they have slain the servants with the edge of the sword; and I only am escaped alone to tell thee.

**16** While he was yet speaking, there came also another, and said, The fire of God is fallen from heaven, and hath burned up the sheep, and the servants, and consumed them; and I only am escaped alone to tell thee.

**17** While he was yet speaking, there came also another, and said, The Chaldeans made out three bands, and fell upon the camels, and have carried them away, yea, and slain the servants with the edge of the sword; and I only am escaped alone to tell thee.

**18** While he was yet speaking, there came also another, and said, Thy sons and thy daughters were eating and drinking wine in their eldest brother's house:

**19** And, behold, there came a great wind from the wilderness, and smote the four corners of the house, and it fell upon the young men, and they are dead; and I only am escaped alone to tell thee.

**20** Then Job arose, and rent his mantle, and shaved his head, and fell down upon the ground, and worshipped.

**21** And said, Naked came I out of my mother's womb, and naked shall I return thither: the Lord gave, and the Lord hath taken away; blessed be the name of the Lord.

**22** In all this Job sinned not, nor charged God foolishly.

**2:7** So went Satan forth from the presence of the Lord, and smote Job with sore boils from the sole of his foot unto his crown.

**3:1** After this opened Job his mouth, and cursed his day.

**2** And Job spake, and said,

**11** Why died I not from the womb? why did I not give up the ghost when I came out of the belly?

**12** Why did the knees prevent me? or why the breasts that I should suck?

**13** For now should I have lain still and been quiet, I should have slept: then had I been at rest,

**6:2** Oh that my grief were thoroughly weighed, and my calamity laid in the balances together!

**3** For now it would be heavier than the sand of the sea: therefore my words are swallowed up.

## What Is Grief?

All of life is a process of grieving. That is, life is a process of establishing primary attachments to significant others, and separating from significant others. To speak of life, in some ways, is to speak of grief. Grief is the tension that holds life and loss together. Grieving experiences are the most profound experiences of life. It is through the process of grieving that we become whole persons.

Grief is essentially our response to loss in life. It is a normal reaction to significant losses. The first such loss is the one we experience at birth, when we are separated from our mother's womb. The process of attachment, loss and grieving are continuous cycles which occur throughout life. Mitchell and Anderson, in their book, *All Our Losses and All Our Griefs*, have developed a frame for our discussion of loss.

There are many types of losses that result in the experience of grief. These losses can be classified under six general headings: relationship, material, psychological, functional, authority/responsibility, and systemic (Mitchell and Anderson, pp. 36-45). When a person experiences grief, it is usually due to at least two of these six types of losses. For example when Job, from Scripture grieves, he is grieving losses in all of the above categories.

The loss of a job involves psychological, authority, material and systemic losses. The loss of a spouse involves social, systemic, identity and material losses. The loss of a leadership position involves relational and systemic losses.

There are three basic stages of the grieving process. First there is the initial shock and numbness associated with the loss. Then there is denial and disorganization. Finally there is the reorganizational stage (Temes, p. 32).

**The Grieving process.** Initial shock or numbness may last from several weeks to several months. It is nature's way of protecting us from experiencing the full reality of the crisis. It is characterized by a person functioning primarily on a mechanical level and by his/her isolating him/herself from others (Temes, p. 32).

During the denial phase of grief, the person doesn't believe what has happened. At this point, anger and guilt are felt. Often the person says that s/he doesn't understand why God would allow this to happen. They search and wail, and search again, scanning their minds to discover what they could have done to prevent the loss from occurring.

During the denial period, there also is a great deal of ambivalence. Typically, the grief-stricken person reviews the "lost" relationship over and over again, and then begins to idealize the other person. The person may see only the good of the "lost" person and ignore his/her "not so good" traits. It may be difficult, at this stage of grief, for the person to internalize the whole person.

As mentioned above, grief is also characterized by disor-

**166**

ganization. Anger may come in greater frequency and should not be stifled. While searching and yearning the grief-stricken person becomes restless and cannot concentrate. The person wants to be fulfilled. He or she is searching for the lost loved one. This stage is also characterized by guilt. In the event of the death of someone who was ill for an extended period, the guilt often relates to a feeling of relief that the person is dead. It can also be related to unresolved conflicts between the person and the deceased, which the person wishes s/he had been able to resolve (Temes, p. 33).

Often, when the deceased has suffered for a long time, the griever experiences some relief that the person's suffering is over. The person may also experience some resentment toward the deceased for having been ill, resentment which wasn't faced before, but which is later a cause of guilt.

Denial may last for many months. It is characterized by loneliness, weeping, depression, loss of sleep and appetite, feeling sorry for oneself and hallucinating. Without a clear understanding, or proper support, the person can lapse into a personality disorder during this stage of grief (Temes, p. 33).

The reorganizing stage of grief begins as acceptance of the loss begins to occur. It is an attempt to review the relationship and complete the emotional ties with the deceased. Along with acceptance comes a redirection of one's energy toward the future. In some cases, this stage begins between the first and second anniversary of the loss.

The grieving person begins to expand his/her social network and develop a few new relationships. The person may even return to old organizations and responsibilities. This reorganizing period may continue for many months and weeks (Temes, p. 33). It is characterized by occasional peacefulness and less intense feelings.

The entire grieving process is not easy. It is very difficult. There is no general time limit. Much of the outcome depends on the strength of emotional coping mechanisms of the individual. The outcome will also depend upon the health of the individual prior to the loss. As mentioned above, there are several types of losses which lead to grief. These losses are discussed in more detail below.

**Relational losses.** The first primary relationship is between mother and child. As mentioned previously, the first relationship loss is the separation of the child from the mother's womb. However, there is a sense of loss that can occur as a result of problems that develop in the relationship between mother and child during infancy and early childhood. These problems themselves become experienced as losses or absences, which can trigger a type of grieving process in the child.

If a mother is too protective and stifling, or non-responsive to the child's needs for nurturance, it can result in the child, on a subconscious level, grieving the absence of a more healthy mother/child relationship. When the child does not get the proper nurturing it leads to anxiety and anger which is the beginning of the grieving process. The person is grieving for a nurturing relationship. Anger, sulking and aloofment are manifestations of the grief, which may extend into adulthood.

This person has not experienced successful attachment and separation into autonomy at the proper time in his/her developmental process. Therefore, the person's entire life involves scanning and seeking a soothing and nurturing primary relationship with others. Early marriages and multi-relationships are all results of an endless quest for the nurturing relationship that was missed during childhood.

If a young child is abandoned early in life, the resulting anxiety can lead to fears of annihilation and loss. Without appropriate coping mechanisms, the child constantly seeks a healthy mother/child relationship in other people. This needy child will have many more crises than will the child who has not been abandoned and who has been given adequate nurturance and allowed to develop into an autonomous being.

**168**

Other typical relationship losses are divorce, graduation, marriage, loss of a job, long vacations, periods of separation from others, unpredictable absences on the part of parents, being a latchkey child and the death of a loved one. After these losses, people experience grief. For many, the loss of the opportunity to share with, touch, argue with, and exchange emotions with significant others can be extremely painful (Mitchell and Anderson, p. 43).

Job, in the Scripture passage, experiences relational losses with the deaths of his children. Keith, in the opening case study, experiences relational losses upon abandonment by his parents, the death of his grandmother and the ending of his marriage in divorce.

**Material losses.** Many adults have significant and powerful attachments to material goods. The loss of objects with sentimental attachments and/or the separation from familial surroundings can lead to grief. Some typical losses in this category are the loss of one's home, a car that is stolen, and a lost or stolen watch or item of clothing which one received from a significant other.

The replacement of the material loss in many cases may only mask the grieving reaction. The fact is that the purchasing of a new item may suppress the feelings of grief. In many cases, the replacement object is never truly adequate.

One example of a person experiencing a material loss is a woman who lived in a house she inherited from her parents. The house burned to the ground, and the fire destroyed pictures and other objects of sentimental value. This woman found it difficult to refer to her new house as home. Another example is a woman whose dog, "Wrex" ran away when she was a child. She was living with her grandmother at the time and was the only child in the home. Wrex became her friend.

In adulthood, she confessed that she never allowed herself to become attached to any other dogs, even those her parents purchased to replace Wrex. Pets are talked about in a relational sense but often treated as objects and replaced. However, this person had grown attached to the pet in a strong relational way and grieved the loss strongly enough not to attempt to replace it. As a result of her inability to replace Wrex, she may suffer from unattended grief.

Pets are treated relationally, in that they are treated as though they are in many ways human beings. However, when pets die, they are treated as objects, in that they are seen as easily being replaced. In one sense the loss of a pet is a relational loss. However in another sense the loss is a material one.

Job experienced a material loss when his property was destroyed by fire. No doubt Keith, in the opening story, experienced a material loss when he was moved back and forth from his parents' home to his grandmother's home and separated from familial surroundings.

**Psychological losses.** A psychological loss is experienced internally. It carries with it a sense of sadness. A loss of an apparent/anticipated gain is experienced as a psychological loss. The resulting is often associated with the loss of an image that was connected to what is lost. Grief may result from the loss of a dream, a possibility, or a significant hope. It may result from the loss of a future life changing event.

The completion of a task or a job promotion can both be experienced as psychological losses, and can lead to grieving. When a politician becomes a professor, s/he may grieve. When one makes the transition from being single to being married, one may grieve. When a man or woman loses a job, s/he may grieve the loss of the image associated with the job.

When a mother or father become grandparents to a child born to an unwed teenaged daughter, the grandparents may grieve. Their grief has to do with the loss of their image as parents of a daughter who would not become a mother-too-soon. Such grandparents (particularly when they are religious) often grieve the lost opportunity to have a son or daughter who did not make the same mistake that they may have made in adolescence.

Job experienced a psychological loss as a result of losing the image and position he had as a wealthy, upright citizen of Uz. He was "demoted", so to speak, from that position to one of poverty, to the status of one who would call forth pity from others.

**Functional losses.** When any bodily function becomes crippled by disease or accident, the affected person grieves. Loss of sight and hearing are both in this category. The grief may be particularly acute when the person experiencing the loss becomes immobilized.

Any type of illness can provoke grief. The onset of drug addiction, AIDS, cancer, and temporary intellectual lapses all cause grief. The grieving reaction is in response to the loss of the sense of "I am self-sufficient" or "I can do it myself." The person experiencing a functional loss may express grief by isolating him/herself, venting anger, or displaying "touchiness" and vindictiveness. All of these behaviors are signs that the person is experiencing grief associated with a functional loss.

Job experiences a functional loss as he becomes ill and sores begin to cover his body, thus incapacitating him.

**Authority, role and responsibility losses.** The loss of one's social status can be internalized as a loss of responsibility, authority or a role. This type of loss is associated with changes in marital status, retirement, the selling of one's business, a demotion on one's job, or a promotion to a new responsibility. The role changes, friends, co-workers, partners and familiar surroundings are gone, and the longing for a previous life style associated with some of the above losses can produce grief.

People who experience this type of loss often express their grief by constantly talking about a previous life style or attempting to hold onto the loss in some way. One example is the widow who cannot bring herself to remove her husband's clothing from a closet so that the closet can be used for something else.

**171**

Job suffers from losing his former status as a parent and successful businessman. He also suffers a sense of loss of his former status as one who had not sinned and was righteous, because his friends continue to imply that his suffering must be due to his having sinned. Keith, in the case study, experienced a loss in his position as the center of attention when he returned to live with his parents after his grandmother's death.

**Systemic loss.** A change or the loss of a relationship with a system or institution often produces grief. The family is one such system of personal relationships. This system brings with it certain responsibilities and duties. When this system changes, and the associated responsibilities and duties change, then a sense of loss may be experienced, and grief may be provoked (Mitchell and Anderson, p. 47).

When a sibling leaves home for college, the military or married life, the family system may call for a drastic change in roles and responsibilities. The style of the family may need to adapt itself to the loss. Various family members may grieve the loss of former roles and the loss of the relationship they had with the sibling who has left.

Other institutions such as prison, mental hospitals, and social organizations are systems from which people can experience a sense of loss. When a person leaves prison or a mental hospital only to return over and over again, the person may be grieving a loss of the relationship to the system.

Other less obvious sources of systemic losses occur when one political party loses an election and the supporters of that party must adjust to a new party in office. New leadership in the church, or a pastor dying, resigning or being transferred may all be experienced by church members as systemic losses (as well as relational losses).

Both Keith and Job suffer from this type of loss. Job, upon losing his children, is forced into a situation where his family system must change from what it once was. Keith experiences this twice, as he is first taken out of his primary family system and forced into another one. Then he is taken out of that system, by the death of his grandmother, and forced into another one (his primary family as it exists eight years after his initial separation from it).

## How to Help People Who Grieve

As mentioned, grieving is a part of life. A key to recovery, however, can be found in the Community of Faith. Within this loving community, the lay person or minister can "partner" with the grieving person. This partnership can provide a productive and healthy recovery route. The Community of Faith can offer the person additional support through its many auxiliaries and activities. The local church can assist in the partnering process.

As counselors, the goal is to successfully "partner" the person through the grieving process. The counselor does not want to inhibit the grieving process, but wants to enable the person to progress through it. This means that the counselor must help the grieving person to: 1) learn to trust again; 2) achieve autonomy; 3) accept a measure of responsibility for coping; 4) put away false gods associated with the loss; and 5) help the person become mainstreamed again.

To be most helpful to a grieving person, the helper needs to understand grief and to understand him/herself as a fellow griever. It is important to understand one's personal responses to grief before partnering with someone who is grieving.

"Partnering" can be an important step in helping grieving persons who become productive again. Ministers, counselors and lay persons all can help in this process. The process matches the grieving person with one or more persons who have worked through their own grief, understand loss and are willing to help. These persons must "contract" (agree to walk together) through the dark tunnel of grief, in honesty and openness to the pain of loss; must reassure one another of confidentiality, and must be committed to venture together through each task and stage of struggle. They should agree not to leave any stone unturned if it might produce a healthier, more responsive person. Gaining awareness of one's self and the fact that most relationships in many ways are at least emotionally incomplete is an important step in the process. Reflecting one's faith, mirroring "the heart of God," and sharing one's own journey through the tunnel of grief will establish the foundation for healing, which is trust.

**Partnering during the initial shock/numbness stage.** At this initial point, what the grief-stricken person needs is emotional distance but physical closeness. They need a sense that people are "sitting with them", as Job's friends finally learned to "sit" with him in silence. The helpers must convey to the grieving person that they are "with" him/her (showing empathy).

During this stage, it is important to encourage the person to perform as many of his/her normal tasks as possible. These tasks can be therapeutic and may include decisions that concern the immediate problem of the loss (Temes, p. 29).

Job's friends made the initial mistake of trying to force Job to make rational sense out of his suffering before he was ready to do so. His wife also tried to encourage him to move forward and take actions that he was not prepared to take. This was not appropriate or helpful to Job.

Within the Community of Faith, the funeral and memorial services that might take place are very powerful rituals that help the person to eventually and successfully interpret grieving as a consequence of human love in a finite world. It also allows them to transcend their circumstances and hear the sacred promises of God.

These "rituals of ending" begin to speak of a new beginning. It is important to have rituals, in the Community of Faith, rather than mere ceremonies. Ritual, as opposed to ceremony, allows the grieving person to transcend the present and connect with the traditions of the past in order to qualify the future. Ceremonies, on the other hand, are mere repetitions of traditions which connect with the past but may not have the sacredness of changing

**174**

the present in a profound way, or of presenting any great hope and vision for the future.

It is important that the rituals of ending bring an interpretation that includes birth, life, death and rebirth on a continuum. The ritual of ending should inform the grieving person that the process of loss, attachment, separation, autonomy and rebirth occurs over and over again until a person is finally reattached, in a perfect way, to God.

**Partnering through the disorganization stage.** As mentioned before, the disorganization stage is characterized by expressions of anger, guilt, searching, wailing and a tendency to idealize the person who is lost. During this stage, the person needs empathetic responses from others. The person needs to mirror a person who cares. They need to be able to ventilate their feelings with a wide range of emotional responses without facing judgment from others.

Angry displays such as shouting and rage are to be expected. The person should not be judged but should be given empathetic support. Again, in order to help the person, the counselor must understand his/her grief and must have processed it, so that s/he can listen and provide "heart-to-heart" support.

Guilt is also characteristic of this stage. Unresolved guilt is a basic problem of grief. Guilt must be experienced and expressed so that the person can learn that loss had nothing to do with the person's wishes, words or hopes concerning the death of the loved one.

It is during this period, in particular, that the counselor needs to understand that the griever needs space and time to grieve. They must be allowed to grieve, free of the counselor's or the Community of Faith's expectations.

Family, friends, lay people and counselors alike must be open and receptive in offering unconditional support. This type of support allows the person to rehearse his/her feelings of doubt, fear and anger over and over. Actually, the person is moving toward a time when s/he can internalize a realistic image of the deceased person, rather than an idealized one. The person then moves away from the problems associated with worshiping the deceased.

Resistance to help may be felt very strongly here, but the counselor and the Community of Faith must continue to encourage. Grieving is a tunnel that one cannot go over or around and which one cannot avoid. One must go through it.

**Partnering through the reorganization stage.** Wholeness or reorganization is experienced with the help of a supportive community and lay counselors. The outcome of this stage is that the person returns to significant commitments and to his/her community. The person, during this stage, makes it through the grieving tunnel to the light.

The counselor might ask responsive and supportive questions. At this time, honest discussions concerning God are important. The person may need to reexamine his/her faith in a supportive community. When the person begins to do this, it is a healthy indication of progress through the tunnel.

As mentioned above, our task as counselors, psychotherapists and lay people alike is to help the person learn to trust again. The healthier we are as supportive persons, the easier it will be for us to respond to the healthy aspects of the grieving process and the griever's responses to us. Genuine concern, positive regard, and unconditional love are all healthy responses to the grieving person.

One of the outcomes of counseling would be that the grieving person achieves autonomy. The counselor's needs must not supersede those of the griever. Therefore, the counselor must be willing to allow the griever to become autonomous and functional. Eventually the griever must achieve a measure of responsibility for what is happening around him/her.

Then the griever must be encouraged to put away false gods. A false god is any object or devotion that is sought and seems to

**176**

offer immediate satisfaction or fulfillment in place of the deceased. The false god is false because it only leads to destruction and a reduction in the quality of life, love and existence. The griever must be encouraged not to fixate on the dead. Real life is with the Spirit of the living.

**Specific helps for relational losses.** The person who is grieving over a relational loss can be helped to establish new relationships within the Community of Faith. There are a number of ways to be helpful.

First of all, several people in the local church can be trained to coordinate ministries to people who are grieving. Deacons, ministers, and lay people can be trained to handle these roles. In fact, it would be ideal if, within every auxiliary, there are a few people who are trained to support people who are grieving.

It is common for people to come to church because they are in pain. Often such people join organizations to mitigate this pain. Trained, Christ-centered people can aid the person's healing process. However, it is important for people to deal first with their own difficulties in the area of grief. During the training process for deacons and others, it is important that the trainee be given the opportunity to explore and deal with his/her personal responses to relational losses and grief.

In developing such opportunities, the local church can invite professional Christian counselors, social workers and psychologists to conduct the training. Perhaps three or four people from each auxiliary could be invited for such training. The goal would be to develop the trainee's proficiency in being "with" and "partnering" people who are grieving. These sessions would provide them with information about the methodology and process of healing. We should understand "partnering" as an agreement ("contract") between the griever and support person to establish a working, supportive, and healthy relationship that will help the griever through the grieving process.

**Specific helps for material losses.** When a person suffers from a material loss, the person needs the opportunity to interpret the loss and ferret out its meaning for the future. In some instances, it may mean helping the person replace the lost object, if the replacement is important for the person's well-being.

A supportive Community of Faith can help a person become aware of the significance of the loss and adjust to the loss. A supportive environment can help the person travel through the stages of the tunnel of grief and see the light at the end of the tunnel.

Rituals of ending are important here, in that the religious motifs of renewal, separation, loss and rebirth all help the person interpret the loss and cope with it. The supportive community can listen to the stories attached to the items or persons that have been lost. The community can help them put the items away, so to speak, and return to normal activity. This process may take many months.

**Specific helps for psychological losses.** Psychological losses often involve the loss of image. For the person who is grieving a psychological loss, the person or thing lost in some way contributed to the image the person has of him/herself. A loss of the person or thing, then, also becomes a loss of that image.

When Job lost his property, cattle, sons and daughters, he also lost the image of being a wealthy citizen of Uz who lived above sin. From the story of Job, we learn that this type of tragedy affects both the just and the unjust. It affects those who belong to the church and those who do not. It affects those who have made a commitment to Christ and those who have not.

The Community of Faith can help a person who is experiencing a psychological loss in the area of image by helping the person develop a new image based on his/her spiritual gifts and the use of those gifts within the body of Christ. At this time, the church must convey to the person the idea that, "I am somebody!" The person must learn that he/she is important to the Lord, with or without the image the person once had. The person needs to be assured of his/her acceptance in the Community of Faith with or without the lost item or opportunity that contributed to a change in psychological image.

To the person who is grieving a psychological loss, the Community of Faith becomes an interpreter of possibilities of new life and hope. The lay person can help interpret the promises and can witness on behalf of the Faith community. This can reassure grievers that they, too, can become new beings. The church counseling service can certainly help in this respect.

**Specific helps for systemic losses.** Some losses involve being separated from an entire system composed of networks of human relationships, procedures, bureaucratic realities, etc. When people become separated from a system to which they have become accustomed, they experience grief.

The church family can help by becoming a new supportive system in the griever's life. The church, in most cases, needs to become much more deliberate about its ability to heal in this respect. Each member of the church needs to understand that s/he is called to the brotherhood and sisterhood of Christ and, if nothing else, must reflect Christ. They must reflect Christ through their ability to be "with" the grieving person. They must be willing to make honest, empathetic statements in support of those who are experiencing loss. They must help the person see the reality of his/her circumstances. This means both the loss and the promise of the future.

The church is one of the most prolific adaptive systems, when it comes to healing. The group within the church which a person joins, can be intentional regarding helping the person to reach spiritual maturity and social maturity as well. To become a supportive system to the person, the group which the person joins can make an effort to make that person an integral part of it. The person should be seen as belonging to a support system.

**Specific helps for losses of authority, roles and responsibilities.** As mentioned, some losses involve a loss of authority which one once had, a loss of a particular role that one had in the community, and/or a loss of responsibilities one once performed. Often this type of loss provokes grief.

There are many creative ways in which the church can come to the assistance of people who suffer from losses in this category. The basic goal here would be to provide the person with a means whereby new authority can be gained, with a new role and new responsibilities within the body of Christ. This is particularly important for Black men whom the world often robs of authority, functional roles and responsibilities.

One way of achieving this would be to establish a job resource bank or network within the church. The church would list jobs to be done in the church and the community. Some of these jobs might be paid positions, whereas some might be volunteer positions. This type of employment ministry would assist people in discovering how their gifts and talents relate to specific careers, jobs or tasks. The church can also write recommendations for the person based on past performance of a voluntary or paid position.

In the process of performing these jobs, the grieving person assumes a new role, new functions and new responsibilities, thereby reducing the intensity of authority, responsibility and role losses. These jobs restore dignity and self-esteem that may have been lost. In this way, the church says to the grieving person that the Community of Faith is for the people, by the people, and with the people, with God as their Shepherd.

The church has sources of power to help people who grieve, but these resources are not always being tapped. They are under-utilized. The church has the ability to build a network through its people in an intentional way, by providing opportunities for employment, reassessment and placement for persons who need help. This kind of ministry goes hand in hand with counseling.

**Summary.** In the final analysis, we are bonded to one another by the human spirit and strengthened by the source of all power--God. Therefore, at all times we are in a three-way connection. Any support or help offered to those in pain, is offered through us from God. No one can heal another, but as we open ourselves up to God's power, healing and renewal become ours.

This chapter has focused on how the local church in general and the lay counselor in particular can help people who are grieving. Grief has been described and six losses leading to grief have been defined. A biblical example of grief has been provided, and ways in which the local church can help the grieving person have been identified. The following is a case study and exercises which allow the reader to apply principles covered in this chapter.

## CASE STUDY

*INSTRUCTIONS: The exercise below allows you to apply principles presented in this chapter to a case study involving a person who is hurting from grief. The first five exercises are "discovery" questions, followed by a summary question. The sixth exercise asks you to summarize and apply information you gained from the first five exercises. The seventh exercise asks you to make personal applications of the principles you learned in this chapter.*

## BRANDY

*It was Christmastime, and Mrs. Blackwell, Superintendent of the Sunday School, was making her usual rounds to see if all of the teachers had arrived. When she got to the teenage class, she noticed that Brandy, the teaching assistant, was absent again. This disturbed Mrs. Blackwell, because Brandy had been showing signs of emotional stress lately, and had missed quite a few Sundays with the students. She hadn't been to the teacher's meetings, either.*

*After church, Mrs. Blackwell decided to pay Brandy a surprise visit. Brandy was happy to see her and invited her in. During the conversation that followed, Brandy broke down in tears. She told Mrs. Blackwell that she was suffering from a hangover. She had been out drinking the night before and felt too sick to teach her class. She said that she didn't want to be this way, but that she couldn't help herself.*

*She said that she, her brother and some friends had been going out to lounges lately, drinking heavily. She had also used amphetamines and had smoked some marijuana. This had been going on, off and on, since she was a teenager. She was now 27 years old.*

*She had made a commitment to Christ, and, for the past year, had stopped drinking and smoking marijuana. However, during the holidays she felt weaker than ever and couldn't prevent herself from yielding to the old desires for drugs. She was disappointed that she could no longer be a role model for her Sunday School students. She felt that she had failed in her attempt to be a Christian.*

*She told Mrs. Blackwell about her search for a relationship with a man and how frustrated she was that most of her relationships ended up being "one night stands". She also told Mrs. Blackwell about her painful childhood. Her mother and father had both become alcoholics, and were unable to take care of her and her brother. The courts had taken them away from her parents when she was 12 years old, and since then, they had been moved from one foster home to another until they had reached the age of 18.*

*At the end of the conversation, Brandy admitted that she needed help but didn't know where to turn.*

## 1. Relationship loss

Brandy suffered from the loss of the relationship between herself and her natural family. It appears that she never attended to the grief she experienced, and is still searching for the nur-

**182**

turant relationship she lost.

a. Hagar, in the Old Testament, suffered a similar loss when she was ostracized from the family of Sarah and Abraham. Who was Hagar? (Genesis 21:9-10)

b. What was the relationship between Hagar and the family of Sarah and Abraham? (Genesis 16:1)

c. Describe Hagar's relational loss. (Genesis 21:1-18)

d. Describe the relational loss experience of Mary Magdalene, Joanna and Mary the mother of James upon discovering the empty tomb. (Luke 24:1-12; John 20:1-20)

e. Describe the relational loss experience of Peter during the crucifixion and later, upon discovering the empty tomb. (Luke 22:45-62; John 20:1-20)

f. SUMMARY QUESTION: How are the loss experiences of Hagar, Mary Magdalene, Joanna, Mary the mother of James, and Peter also psychological, authority/responsibility, systemic and functional?

## 2. Functional loss

Alcoholism and drug dependency have eroded Brandy's ability to function as she once did as a Sunday School teacher. She also appears to be grieving the loss of her once-found independence from these drugs.

a. Samson, in the Old Testament, suffered a functional loss. Who was Samson? (Judges 13:2-5, 24)

b. What was Samson's relationship with the Philistines? (Judges 14:1-20)

c. Describe Samson's functional loss. (Judges 16)

d. Describe the Apostle Paul's functional loss on the road to Damascus. (Acts 9:3-9)

e. What was the outcome of Paul's loss experience? (Acts 9:20-29)

f. SUMMARY QUESTION: In what ways are the stories of

Samson and the Apostle Paul also examples of systemic and functional losses?

## 3. Psychological loss

Brandy's decision for Christ provided a new image of herself as someone who was loved by Christ and worthy to be loved, and as someone who didn't need the false support of drugs and alcohol. Her compassion for her students caused them to see her as a good role model. However, her return to drinking caused her to suffer the loss of this image, and its replacement with a negative one.

a. Elijah suffered a similar loss of image as he fled from Jezebel. What was Elijah's image of himself before his flight from Jezebel? (1 Kings 17) What was Elijah's image before the people? (1 Kings 18)

b. What was the threat that Elijah faced from Jezebel? (1 Kings 19)

c. Describe Elijah's image of himself as he fled from Jezebel. (1 Kings 19:1-4)

d. The Apostle Peter also suffered psychological loss. What image did Peter have of himself prior to his denial of Christ? (Matthew 16:21-22; 17:1-5)

e. What type of image loss did Peter experience following his denial of his relationship with Christ? (Mark 14:66-72; Luke 22:55-62; John 18:15-18, 25-27)

f. SUMMARY QUESTION: To what extent are the stories of Elijah and Peter also examples of the threat of functional or role/responsibility losses?

## 4. Authority/role/responsibility loss

As a Sunday School teacher, Brandy had a certain amount of authority and responsibility. Now that she isn't teaching anymore, she is experiencing a loss in this area and is grieving from it.

a. Saul, in the Old Testament, also suffered from a loss of authority, role and responsibility in Israel. Originally, what role did Saul play in Israel? (1 Samuel 11; 12; 17:1-2; 19:1-2; 13:1)

b. What caused Saul to lose his position in Israel? (1 Samuel 13:13-14)

c. Describe Saul's unattended grief, and the behaviors to which it led. (1 Samuel 16:19-23; 18:10-11, 17-18; 19:9-11)

d. Describe the disciple's functional loss upon the death, burial, resurrection and ascension of Jesus Christ. (Luke 15:11-32)

e. How did the Great Commission help the disciples cope with their grief? (Matthew 28:18-20)

f. SUMMARY QUESTION: In what sense are the losses of Saul and the disciples also examples of relationship and systemic losses?

## 5. Systemic and material losses

In being transferred from one foster home to another, Brandy and her brother were separated from one family system after another. As they left each system, they experienced a loss of that system. They also experienced material losses, having to do with objects such as furniture and bedrooms that they had to leave behind.

a. Ruth, Naomi and Orpah also suffered from systemic and material losses. What was Naomi's initial systemic loss? (Ruth 1:1) What was the second one? (1:3) What was her third? (1:5) What was her fourth? (1:6)

b. Compare Ruth and Orpah's systemic losses with those of Naomi. (Ruth 1:8-22)

c. In what ways were the losses of Ruth, Naomi and Orpah also material losses? (1:8-22)

d. Zacchaeus also suffered a systemic loss when he decided to climb down from the tree and meet Jesus. (Luke 19:1-10) Describe his systemic loss.

e. In what way was Zacchaeus' loss also a material one? (19:8-10)

f. SUMMARY QUESTION: In what sense are the losses of Ruth, Naomi, Orpah and Zacchaeus also relational and functional losses?

## 6. SUMMARY EXERCISE

What are some specific ways that your Sunday School could provide support to people who are grieving from relational, psychological, systemic, material, and functional losses?

## 7. PERSONAL APPLICATION

Do you know someone who is grieving? During which stage of the grieving process is the person? How can you "partner" with him/her so that eventually the person will see the light at the end of the tunnel?

# CHAPTER EIGHT

# GUILT

## Rev. Zenobia Brooks

*Good Shepherd Lutheran Church had recently in-stalled a Women's Crisis Center with a 24-hour telephone counseling service. The telephone counsel-ing service was run by volunteers from the church, who received telephone calls in their homes. One night Sister Marshall, one of the volunteers, got a call from Bernice.*

*Bernice wept as she told Mrs. Marshall that her boyfriend was out and she didn't know where he was. She said her boyfriend was a drug dealer. She wasn't on drugs herself, but she gave most of her money to her boyfriend. She felt that she couldn't assert herself in the relationship or she would lose him. She men-tioned that he always brought up the fact that she had once been involved with his brother before she started dealing with him. She knew her relationship with this man was not good for her, but she couldn't seem to pull away from it.*

*Mrs. Marshall invited her to come in for short-term counseling. In the weeks that followed, Bernice told Mrs. Marshall quite a bit about her early life.*

*Bernice had been abandoned by her mother at four years of age, when her mother was 16 years old. Her mother left her with Bernice's father and told her she didn't want her because Bernice was interfering with her social life. It wasn't long before the brother of her father's new wife had sex with Bernice while he was babysitting for her, even though Bernice was only seven years old at the time.*

*At the time, Bernice didn't know it was wrong, so she participated. She never told anyone, but kept this secret until she was 23 years old. She shared it for the first time during her counseling sessions with Mrs. Marshall. Bernice blamed herself over and over for what had happened. She said it wouldn't have happened if she hadn't had such a well-developed body for her age.*

*Today, although she had finished cosmetology school and had taken classes at a community college, she could not bring herself to look for a job in her field. She was depressed, but she didn't know why she couldn't "pull out of it."*

Bernice is suffering from the effects of guilt. She probably first began to feel guilty when her mother told her she didn't want her and said that Bernice's birth interfered with her happiness. This sense of guilt about her very existence was probably aggravated by her sexual encounter with the brother of her stepmother. She felt guilty that she had participated in this affair at such a young age, and again believed that her personal existence itself was responsible for someone else's sinful behavior (i.e., her body was too well-developed).

As a 23-year-old woman, she didn't realize that the guilt she had been carrying all of her life could be one of the reasons that she finds it difficult to deal appropriately with her current boyfriend. This chapter focuses on how to help people such as Bernice deal with guilt.

## An Example of the Effects of Guilt in Scripture

A woman who was very similar to Bernice, in the above case study, is the woman at the well, whom Jesus encountered in Samaria. Like Bernice, this woman thirsted for truth. Like Bernice, she had been attempting to quench her thirst through unhealthy relationships with men. No doubt she felt guilty about these relationships but could not break away. She did not realize that she could be free from her guilt and sins by trusting Jesus Christ.

### from Scripture

**John 4:5** Then cometh he to the city of Samaria, which is called Sychar, near to the parcel of ground that Jacob gave to his son Joseph.

**6** Now Jacob's well was there. Jesus therefore, being wearied with his journey, sat thus on the well: and it was about the sixth hour.

**7** There cometh a woman of Samaria to draw water: Jesus saith unto her, Give me to drink.

**9** Then saith the woman of Samaria unto him, How is it that thou, being a Jew, askest drink of me, which am a woman of Samaria? for the Jews have no dealings with the Samaritans.

**10** Jesus answered and said unto her, If thou knewest the gift of God, and who it is that saith to thee, Give me to drink; thou wouldest have asked of him, and he would have given thee living water.

**11** The woman saith unto him, Sir, thou hast nothing to draw with, and the well is deep: from whence then hast thou that living water? **12** Art thou greater than our father Jacob, which gave us the well, and drank thereof himself, and his children, and his cattle?

**13** Jesus answered and said unto her, Whosoever drinketh of this water shall thirst again:

**14** But whosoever drinketh of the water that I shall give him shall never thirst; but the water that I shall give him shall be in him a well of water springing up into everlasting life.

**15** The woman saith unto him, Sir, give me this water, that I thirst not, neither come hither to draw.

**16** Jesus saith unto her, Go, call thy husband, and come hither.

**17** The woman answered and said, I have no husband. Jesus said unto her, Thou hast well said, I have no husband:

**18** For thou hast had five husbands; and he whom thou now hast is not thy husband: in that saidst thou truly.

**19** The woman saith unto him, Sir, I perceive that thou art a prophet.

**25** The woman saith unto him, I know that Messias cometh, which is called Christ: when he is come, he will tell us all things.

**26** Jesus saith unto her, I that speak unto thee am he.

**28** The woman then left her waterpot, and went her way into the city, and saith to the men,

**29** Come, see a man, which told me all things that ever I did: is not this the Christ?

## What Is Guilt?

Guilt is a feeling that is very similar to anger, fear and shame. However, guilt makes one feel trapped by negative forces. It causes a person to feel out of control. It keeps a person in darkness and it makes a person feel worthless. It is a bondage.

*Roget's Thesaurus* uses the following synonyms for guilt: criminality, reprehensibility, blameability, blameworthiness, and reproachability. *Webster's New Collegiate Dictionary* defines guilt as: "guilty conduct. The fact of having committed a breach of conduct. Violating a law that involves a penalty. A feeling of culpability for the offense."

Guilt can be associated with something that one has done, or it can be associated falsely with something that one has not done, or with something over which one does not have control.

**False guilt**. Often people feel guilty about things over which they have no control. Perhaps they may have done things before they knew any better. However, after getting to know Christ, they still carry guilt about these things and find it difficult to accept God's forgiveness.

In other cases, this type of guilt is the direct result of emotional, physical and mental abuse which one received in childhood from a parent or some other adult. This type of abuse occurs within parent/child relationships more frequently today, with the increase in "babies having babies." Teenage parents are usually not at a developmental stage where they can provide the type of nurturance that children require. The child then becomes a victim of the teenage parent's environment and immaturity.

Such teenage parents often neglect their children physically by not taking care of some of the child's most basic needs (cleaning, feeding, holding, etc.). In other cases, they say things to the children which cause the children to feel worthless and guilty for having been born. Mental abuse occurs when parents do not educate children so that children learn to cope with their environments and grow into healthy, well-adjusted adults.

Adolescent parents are not usually equipped to educate their children in wisdom, in the ways of God and in preparation for the world. They cannot teach the children how to care for themselves because they, as parents, do not yet fully know how to care for themselves. Often the teenage parent was born into a situation that was very similar to the one in which they have brought their own child. In many instances, they too, were born to immature teenage parents.

In some cases, grandparents, parents and children of teenage parents are all forced to live in poverty due to lack of skills, education and opportunities. The grandparent cannot help the parent mature beyond the grandparent's level of maturity. Neither can the parent help the child mature beyond the parent's point of maturity. Most teenage parents cannot grasp the type of responsibility that is necessary to raise a child. They usually do not know what responsibility is, because they have not been taught responsibility. They are still seeking someone who can take care of them.

Often children who are neglected by teenage parents become the victims of sexual abuse. When a child becomes a victim of sexual abuse, and reports it to an irresponsible parent, sometimes the child is taught to blame him/herself for the abuse. Often the child is told that she should have "kept her dress down", or she shouldn't have been sitting in a particular way. In short, the child is often taught that his/her own body is responsible for the abuse. Often mothers and grandparents, involved with sexually abusive men, will either deny or hide the problem. The children in these situations often develop a false sense of guilt and related shame.

One of the results of this cycle is that children can almost "inherit" a sense of guilt that is passed down through the generations. The child feels guilty for having been brought into the world and feels that only bad things are intended to happen to him/her. S/he may feel "wrong" for being here and may feel that a life of poverty and/or sexual abuse is a just reward. They may also develop the unconscious notion that poverty is a condition from which they do not have permission to escape.

**Real guilt.** In other instances, guilt is brought on by something that a person has actually done. No one has to be taught how to sin. We are born with this knowledge. The Bible says that the heart can be desperately wicked, and beyond humankind's ability to understand (Jeremiah 17:9). The Bible also says that we are born into sin from our mother's womb (Psalm 51). For example, Cain did not have to be taught disobedience, jealousy, murder or lying (Genesis 4:1-11).

When Cain gave in to sin, it ruled him, just as it can rule anyone (Proverbs 15:13-15). Cain's sin bore bad fruit. Sin always bears bad fruit. Often, even though sin is ruling a person, that person may not understand the full magnitude of the act.

**192**

This was the case with Eve, Cain's mother. She thought the punishment for her sin could be a mere sudden death, coming to her from God. She did not realize she had ushered death into the world, and that her sin would cause death to pass to future generations.

Neither Eve nor her son appear to have fully understood guilt. They did not understand the consequences of the bad fruit they had borne. There is no cure for the type of guilt that comes from actually disobeying God, except repentance and the acceptance of God's grace and forgiveness. This type of guilt is a reality, and it is something that everyone has experienced at one time or another. That is why God paved the way for our forgiveness by sacrificing His Son (John 3:16).

## Helping People Who Feel Guilty

The primary goal for the counselor of a person who feels guilty is to lead that person into a loving relationship with the Lord. However, that goal is not likely to be accomplished until a relationship of trust exists between the counselor and the counselee. Counseling must take place within an environment where the counselee is free to share his/her most intimate feelings.

In order to create this environment, the counselor must call on the Holy Spirit of God. S/he must become a good listener and be prepared to teach the counselee about hope and faith. The counselor must also be prepared to refer the counselee to other resources when these resources can provide support that the counselor is not prepared or trained to give. Above all, the counselor must be truthful.

**Listening and clarifying feelings.** As the counselee talks, the counselor should listen for general, but key words. S/he can listen for words that are not descriptive, and then help the counselee expand upon the words by "breaking them down" and defining them. For example, a counselee might say, "My husband is driving me crazy. He makes me feel dirty." In response to this type of comment, a counselor might ask what the counselee means by "crazy," in order to clarify the counselee's feelings. S/he might also ask the counselee to explain exactly what her husband does that makes her feel "dirty."

The counselor can achieve this by asking, "What did you mean when you said...?" The counselor can also ask for examples. Listening and clarifying are not easy tasks. They require patience and practice.

**Calling on the Holy Spirit in prayer**. The Lord said He would send the Comforter (14:16) who is the Holy Spirit (14:26) and that the Comforter would teach us all things (John 15:26-27; 14:26). Therefore, it is important for the counselee to make contact with the Holy Spirit through prayer. Scriptures can be used to teach the counselee about prayer.

Psalm 23 is excellent for this purpose. This Psalm helps the counselee see the presence of God in every situation. Another passage that is useful in illustrating the importance of calling out to the Lord in prayer is the story of the woman with the daughter who was vexed with spirits (Matthew 15:21-28). When Jesus encountered this woman, it was not the most pleasant period of His ministry. He had recently heard the news of the beheading of John the Baptist (Matthew 14:3-12; Mark 6:17-29), and it was just after He had fed five thousand people from a few loaves of bread and fish (Matthew 14:15-21; Mark 6:35-44; Luke 9:10-17; John 6:1-14).

When His disciples became aware of the woman with the demon-possessed daughter, their first response was to tell Jesus to send her away. They did not want to deal with a person who was vexed with a spirit (Matthew 15:23). However, Jesus listened to the woman and interacted with her until she was able to express her faith in Him.

He listened and allowed her to state her need for help (15:25) and her willingness to ask for this help even when Jesus said that He was sent only to the lost sheep of Israel (15:24). He allowed her to worship Him (15:25), and to cry out to Him. Jesus allowed her to elaborate on her feelings of being considered an "outsider" among privileged Jews (16:24). Finally, she was allowed to express the fact that Jesus was her Lord, regardless of what anyone else might think (15:27-28). It is this faith that caused Jesus to heal her daughter.

It was important for the woman to accept who she was, within the society of that time, and to recognize that a person such as herself needed a healer. It was important for the woman to know she could not be healed by Jesus' disciples, but that she had to come to Jesus Himself for healing. She had to recognize that she wasn't there because she was whole.

She was there because she was broken. She had to know that she had to lean on the grace of Jesus. She had to recognize that Jesus would not be prejudiced against her and would heal her. All of this was achieved because Jesus listened and helped her clarify her situation, her feelings and her motives for being there.

**Introducing the counselee to Jesus Christ.** Of course, in order to appreciate prayer and the presence of the Holy Spirit, the counselee will need to be introduced to Jesus Christ (John 3:16). Then the counselor can share Jesus' teachings about prayer (Matthew 6:6-13). Whenever possible, the counselor should compare the counselee's situation with those of people who experienced healing and who witnessed the miracles of our Lord. The story of the man at the Bethesda pool is an appropriate passage to share (John 5:5-9). This story illustrates how Jesus healed the man after the man indicated he really wanted to be healed and took the action that resulted in the healing.

During the process of leading a person to Christ, it is important to ask key questions such as: "Do you believe? Do you believe that Jesus is the way to eternal life and happiness?" These and other questions can be posed, and such Scriptures as John 3:16 and Hebrews 11 can be used to lay the foundation for faith and hope.

It is critical that the person recognize it is Jesus, and no one else, who can heal. Jesus is the Way, the Truth, and the Life

(John 14:6). The way to healing is Jesus, not Jesus' disciples. For example, when the disciples were given the Scripture regarding Jesus being the Way, they were completely confused. Doubting Thomas and the others could not grasp the full meaning of this. They did not want Jesus to go away (14:5). Often there are many "doubting Thomases" within our congregations. Therefore, the counselees must recognize that it is to Jesus they are turning, not to the counselor, not to the pastor, and not to the people at the church.

The counselee who feels guilty must be shown that it is not the counselor or other disciples who are the source of the Truth. Jesus Himself is the source, and the counselee is not coming to the counselor for help, but to Christ. The counselor is like a tour guide in a foreign country. S/he is merely taking the counselee to Jesus.

**Recognizing true motives**. Part of the process of reaching the point where one cries out to the Lord is recognizing one's true motives. This was what Jesus was doing when He led the woman (with the demonpossessed daughter) into clarifying exactly why she was coming to Jesus. Did she have motives of distracting Him from the lost sheep of Israel? Did she merely want her daughter to be healed? Or did she recognize Jesus as her Lord and the source of all good things for everyone?

Often the link between wholeness and brokenness is made when the person becomes aware of his/her true motives and can see whether the motives are for good or evil. Being confused about one's motives is often at the root of guilty feelings. Frequently people believe that they have evil motives, when the motives in themselves are good ones. However, often intentions are evil, and the counselee can be helped by recognizing this and repenting.

**Forgiving and being forgiven**. The person should be shown that, in order to receive forgiveness for one's sins, one must also be willing to forgive others (Matthew 6:14). This is particularly true when the person is experiencing anger and guilt over having

**196**

been sexually abused as a child. During the course of counseling Bernice, in the introductory story to this chapter, discovered that she had so much anger against her mother, father and the brother of her stepmother, that she could not forgive them. She found she could not forgive her stepmother for the fact that, as a child, she was treated differently from the other children.

All of this anger had to be faced, and she had to learn to forgive these people before she could fully experience the forgiveness of God--the forgiveness that would pave the way for eliminating her feelings of guilt.

**Exercising faith**. The counselee must be shown that the Christian life is one of faith. It is similar to an object lesson that I often use in Youth Church to teach children about faith. I begin by blindfolding a youngster and asking him or her to fall back into my arms. At first the child has quite a bit of trouble doing this. However, once it is done the first time, the second time is much easier because the child knows that I am not going to let him/her fall or be hurt.

The counselee needs to know that Jesus Christ has a good track record. Jesus will not let them perish. Hebrews 11 is an appropriate chapter for pointing out the many people who exercised faith in God, and the diverse situations in which they found themselves. The counselee needs to know that faith is the substance of things hoped for.

**Being truthful**. The counselor must be prepared, when necessary, to point out to the client when a given behavior is actually wrong, so that the counselee can have an opportunity to repent and free him/herself from the guilt that could result from such behavior. Parenting also becomes counseling in this respect. Parents must show children when they are doing something that is actually wrong, and must provide the child with the opportunity to apologize and repent.

This is a very critical process in a child's development. If a child does something that is wrong (lying, stealing, cheating, etc.), the child must be shown the behavior is wrong. They must be led to an understanding of why they did it, and they must be shown the importance of saying they are sorry. They also need to be shown the importance of asking forgiveness from the Lord. If a parent is responsible in this way, the child is less likely to suffer from guilt. The child can be spared of the danger of growing into adulthood with feelings of guilt about things they have done that have never been resolved. As early as possible, the child needs to know that all s/he needs to do is ask forgiveness and repent. S/he does not need to carry around guilt about past sins, but merely repent.

When children have not had this experience, they often develop problems. They have to learn the difference between bad fruit and good fruit. They need to know the dangers of bad fruit. Otherwise, sin and guilt will soon dominate them. If they are not shown the difference between good and bad fruit, they may become confused about the difference between right and wrong.

This is one of the reasons that gang members, pimps, prostitutes and dope dealers appear not to have consciences. Their behavior is a result of being fed bad fruit rather than good fruit. No one took the time to tell them the difference between the two, the dangers of bad fruit, and the necessity and effectiveness of repentance. However, it is noticeable that children who accept Jesus Christ as their Saviour, who are raised in the church and have a God-countenance about them, do not exist for very long as gang members, pimps, prostitutes, etc. (Proverbs 22:6). It is so important to teach children the truth at an early age.

**Making referrals**. Often counselees feel guilty that they are unable to provide for themselves or their families. In these cases, often the counselee has unmet physical and educational needs. When this is the case, the counselor must be prepared to use other resources outside of the counseling setting. These would include human resources within the church and professional agencies outside of the church.

If people are homeless, they need to be referred to a shelter. If

**198**

they need food, they need to be referred to a food pantry or to a ministry in the church which provides food in times of emergencies. If they need medical care, they need to be directed to agencies which will provide this.

If they cannot read or write, they need to be directed to one of the many adult education programs which exist in public schools, community colleges, churches, libraries and civic organizations (2 Timothy 2:15). Counselors should avoid restricting their help to a "pie in the sky" approach which ignores counselees' present physical and emotional needs.

The counselor should also familiarize him/herself with the auxiliaries at the local church the counselee attends. Some counselees may be able to benefit by becoming a part of an auxiliary and working through that auxiliary to help others and themselves. Auxiliaries can provide friendships and can be a means whereby gifts can be developed and used in the service of the Lord.

The local church has a very important role in healing. Often the counselee's problem can be "prayed through" in the Community of Faith. Being healed is a process. It doesn't always happen overnight. We must remember that the Black church has always been a center of healing in the Black community.

In the days when we did not have access to various health care agencies in the community, our people have come to the Black church and have been healed. Miracles have always happened within the church. Contemporary ministry can continue this tradition during times when social resources are being eliminated and when conservative legislators are attempting to turn back the clock on civil rights. Many hurting people will come to the churches. We must be prepared to help them within the Community of Faith.

**Summary.** This chapter has focused on helping people who feel guilty. It has distinguished between false guilt and real guilt and the types of situations that lead to feelings of guilt. The chapter has provided guidelines for helping people who feel guilty.

These include listening and clarifying the counselee's feelings, calling on the Holy Spirit in prayer, introducing the counselee to Jesus Christ, and helping the counselee deal with true motives. These also include learning to forgive and experience forgiveness, recognizing the importance of faith, and being truthful. It also pointed out the importance of using social agencies outside of the local church when necessary. Finally, the chapter underscored the healing ministry of the local church and the historical healing ministry of the Black church.

The following exercise provides the opportunity to apply these principles to a case study.

## CASE STUDY

*INSTRUCTIONS: The exercise below allows you to apply principles presented in this chapter to a case study involving a person who feels guilty. The first five exercises are "discovery" questions, followed by a summary question. The sixth exercise asks you to summarize and apply information you gained from the first five exercises. The seventh exercise asks you to make personal applications of the principles you learned in this chapter.*

## TANISHA

*Late one Friday afternoon, Mrs. Jackson, a social worker at the Department of Social Services, received a call from a little girl who seemed very nervous. The little girl was from the family of one of Mrs. Jackson's clients. Tanisha told Mrs. Jackson that she was frightened. Her uncle was going to come home soon, and she was afraid he would force her to have sex with him again.*

*She said that she had told her grandmother, but her*

*grandmother wasn't doing anything about it. Tanisha was one of six children. All of the children had been abandoned by their mother and left with their grandmother.*

*In the following weeks, Mrs. Jackson went through the appropriate procedures for removing Tanisha and her brothers and sisters from their grandmother's home. The children were all placed in foster homes. Tanisha was placed in the home of one of the ladies at Mrs. Jackson's church who kept foster children.*

*Mrs. Brand, the woman who took Tanisha in, informed Mrs. Jackson that Tanisha told her she was the fourth child to have been sexually abused by this one uncle. The little girl was very frightened and withdrawn.*

*Although Mrs. Brand realized that much damage had already been done, she encouraged Tanisha to sing in the Children's Chorus, and she proceeded to get Tanisha enrolled in the church's tutorial ministry.*

*Shortly afterward, the choir director informed Mrs. Brand that, at choir rehearsal, Tanisha began to cry uncontrollably. When the choir director asked her what was wrong, she told him she believed that God was going to punish her and send her to hell for her sins. The choir director tried to talk to her about salvation, but felt that Tanisha was too upset to concentrate on what he was saying. He thought that her behavior was very unusual, so he called it to her foster mother's attention.*

## 1. False guilt

Many people carry false guilt that is connected with incidents over which they had no control. Others carry false guilt connected with things for which God already forgave them when they became Christians.

a. Is there any scriptural basis for sexually abused persons to feel that they are the ones who sinned, just by being sexually abused? (Ezekiel 18:1-4, 19-24, 30-31)

b. Is there any scriptural basis for a child believing that s/he sinned by being born? (Psalm 139:13-17)

c. Is there any scriptural basis for continuing to feel guilty about sins committed before one was saved? (Jeremiah 31:34; Romans 10:8-11)

d. How does one break the habit of harboring guilt about sins committed after one has been saved? (Romans 6:1-11; 1 John 1:19)

e. How does a believer know that God has forgiven him or her? (1 John 1:10; 2:13-16, 19)

f. SUMMARY QUESTION: How can a counselor use the information from questions a-e above to help a counselee who carries false guilt?

## 2. Calling on the Holy Spirit in prayer

The Holy Spirit has a role in freeing people from guilt.

a. What is one type of power that has been manifested through God's Spirit? (Genesis 1:1-5; 2:7; Job 33:4; Acts 3:1-10)

b. What is another type of power that is manifested through God's Spirit? (Psalm 104:30-31; Isaiah 32:14-15; Acts 2:1-2, 38-41, 47)

c. What is another type of power that is manifested through God's Spirit? (Exodus 31:1-11; John 16:13-15)

d. What is yet another type of power that is manifested through God's Spirit? (Numbers 11:16-17; John 14:16-18)

e. What is yet another type of power that is manifested through God's Spirit? (John 3:5-6; Galatians 5:22; 2 Corinthians 3:3; 1 Corinthians 6:11)

f. SUMMARY QUESTION: How can a counselor use the information from questions a-e above to prepare a counselee to call out to God in prayer?

3. **Leaning on God's grace**

It is important for persons who feel guilty to accept the fact that Jesus Christ died so that we could be forgiven for our sins.
a. Does Jesus really understand a human being's struggles with sin? (Hebrews 4:15-16; 2 Corinthians 12:9)
b. What has Christ done to help people who struggle with sin? (Hebrews 6:19-20; 7:25-27; 9:27-28; John 3:16)
c. How is one saved from bondage to sin? (Acts 16:31; Ephesians 2:8; Romans 10:9; 1 John 4:15)
d. Can we earn God's forgiveness? (Ephesians 2:5, 8)
e. What does the phrase "grace of God" mean? (1 Corinthians 1:3-7; 15:9-10; Acts 11:21-23)
f. SUMMARY QUESTION: How can the counselor use the information from questions a-e above to help a counselee lean on the grace of God for forgiveness from sin?

4. **Forgiving**

Forgiveness among believers plays an important part in the healing ministry of the Community of Faith.
a. Can a Christian really experience the love of God as long as s/he harbors resentment and hate against another person? (1 John 4:20)
b. Is it important to "forgive and forget"? (Luke 17:3)
c. Is there a relationship between forgiving and being forgiven? (Luke 6:37-38; Mark 11:25-26)
d. Why should we be enthusiastic about forgiving others? (Matthew 18:21-35)
e. Are people who struggle with sin "out of place" in the House of the Lord? (John 8:1-11; Romans 3:23)

f. SUMMARY QUESTION: How can the information from questions a-e above be used to prepare those who want to serve in a local church's prison ministry?

## 5. The role of faith in healing

People can be healed of emotional problems, if they exercise faith in God.

a. What is the basis for having faith in Jesus' power to heal emotional problems? (Mark 1:23-26; 5:1-13; Luke 4:33-35; Matthew 8:28-32)

b. Is there any basis for believing that the Community of Faith can be used by the Lord to heal emotional problems? (Acts 8:6-8; 16:16-18)

c. Who exercised the faith that resulted in some of the demon-possessed men in Galilee being healed? What does this suggest about the role that faith plays in the counseling process? (Matthew 9:32-33; 12:22; Luke 11:14)

d. What is the relationship between faith and healing? (2 Chronicles 7:14; Hebrews 11:1-3)

e. Describe the Lord as healer. (Hosea 11:1-11; Psalm 23)

f. SUMMARY QUESTION: How can a counselor use the information from questions a-e above to help a counselee understand the role of faith in healing?

## 6. SUMMARY EXERCISE

What types of services can the local church provide for people who are suffering from false guilt? Are there ways that the church can help those who have been sexually abused in childhood? Are there ways that the local church can help people who are suffering from real guilt? How about those who are currently in prison? If the church developed a prison ministry, how would counselors in the prison ministry use the information from exercises 1-5 above to help those who are incarcerated?

## 7. PERSONAL APPLICATION

Are you carrying a burden of guilt? Is it false guilt? Is it guilt related to something for which you have already been forgiven? If so, take your burden to the Lord and leave it there.

# CHAPTER NINE

# INSECURITY

## Dr. Dwight Perry

*Mr. and Mrs. Kennedy sat quietly as Deacon Pearson introduced himself. The couple had signed up for counseling, expressing on the sign-up sheet that they were having marital problems.*

*Mrs. Kennedy began by complaining that Mr. Kennedy never listened to her. When Deacon Pearson probed a little further, he discovered that Mr. Kennedy agreed he did not listen when Mrs. Kennedy tried to give him advice. Mrs. Kennedy complained because she felt the advice was important, seeing that it related to the well-being of the children and the security of family finances.*

*In the weekly sessions that followed, Mr. Kennedy gradually opened up and talked about himself. He said he had a master's degree in business administration and was the only Black manager in the Fortune 500 accounting firm where he worked. In describing his work situation, he said he never really felt appreciated on his job. He got very little feedback on projects that he completed, even when, due to his expertise, the projects had brought thousands of dollars into the firm.*

*He mentioned that he was rarely invited to social*

*events with the other, white male accountants, and he usually ate lunch alone. When it came to promotions, he had been passed over many times. Recently a younger white woman whom he had trained was promoted over him and now made decisions which affected the direction of his projects.*

*He had developed the habit of constantly comparing himself to this woman and to other men, particularly the white men with whom he worked. He compared himself to them in minor as well as major details. He even said the reason that Mrs. Kennedy was complaining was actually because he didn't have as much money as other men and was not driving a "flashy car." As he talked, Deacon Pearson was reminded of how competitive Mr. Kennedy seemed to be at church. He remembered how he argued in meetings, always needing to get the final word, seemingly regardless of the issue being discussed.*

*Further exploration revealed that Mr. Kennedy grew up the only boy in a family of four girls and a mother. His father had abandoned the family when he was still an infant, so he didn't remember him. He couldn't remember ever knowing any adult men whom he considered positive role models.*

*Lately, arguments with his wife had escalated to the point that they were bitterly arguing before the children. Mrs. Kennedy said Mr. Kennedy had radical mood shifts, from total withdrawal from the family, to nearly violent temper outbursts. She had begged him to come with her to counseling, and he had consented, feeling that the situation was quickly getting out of hand.*

Mr. Kennedy is suffering from insecurity. The insecurity probably began within his family, where he had been abandoned by his father, and where he lacked the opportunity to observe a healthy relationship between a woman and a man. His experiences on his job no doubt contribute to his feelings of insecurity. These feelings of insecurity no doubt affect the way he relates to his wife.

## An Example of Insecurity in Scripture

A classic example from Scripture of one who did not deal properly with the emotion of insecurity is Saul, the king who preceded David. Saul compared himself with others, and if he felt that someone had more ability than he did, he became insecure. He could not properly appreciate his personal greatness because he was obsessed with the greatness of David, who seemed to outshine him.

## from Scripture

**1 Samuel 9:1** Now there was a man of Benjamin, whose name was Kish, the son of Abiel, the son of Zeror, the son of Bechorath, the son of Aphiah, a Benjamite, a mighty man of power.

**2** And he had a son, whose name was Saul, a choice young man, and a goodly: and there was not among the children of Israel a goodlier person than he: from his shoulders and upward he was higher than any of the people.

**18:6** And it came to pass as they came, when David was returned from the slaughter of the Philistine, that the women came out of all cities of Israel, singing and dancing, to meet king Saul, with tabrets, with joy, and with instruments of music.

**7** And the women answered one another as they played, and said, Saul hath slain his thousands, and David his ten thousands.

**8** And Saul was very wroth, and the saying displeased him; and he said, They have ascribed unto David ten thousands, and to me they have ascribed but thousands: and what can he have more but the kingdom?

**9** And Saul eyed David from that day and forward.

**209**

**10** And it came to pass on the morrow, that the evil spirit from God came upon Saul, and he prophesied in the midst of the house: and David played with his hand, as at other times; and there was a javelin in Saul's hand.
**11** And Saul cast the javelin; for he said, I smite David even to the wall with it. And David avoided out of his presence twice.
**12** And Saul was afraid of David, because the Lord was with him, and was departed from Saul.

## What Is Insecurity?

Insecurity is a feeling of never "measuring up." It is the feeling that a person is not "as good as" other people. Among the most common signs of insecurity are: a) a tendency to rely on outward appearance in order to determine personal worth of oneself and others; b) an oversensitivity to the thoughts and opinions of others; c) an intense inner need for acceptance; d) frequent emotional "roller coasters"; e) a drive to be in control of every life circumstance.

**Reliance on the outward appearance.** Like Saul, insecure people have a tendency to rely on the external. When evaluating themselves and others, they consider such factors as how much money they make, how many cars they have, and the type of job they have. They focus on these outward symbols of success, rather than on what God thinks of individuals. They compare themselves with others in these respects and often see themselves as "coming up short."

In other cases, they compare themselves with another person in the one respect that they feel they do not "measure up," but ignore the areas where they may, indeed, be "taller" than the other person. Saul did this when he compared himself to David, the shepherd boy. The Israelite people in general were relatively small people in stature whose average height was around five feet tall. However, Saul was what would be considered tall, dark and handsome (1 Samuel 9:2). He was at least a foot taller than

other Israelites. He must have been an imposing figure.
Even with his imposing stature, however, he was unsure of
himself, and seemed to "come up short" when he compared
himself to David, the shepherd boy, who was actually much
shorter than he was (1 Samuel 16:7). Saul didn't seem to know
that one's outward appearance is not the basis of one's self-
worth. Insecure people don't seem to realize that someone may
care about outward appearance, but God looks on the heart (1
Samuel 16:7).

Another form of outward appearance overly valued by the insecure person is skill and ability. Insecure people focus on the
skills and abilities of others and use these as a basis for evaluating a person's worth. When comparing themselves to others,
they often fear they are not as skillful as others or they do not
have the same ability as others.

Saul, for example, had grown to compare himself with others
on the basis of his own ability. At one time, he rarely met
anyone who had as much ability as he did. After all, Saul had become king when he was only thirty years old, and he had reigned
over Israel for 42 years (1 Samuel 13:1). He and his son had successfully attacked the Philistines many times, and were admired
throughout Israel because of this (chapters 11 and 12). Saul,
being a soldier by vocation, was indeed a man of action.

When Saul met David, who seemed more skillful, he became
greatly alarmed. He seemingly forgot that his impending decline
was due to his disobedience of God, rather than his natural skills
and abilities (13:12-14). Instead, he seems to have felt that his
problems had to do with the personal skill and power he pos-
sessed in relationship to others. Saul's sin was that he trusted
more in his personal valor than in God. This sin caused Saul to
operate independently from God. These actions laid the
groundwork for his kingdom being taken from him (13:14).

Insecure people also overvalue another form of "outward appearance"--the social position or occupation that one has. Insecure people often use this as an indication of personal worth.

Saul had this problem. Too much of his personal identity was associated with the position he held in Israel. Saul became extremely insecure as he realized that his position of prominence was not unshakable. That is why he wanted to kill David in order to prevent this from happening (19:1).

Mr. Kennedy, in the case study at the beginning of this chapter, also overvalues outward appearances. While it is true he is being unfairly treated on his job, and the treatment is probably due to racial discrimination, because he is insecure, he is unable to separate himself from the situation itself. Instead he constantly compares himself to other white workers in terms of money they have, skills they may or may not have, and cars they may or may not drive. In other words, he has internalized the idea that his problems are due to his personal deficiencies rather than outward circumstances and possibly racism.

In his heart, he probably really believes he is being passed over because he does not "measure up." "Not measuring up" in some respect or another has become the basis of Mr. Kennedy's evaluation of his own personal worth.

Like Saul, Mr. Kennedy blames his outward appearance for some problems that are caused, not by his own appearance, but by problems he may be experiencing inside of himself. He is unable to accept that his personality (radical mood shifts, inability to receive counsel from his wife, and constant arguing) may be the cause of the difficulties between him and his wife. He is unable to see this because he believes his wife could not be unhappy with him unless it had to do with his financial status. After all, people are loved or unloved on the basis of what they have, he thinks.

**The need for acceptance.** Insecure people exhibit a need for acceptance that is beyond an appropriate range of needing approval from others. Needing approval and affirmation from others is normal. It is God who has made people so that they need affirmation from others. However, reality dictates that very few people will provide affirmation and acceptance of any one person. Therefore, most people learn very early that one does not always receive acceptance from others, and most people become adjusted to this reality. However, the insecure person does not.

Mr. Kennedy seems deeply disturbed by the fact that he is not invited to lunch or social gatherings with the men from his firm. Although there is every indication that much of this rudeness could be due to problems which the other men possess, Mr. Kennedy seems, on an emotional level, to have attributed this to some personal deficiency. Mr. Kennedy's way of thinking contributes greatly to his personal sense of insecurity.

**Oversensitivity to others' thoughts and opinions.** The insecure person, because of an overbalanced need for acceptance, can become overly sensitive to how others respond to him or her. Insecure people are frequently almost in bondage to others' thoughts and opinions.

Saul had this type of bondage. When he heard the women singing about David, he was so in need of their acceptance and approval that he began to resent David for getting it instead. This jealousy, over what he perceived as a lack of approval from the women, drove him to try to murder David.

Mr. Kennedy, within the context of his job, has also become obsessed with others' thoughts and opinions. The objective fact of bringing thousands of dollars into the company, and the objective reality of the quality of his work are not enough. For some reason, he still needs to hear his superiors' thoughts and opinions about his performance on these projects.

**The emotional "roller coaster."** Insecure people live on what could be called an emotional "roller coaster." Often their emotional responses to how they think they are perceived by others fluctuate from withdrawal to anger. This results in a great deal of emotional insecurity in relationship to others.

Saul can also be seen on an emotional "roller coaster." One day, he wants David to play for him on his harp (1 Samuel 16:19-23). Shortly thereafter, he is seen throwing a javelin at

David (18:10-11). Then he is seen offering David his daughter (18:17-18). Very soon thereafter, he is seen throwing a javelin at David again (19:9-10), and then sending messengers out to find David and kill him (19:11).

While Mr. Kennedy has not become as violent as Saul, his radical mood shifts are similar to those of Saul. These extreme mood shifts lead to arguments and can eventually threaten his relationship with his children and the marriage itself.

**The need to control**. The person who suffers from insecurity has an overwhelming drive to be in absolute control over life's circumstances. Like Saul, most insecure people gain their sense of wholeness by knowing that everything in life is "moving along as planned." If any deviations occur, the insecure person may become alarmed. Saul had planned to be king most of his life and remain at the center of Israel's affections. When it seemed this plan would not become a reality, Saul became alarmed and irrational.

Mr. Kennedy has such a need to be in control. To him, any indication that he is not absolutely controlling his wife is a threat to his authority. Therefore, he cannot receive advice from his wife, even when the counsel relates to the well-being of himself and their family.

## Dealing With Insecurity

To help the insecure person, the counselor will need to guide the person into understanding the benefits of failure. The counselor will need to bring the person into an awareness of the supernatural love of God. Then the insecure person will be in a better position to rely on that love to establish loving relationships with others. The person must be encouraged to study the Scriptures diligently, to pray, to attack the lies of Satan, and to properly relate to the counseling situation.

**The benefits of failure**. One of the biggest threats to the insecure person is the fear of failure. However, the person can be shown how failure, whenever it comes, can be the back door to success, as Erwin Lutzer once wrote. In so many instances, God closes one door so that another one can be opened. Often a person discovers more about him/herself through failure than s/he could have learned if the failure never occurred. This new knowledge can be the basis of success in a new situation.

Once this fear of failure is neutralized by positive thinking, the person has laid the groundwork for focusing away from abilities, outward appearance, position held in life, etc., as shields against "failure" (i.e., some plan or another not materializing). Instead, the person focuses on the future, learns why a given plan did not materialize, sets up new goals under the direction of God, and pursues them with the newly found knowledge gained from this "failure" experience.

The person does not see life in terms of "failure," but leaves his life in the hands of the Lord (Job 1:20-22), knowing that all things work together for good to those who love the Lord and are called according to His purposes (Romans 8:28).

For example, Mr. Kennedy, in the introductory situation, can focus away from how others are treating him in his current job situation, to learning as much as he can from this situation so he can use it on another job or in the establishment of his own accounting firm. While he is experiencing the circumstance, he can seek God for what he is to learn from it, and seek God for knowledge of how to circumvent some of the barriers. He can look for the good that he is going to get out of this situation, because he knows that things work together for good.

Mr. Kennedy can stop seeing himself at the mercy of others, because he soon realizes that, if he is a Christian, he is called according to God's purposes (Romans 8:28).

**God's love.** The ultimate goal of counseling the insecure person would be that the person would experience the supernatural revelation of God in a new way. It is only the assurance of God's unconditional, unmerited love that can give anyone the inner stability one needs to be secure and stable. It is the supernatural love of God that enables a person to accept others. As Dionne Warwick once sang, "What the world needs now is love sweet love! That's the only thing that there's just too little of."

The counselor can also guide the insecure person in establishing loving relationships with others, based on the new experience of God's love. Love relationships are one of the primary vehicles that God uses to build His love into our lives and develop within us more inner strength and security about our lives.

Mr. Kennedy, in the opening case study, can be guided through Scriptures which provide the basis for him to know he is loved of God, and that God's love is not conditional, based on Mr. Kennedy's outward appearance, possessions or skills and abilities. Then he must be shown the importance of cultivating a God-centered loving relationship with his wife, children, and brothers and sisters at church. These relationships need not be based on status symbols that Mr. Kennedy has or does not have.

**Scripture study**. Diligent study of Scripture can reveal one's personal worth before God. Psalm 139 is an example of a Scripture focused on self-worth. This Psalm says that all of God's creations are fearfully and wonderfully made. What better basis is there for feeling secure as a person!

There is a need for insecure people, particularly Black people, to be able to use the Word of God as a basis for sharply contrasting what God thinks of them with what the world projects to them about themselves. It is important for them to realize that the Son of God Himself came to earth to die for them individually and as a group. His love goes beyond anything humankind can fathom. His love does not depend on superficial status symbols, manufactured by the world system, and headed by the evil one.

**The importance of wise counsel**. Everyone needs people with whom they can talk. This is particularly important when dealing with fears leading to insecurity. Some need this more than others. However, we live in a culture which says it is a sign

**216**

of weakness to turn to a friend or relative for counsel. This is particularly true when the person needing counsel is a man. However, often counseling is needed, and in many instances professional counselors and pastors should be sought for this help.

Mr. Kennedy, in the introductory case study, seems to reject counsel from his wife. This type of attitude toward advice could reflect itself in the counseling sessions with Deacon Pearson. Mr. Kennedy may also feel insecure if he receives counsel from another man. This needs to be discussed in the counseling sessions. It needs to be pointed out that seeking wise counsel, and properly considering the counsel of one's wife can be a strength rather than a weakness. Many scriptural passages emphasize the importance of God's wise counsel: Psalm 73:21-26; Proverbs 11:14; Isaiah 28:29; 30:1; 11:1-4. This wise counsel can come from brothers and sisters in the Lord, from wives, husbands, family members, and from pastors and ministers whom God has placed in positions of authoritative support.

**Prayer.** Unless the Lord builds the house, the laborers labor in vain. Unless the Lord watches the city, the watchman stays awake in vain (Psalm 127:1, 2). Ultimately, only God can provide healing in various areas of one's life. Therefore, prayer is essential in overcoming insecurity.

Insecure people, such as Mr. Kennedy, might be encouraged to develop a prayer list of various insecurities. He might, in the course of praying, ask God to make him more intimately aware of God's love for him, and the love of God's people for him.

**Attacking Satan's lies.** It is important to consciously attack the lies of the enemy. David Breese, in *Satan's Ten Most Believable Lies*, shares how Satan, the enemy of God's people, loves to accuse the brethren day and night. Thus the battle against Satan involves preventing him from pulling down God's people (2 Corinthians 10). The Christian must fight against various false strongholds that the evil one wants to build in the mind.

For example, Mr. Kennedy has come to believe many things

suggested to him by the evil world system in which he lives, and of which Satan is the head (Ephesians 2:2-3, 12). This world system has told Mr. Kennedy his personal worth depends on how others assess him. It has told him that, when others do not provide him with the appropriate affirmation and feedback, something is wrong with him. The world system has told him that all conflicts between himself and others can be attributed to the possessions and status symbols that he does or does not have. The world system has blinded him to the presence and love of God in his life.

The beginning of healing for insecure people such as Mr. Kennedy is to reject Satan's lies and accept God's love. More healing will take place as such people study the Word of God and appropriate God's promises for their lives.

**Summary.** This chapter has focused on the problem of insecurity, and how counselors can help people who feel insecure. It has presented several signs of insecurity, including reliance on outward appearances, an extreme need for acceptance, overconcern for others' thoughts and opinions, and emotional "roller coasters". In combating insecurity, it has been suggested that the insecure person develop a new attitude toward failure, accept God's love rather than the ideas of representatives of the evil world system, study Scripture, pray, and use Scripture as a basis for attacking Satan's lies.

It is indeed our prayer in closing that Christian people everywhere resist the tendency of the evil one to destroy us through insecurity.

## CASE STUDY

*INSTRUCTIONS: In the following story, John is experiencing insecurity. The exercises will lead you into an in-depth study of John's problem, based on the principles that were introduced in this chapter.*

*The first five exercises consist of a series of "discovery" questions, followed by a summary question. The sixth exercise asks you to summarize and apply information you gained from the first five exercises. The seventh exercise asks you to make personal applications of the information you have received.*

## JOHN

*When John entered his brother Paul's home, it seemed that all of the sadness of the months before came over him at once. His voice broke, and tears entered his eyes as he sat on the couch across from his brother and began to talk. By now, his family had heard the news. John had been dismissed from his position as pastor because he had falsified information on his employment application. He had told the congregation that he graduated from seminary, but he hadn't. A member found out from a former classmate and took the matter to the church authorities, after spreading rumors related to it all over the church. The church authorities verified the story and then asked John to leave his position.*

*John told Paul that seminary had been very difficult for him and he had been asked to leave in his final year, because he failed all of his classes. He was informed of his dismissal from the school just before graduation exercises. He had lied to his parents in order to prevent them from coming to the graduation exercises and not seeing him there. He never told the church he hadn't graduated, rationalizing that he had finished four years of seminary, which was really the requirement for the job.*

*As John talked, his brother recalled earlier times in their lives when both he and John had been pressured by their father to enter the ministry. Their father was*

**219**

*an ordained minister. Paul remembered how he had dropped out of seminary, deciding that the ministry was not his calling. He remembered how devastated his parents had been, and how John, his younger brother, had entered the seminary, hoping not to disappoint his parents as Paul had done.*

*As John talked, Paul said a quiet prayer, hoping he would be able to help John through the traumatic experience he was describing.*

## 1. The benefits of failure

Insecure people such as John can be overwhelmed by what appears to be a failure on their part. However, a Christian can see what others call failure in a different light.

a. Will God fail to keep his promises? (Deuteronomy 31:6)

b. If something doesn't turn out right, what does that mean? (Romans 8:28)

c. Failure is really adversity. What are some outcomes of adversity for the person who loves the Lord? (Genesis 30:27; Romans 5:4; Hebrews 5:8)

d. What can a child of God expect to happen during a time of adversity? (Isaiah 30:19-21)

e. What attitude should a child of God have toward adversity? (Job 1:20-22)

f. SUMMARY QUESTION: In what ways could a counselor use the answers to a-e above to help a person such as John accept the fact that s/he doesn't do well in a particular college or career?

## 2. God's love

The world tells people such as John that personal worth is based on the extent to which one meets the expectations of parents and others. However, God's love is the only real basis

for a Christian's acceptance of him/herself.
a. In what way is God different from the authority figures on our jobs? (1 Corinthians 13:8-13)
b. What is the relationship between our personal deficiencies and God's love? (Proverbs 10:12)
c. Why is it important for a Christian to cultivate loving relationships with family and church, rather than becoming totally absorbed in solving problems of racism on jobs? (Proverbs 15:17)
d. In what ways does God's love help us become the best persons that we can be? (Jeremiah 31:3)
e. What role does the church play in helping people experience God's love? (1 John 4:7-12)
f. SUMMARY QUESTION: How can the answers to a-e above be used to help an insecure person cope with lack of acceptance from others? How can these Scriptures be used to help a person deal with a demanding, rejecting parent?

## 3. God's opinion of human beings

Insecure people are often in bondage to others' opinions and thoughts. However, God's opinion of a person (as reflected in His Word) is usually in stark contrast.
a. In whose image have human beings been created? (Genesis 1:27)
b. What is God's opinion of human beings, as He created them to be? (Genesis 1:31)
c. What is another indication of God's opinion of human beings? (Psalm 139:13-18)
d. How does God see those who believe in Him? (Exodus 19:6; 1 Peter 2:5, 9)
e. What is the best evidence of God's opinion of human beings? (John 3:16)
f. SUMMARY QUESTION: Using the answers to a-e above,

how does God's opinion of a person contrast with those held by racists and others who judge people by outward appearances?

## 4. The importance of wise counsel

Some insecure people try to fight insecurity through achieving academically, earning money, joining prestigious clubs, and being seen with the right people at the right time. However, the Bible says that one of the best ways to fight insecurity is with wise counsel from Himself and godly people.

a. In what ways does the Lord help a Christian deal with oppression on his/her job? What role does wise counsel play? (Psalm 73:21-26)

b. What are some reasons a Christian should not attempt to deal privately with thoughts that come as a result of oppression and adversity, without the help of other Christians? (Proverbs 11:14)

c. On what basis will people be judged by the Lord? What role will wise counsel play? (Isaiah 11:1-4)

d. What role does the Holy Spirit play in providing wise counsel? (John 14:15-21; 15:26)

e. In what ways can the church provide an environment where people can become confident (Psalm 108:35-43)

f. SUMMARY QUESTION: Considering the answers to a-e above, what role does prayer, Scripture study and fellowship with believers play in fighting insecurity?

## 5. Attacking Satan's lies

Satan has a special package of lies for insecure people. However, for the insecure person to maintain a positive attitude, it is necessary to attack Satan's lies with the Word of God. Refute the following lies of Satan, using the Scriptures suggested and any others that you know.

a. Lie #1: A person should be "sized up" based on outward appearances such as: job, expensive clothing, skin color, place of residence, family connections, educational achievement, and what white people give them. (Isaiah 28:29; 30:1)

b. Lie #2: Only "high class" people (in the world's terms) should hold positions of leadership (such as deacon) in the church. (Romans 12:2; 1 Corinthians 11:18; Revelation 20:11-12)

c. Lie #3: It is important for a man to be #1 in everything he does. He must look the best, maneuver the best, and have the most things. (2 Corinthians 10:12; 1 Corinthians 12)

d. Lie #4: A real man is one who can control others at all times, particularly his wife. (1 Peter 5:1-7; Proverbs 15:33; Ephesians 5:21-33)

e. Lie #5: Corporate America is the center of the universe. It is where the action is. (James 1:17; Hebrews 12:9; Matthew 28:18)

f. SUMMARY QUESTION: How can each of the above lies play a part in causing a person to become insecure about who they are? How can a counselor use the answers to a-e above to help such an insecure person?

## 6. SUMMARY EXERCISE

In what ways can the local church minister to people dealing with insecurity related to oppression on their jobs? Are there special support groups that can be formed? In what ways can the local church help individuals form a view of themselves that reflects God's love rather than others' opinions?

## 7. PERSONAL APPLICATION

Are you insecure? If so, meditate, during your prayer time, on some of the Scriptures presented in this case study. Then ask the Lord for wise counsel so that you can form a better opinion of yourself.

# CHAPTER TEN

# LONELINESS

## Beverly Yates

*Carmen and Jewell left the nurses' station together, at the end of the work day. As they walked down the corridor toward the parking lot, Jewell began telling Carmen how lonely she was. She said that she was afraid to go home to her empty apartment. She had moved to Atlanta from Ann Arbor three years ago, after completing both a master's degree in nursing and a professional physician's assistant program. Her brothers and sisters still resided in Michigan. In all of this time, she hadn't really made any friends.*

*As the only Black woman at the hospital holding a position as prestigious as that of a physician's assistant, both Black and white nurses seemed to feel uncomfortable with her, and most did not respond to her attempts to form friendships with them.*

*She had recently left a local church that she had joined, feeling unloved, after attempting to form a new health care ministry there and not getting any cooperation from the church nurses. She felt that they were uncomfortable with her because she had professional nursing skills, and they were not accustomed to accepting leadership from a younger woman. She really didn't feel that she "fit in" at the church.*

*Relationships with men had also failed. Most men she had dated were accustomed to having sexual relations soon after their first dates. When she refused, they said that the reason she wouldn't do it was because she felt she was better than other women and the men she dated, since she had a college degree. She had become very depressed and had recently started smoking reefers.*

*Sometimes, when she was alone in her apartment, she was frightened by thoughts of suicide. She said she reached out to Carmen because Carmen seemed different from the other nurses, and she needed to talk with someone who would listen.*

Jewell, in the above story, is hurting as a result of loneliness. Loneliness is a condition common to all human beings. People from all walks of life, young, middle-aged, and elderly, pass through the gates of loneliness. Moreover, most Christians both work and live around lonely people who may never have accepted Jesus Christ as their personal Saviour, or are not connected to church families.

This chapter focuses on how to help lonely people. It is for those who want to be able to lead lonely people into a relationship with the Lord, and for those who want to lead lonely Christians into more meaningful relationships with the Community of Faith.

## An Example of Loneliness in Scripture

A position of leadership can be a lonely place. It was for Elijah, in Scripture. In fact, because of his attempts to lead the Israelites into worshiping the one true God, he was ostracized. His life was threatened by Ahab and Jezebel, who wanted the Israelites to worship Baal rather than the true God. In his flight from Jezebel, Elijah became so despondent that he wanted to die.

## from Scripture

**1 Kings 19:1** And Ahab told Jezebel all that Elijah had done, and withal how he had slain all the prophets with the sword.

**2** Then Jezebel sent a messenger unto Elijah, saying, So let the gods do to me, and more also, if I make not thy life as the life of one of them by tomorrow about this time.

**3** And when he saw that, he arose, and went for his life, and came to Beersheba, which belongeth to Judah, and left his servant there.

**4** But he himself went a day's journey into the wilderness, and came and sat down under a juniper tree: and he requested for himself that he might die; and said, It is enough; now, O Lord, take away my life; for I am not better than my fathers.

**5** And as he lay and slept under a juniper tree, behold, then an angel touched him, and said unto him, Arise and eat.

**6** And he looked, and, behold, there was a cake baked on the coals, and a cruse of water at his head. And he did eat and drink, and laid him down again.

**7** And the angel of the Lord came again the second time, and touched him, and said, Arise and eat; because the journey is too great for thee.

**8** And he arose, and did eat and drink, and went in the strength of that meat forty days and forty nights unto Horeb the mount of God.

**9** And he came thither unto a cave, and lodged there; and, behold, the word of the Lord came to him, and he said unto him, What doest thou here, Elijah?

**10** And he said, I have been very jealous for the Lord God of hosts: for the children of Israel have forsaken thy covenant, thrown down thine altars, and slain thy prophets with the sword; and I, even I only, am left; and they seek my life, to take it away.

**11** And he said, Go forth, and stand upon the mount before the Lord. And, behold, the Lord passed by, and a great and strong wind rent the mountains, and brake in pieces the rocks before the Lord; but the Lord was not in the wind; and after the wind an earthquake; but the Lord was not in the earthquake:

**12** And after the earthquake a fire; but the Lord was not in the fire: and after the fire a still small voice.

**13** And it was so, when Elijah heard it, that he wrapped his face in his mantle, and went out, and stood in the entering in of the cave. And, behold, there came a voice unto him, and said, What doest thou here, Elijah?

**14** And he said, I have been very jealous for the Lord God of hosts: because the children of Israel have forsaken thy covenant, thrown down thine altars, and slain thy prophets with the sword; and I, even I only, am left; and they seek my life, to take it away.

**15** And the Lord said unto him, Go, return on thy way to the wilderness of Damascus: and when thou comest, anoint Hazael to be king over Syria:

**18** Yet I have left me seven thousand in Israel, all the knees which have not bowed unto Baal, and every mouth which hath not kissed him.

## What Loneliness Is

Loneliness is a state of living in a solitary mode or place. It is the experience of being confined, to the extent that meaningful relationships with other human beings are impossible, or at best inadequate. People experience loneliness when they are isolated from other persons. Loneliness is the prelude to depression, and to more serious mental problems. People who suffer from loneliness display some of the following characteristics. These characteristics can be seen in Elijah the prophet as he fled, alone, from Ahab and Jezebel:

1. A sense of loss resulting from being cut off from loved ones (1 Kings 9:3-4, 11b-12a).

2. Lack of communication with "significant others" (19:14).

3. Lack of enthusiasm (19:4).

4. Boredom (19:4).

5. Self-pity (19:4, 10, 14).

6. Fear (19:3, 14).

7. Anger (19:4).

8. Self-consciousness (19:13).

Among the effects of loneliness are: low self-esteem, lack of confidence in oneself and in others, the belief that no one cares, and the belief that one is not worthy of attention from others.

**Everyday experiences of loneliness.** There is nothing wrong with being alone, sometimes. Being alone doesn't necessarily mean that one is lonely. Being alone is human and natural. Many everyday experiences place people in positions where they must act alone. Have you ever witnessed a group of people receiving degrees or diplomas? Each graduate is awarded the certificate of his/her accomplishment separately.

Recently my husband and I assisted our 13-year-old daughter Sara in her struggle to learn the United States Constitution and to pass a related test as a requirement for graduation from elementary school in Chicago. We would gladly have taken the test for her, but she had to pass it all alone.

Most important decisions of life must be made alone. While others may advise, teach, and guide, most of life's major decisions are made alone. Decisions related to marriage, profession, vocation, and parenthood, are made alone. Life is a lonely journey in spite of the abundance of men and women and boys and girls around us. Many of life's experiences and achievements are carried out alone, with each person dependent on God and his/her own efforts and abilities.

We must be supportive and interested in one another, but the lonely climb to success or failure is borne by each of us apart from anyone but God.

Some loneliness can be very painful, and people who experience painful loneliness can require help and support from others, in order to prevent loneliness from leading to mental illness.

**The painfully lonely in Scripture**. Job is an example of a painfully lonely person (Job 1:21). Afflicted by Satan, Job experienced the loss of his property and his children, and then began to experience the loss of his health as boils began to cover his body. Although Job had friends, they were of little assistance. Job also had a wife, but she also was of no assistance; she encouraged him to curse God and die (Job 2:9-10). Job, although surrounded by people, was a very lonely man.

David, a man after God's own heart, was also a painfully lonely man. His response to his loneliness was to sin, by initiating an adulterous relationship with Bathsheba. Then that sin caused further loneliness, causing him to be cut off from fellowship with God because of his lust and sin (2 Samuel 11). One sin led to another until David was responsible for the death of his friend Uriah (2 Samuel 11:24). In Psalm 51, one can easily visualize David's (the author) loneliness as he cries out to God for forgiveness, cleansing and renewal. He needed to do this before he could experience fellowship with God again.

**Modern, famous, but painfully lonely people**. Today, painful loneliness is experienced by both the rich and the poor, those who are well-known and by those who are relatively unknown. On the cover of the April, 1988 issue of *Sports Illustrated* is a picture of Muhammad Ali, an example of a famous but lonely person. Ali, perhaps the greatest professional boxer since Joe Louis, is pictured in the expressionless black and white photo. His once bright, confident smile is gone, and his eyes have a look of hopelessness. Ali has Parkinson's disease.

The interview with Ali, in the magazine, provides evidence that this once popular man is alone. Gone are the people who once cared for every need: wives, personal physicians, managers, trainers, cooks, bodyguards, and masseurs. Most are involved with others now. The interviewer, Gary Smith wrote: "The Champ and his followers were the greatest show on earth, and then the show ended. But life went on." Singer Michael Jackson has also been portrayed as a very lonely person. In the biography of Michael Jackson by Jacqueline Kennedy Onassis, he appears, in spite of his talent, popularity, and riches, to have few close relationships with people. One can see that the experience of being lonely appears to be a universal and common part of human existence.

**Recognizing the painfully lonely in our midst.** Loneliness is also experienced by common people. There are many people who, due to the circumstances in which life has placed them, experience loneliness. One example is the senior citizen. The fastest growing segment of America's population today are senior citizens. Due to improved living conditions, better nutrition and generally improved access to health care in our nation, more people are living longer. Senior citizens probably constitute the largest group of lonely people in our midst.

Among these seniors are widows, separated from their adult children, living alone, and lacking transportation to church. Also among them are former pastors, ministers, deacons, deaconesses, trustees and others who once helped to build our churches but are now confined to nursing homes.

Our seniors often live alone, after retirement, on fixed incomes. Most are proud. Many are not helpless. However, many are inactive. Many, in spite of the availability of excellent doctors and the knowledge of medical remedies for most ailments, still suffer from various diseases of the aging process.

One doesn't need to be a senior citizen to be lonely, though. College students living on campuses are often very lonely people. Every year young people leave our homes and churches bound for new experiences in colleges, universities and the armed forces. Away from home, they encounter many new and disturbing problems, which can lead to feelings of loneliness.

I once experienced this type of loneliness. I experienced it when, some years ago, I entered Cook County School of Nursing in Chicago to fulfill my dream of becoming a registered nurse. My family, for the most part, lived in Michigan. Upon entering school I was assigned a room on the 14th floor of the nurses' residence overlooking the vast west side of Chicago. Although I was involved in a course of study that challenged my young mind and body, I was lonely.

I missed the sights and sounds of home. In the dormitory there were no noisy brothers and nosy sisters around to "bug me"! In addition, there were some problems that had to do with being Black. I always felt that the white girls avoided me because I was Black. I felt that most of the Black girls didn't like me because I had light skin and long hair. I remember crying myself to sleep many nights because I felt alone and unloved in a strange environment.

Troubled teenagers are also frequently found among the lonely. Such teenagers are usually somewhere within our midst. They are in our churches, families, and communities surrounding the churches. Some are very young and pregnant. Others have various addictions, and some have deadly diseases such as AIDS. Others (many of whom were at one time a part of our churches), are either imprisoned or detained in juvenile detention facilities. Because they are troubled, such teenagers often experience hostility and ridicule from others, to the extent that they rarely get the opportunity to discuss their real feelings about the problems they face.

Then there are people among us who are suffering from various terminal illnesses. Often such people are confined to hospitals for chemotherapy and other treatments, and they usually face these problems alone. Struggling with the realities of death is usually a very lonely experience.

Among the lonely are the divorced and separated. People who are experiencing separation from spouses, for one reason or another, are often very lonely people. It is very difficult to recover from relationships that have failed. It is difficult to take the chance to establish new relationships with new people.

Married people can also be very lonely. Many singles believe the only answer to loneliness is marriage. However, singles who envy married people are frequently unaware of the many failures in intimate relationships that result in the loneliness of a married person. One example is the married woman who must work and take care of her family, for financial reasons. Such women rarely get the time they need to be alone.

Such women soon begin to feel sorry for themselves, one of the signs of loneliness. They often feel misunderstood and alone in their roles within the family, unable to communicate their real feelings or needs to anyone, for fear of being misunderstood. This is particularly true of many professional Black women who try to meet the demands of church life, careers and families.

Such women are often expected to focus on others' needs and deny their personal needs. If they do not do this, they are often made to feel guilty. Few people recognize the needs of such women to be served and heard.

Other painfully and obviously lonely people are among "latchkey children", the homeless, the hungry, the thirsty, the poor, the imprisoned, the single, the single parent, the orphan, the doctor's wife, the pastor's wife, and missionaries living in other countries (Matthew 25:34).

## Dealing with Loneliness

Often lonely people reach out for help from Christians they know. These Christians could be persons with whom they work, neighbors, people who are responsible for follow-up of Sunday School absentees, people who handle sick visitation, people who teach Bible study classes, the church secretary, the church janitor, the deacon, the trustee, or the "bench member" who sits beside them every Sunday.

Following are guidelines for helping people who are lonely.

The guidelines can be used as information for dealing with personal loneliness as well.

**Recognize and understand feelings of loneliness.** Not everyone who is experiencing loneliness recognizes that is their problem. Jewell, in the story at the beginning of this chapter, did acknowledge that loneliness was her root problem. However, this isn't always easy to do. It is important for a person who reaches out for help, to recognize some of the basic signs of loneliness. These have been presented earlier. They include a heightened sense of boredom, lack of concentration, hypersensitivity, a heightened sense of self-awareness, and self-pity. Such feelings often follow a separation of some type (death of a loved one, divorce, etc.).

In order for the lonely person to accept the reality of loneliness, he or she needs to realize that loneliness is not unusual. Being alone does not mean that the person is a bad person, or that the person is not worthy of being loved.

Once the counselor, friend or lay leader gets the person to acknowledge that loneliness is the problem, then the counselor and counselee are in a position to work on solutions.

**Establish a relationship with Christ.** The most important decision of one's life is whether to accept or reject Jesus Christ as Saviour and Lord. This decision is so important because one's acceptance or rejection of Jesus Christ determines whether one will be a part of God's kingdom and the Community of Faith on earth (John 3:3). Belief in the Lord Jesus Christ's death, burial and resurrection is an "insurance policy" against perishing (John 3:16) as a result of loneliness or anything else. One should not allow past sins to keep one from accepting Christ and joining the Community of Faith, for all have sinned and fallen short of God's glory. Therefore, everyone needs to be saved (Romans 3:23).

Refusing to accept Jesus Christ as Saviour is a sin, and the wages of this decision is spiritual death (Romans 6:23), one symptom of which is painful loneliness. A person can escape from the pain of loneliness. The escape begins with salvation and confessing that Jesus Christ is Lord (Romans 10:9, 10).

While a counselor may not want to rush into counseling about salvation at the beginning of the counseling sessions, the lonely person must ultimately be shown that only Christ has the power to rescue the person from painful loneliness. It is only by abiding in Christ that we receive the power to handle the sometimes overpowering effects of loneliness (John 15:4, 5). Human relationships have their place, but only faith in Jesus Christ, God's Son, can satisfy the innermost part of our being. God created us to need fellowship with Him. People begin to deal with loneliness as a result of spiritual development after salvation. The pace at which this occurs varies with the individual.

In my personal situation, after many hours alone with God in meditation and prayer, I learned to appreciate the presence and power of the Holy Spirit. I now know that, when God allows illness, the loss of a job, or the loss of friends to occur, I will not be alone. God, through His Holy Spirit will always be there.

People who want to help lonely people should begin by informing them about the love of God and how God gave His only begotten Son for them. Once the lonely person has accepted Christ, then the counselor or friend should encourage them not to despair when hard times come. They can practice turning their eyes toward Jesus and being sensitive to the Holy Spirit within them.

For example, in the case of Jewell in the story at the beginning of this chapter, the first place to begin to deal with her life's challenges and with the related problems of loneliness, is to get to know Jesus Christ and then learn to cultivate an intimate relationship with Him.

**Become more aware of the presence of God.** One of the facts about loneliness is that it is more a feeling than a reality for the Christian. The Christian realizes that God is always present and the Holy Spirit of God is within. The Christian knows that God will never leave him/her or forsake him/her (Hebrews

13:5).

Recall that, in the story of Elisha, God came to him in the midst of his painful loneliness. God sent an angel to minister to him. God spoke to Elijah in a still small voice, after Elijah had experienced an earthquake, wind and fire. After that experience Elijah was willing to obey the voice of God.

If the Christian is not aware of God's presence, s/he can become vulnerable to Satan. Satan loves to tempt people when they are alone. The counselor can show the lonely person how Satan tried to tempt Jesus when He was in the wilderness, alone and hungry (Matthew 4:1-11). However, Jesus did not compromise Himself or fall prey to Satan as David, the Psalmist did in his affair with Bathsheba, and as many people do when they are alone and feel needy.

When people are alone, the devil will lie to them and tell them that illicit sex, stealing, drugs and alcohol are the keys to ending their loneliness. Billboard ads suggest this as they advertise alcohol and illicit sex as cures for loneliness. It is important for the Christian who is feeling lonely to learn to practice God's presence through prayer, Bible study and meditation (Matthew 5:6). Singing songs of praise and thanksgiving also helps to bring one into the awareness of the presence of the Holy Spirit (James 5:13). These are the best weapons against Satan, who uses loneliness to tempt Christians into sin (Ephesians 6:10-18).

Practicing the presence of the Lord also involves waiting on the Lord and being of good courage.

**End painful loneliness by helping others**. It appears from God's perspective of life on this planet that we need meaningful relationships with other humans. Moreover, the Bible says that whatever we want others to do for us, we should be willing to do for them (Matthew 7:12). Therefore, one of the perfect solutions for loneliness is for the lonely person to find ways to help other people end their loneliness and help other people meet needs that they may have. Churches, charities, civil rights organizations, and other groups have many opportunities for helping others.

However, one of the most important ways of ending painful loneliness is by helping others through the Community of Faith. The Bible says that a place has been set aside in the Community of Faith for every believer (2 Corinthians 12), and that there are many different ways their gifts can be used there. The counselor or friend should help the lonely person find ways to use their talents and skills within the Community of Faith, within the Black community, and within the community at large.

For example, with Jewell, in the story at the beginning of this chapter, it is important that she locate a local church in which she feels welcome and comfortable. It is important that the church welcome people such as Jewell and allow them to use their gifts in the Community of Faith. She needs to be affirmed and loved in the same way that any other member of God's family needs to be loved, regardless of her educational background (1 Corinthians 12:23, 25).

In relationship to this, the counselor must show the counselee that some forms of loneliness are self-inflicted. They are brought on and sustained by oneself. In the April, 1988 issue of *Ladies Home Journal*, Pastor Charles Meyer, Director of Pastoral Care at St. David's Community Hospital in Austin, Texas said that a person can be alone without being lonely. However, loneliness can be brought on by oneself. That type of loneliness can be present when a person is alone or when s/he is with a group of people.

To take the steps necessary to end loneliness, one must recognize that some of it has been brought on by oneself. For example, Jewell, in the story at the beginning of this chapter, has brought some loneliness on herself by refusing to locate another church where she feels more comfortable, and by refusing to determine where, and in what circumstances, she can meet men who are saved and have high moral standards.

**Consider marriage**. God intends for some people to marry. Marriage, if intended by God, is one of the ways in which loneliness is alleviated. Therefore, single people of all ages should be encouraged to consider this as a possibility, if they sense God leading them in this direction.

God instituted and sanctions marriage (Hebrews 13:4). God has said that prolonged periods of loneliness are not good. After saying this, He created a partner for Adam (Genesis 2:7-24). The Lord had sensed Adam's loneliness.

The birds and beasts had been considered as suitable companions, but they were not sufficient to meet Adam's needs. The Bible seems to indicate that for Adam even the presence and fellowship of God were inadequate. He truly needed Eve. God made him that way. It is important to recognize that God did not create another man for Adam's companion but created a unique creature similar to Adam, yet very different. He formed woman and held the first wedding ceremony. God intended marriage to be one answer to loneliness.

Of course not all Christians will or should be married (Matthew 19:11-12), but marriage is certainly one solution to the problem of loneliness. It is an option that God leaves available for Christians (1 Corinthians 7:1-9). All marriages are not solutions to loneliness either. Problem marriages can trigger painful experiences of loneliness. Therefore, it is important to listen to the voice of the Lord and allow Him to lead you to a marriage partner. Once in marriage, one must still listen to the Lord's voice in order to stay within the marriage and help it develop into what it needs to be. Marriage is not the "end-all" or "be-all." Only the Lord is.

**Be grateful!** As mentioned above, lonely people are prone to feel self-pity. In this state of mind, one feels that because one is alone one is not loved. To turn these feelings around, the counselor, friend or lay leader might encourage the lonely person to count his/her blessings. The counselor might even remind the counselee of the lyrics of the song, "Count Your Blessings." This can be the starting point for an exercise, whereby the counselee actually lists on a sheet of paper all of the wonderful things that God has done for him/her:

"Count your blessings. Name them one by one!
Count your blessings. See what God has done!
Count your blessings. Name them one by one!
And it will surprise you what the Lord has done!" *(National Baptist Hymnal,* p. 30)

**Use time productively and creatively.** It is possible to spend enjoyable time by oneself. However, this does require filling time creatively. To do this, it is necessary to determine who you are, what you need, and what you want.

The counselor can encourage the lonely person to embark on personal self-help projects, in areas the counselee perceives that s/he wants to improve. Many courses at local colleges, continuing education centers, "discovery centers," the YWCA and YMCA, and churches are designed for this purpose. They are also good places to meet friends.

**The role of the church.** The church can't meet everyone's needs for fellowship all the time. However, God sent His Son to redeem and call out a people who would minister to one another in their needs (1 Corinthians 12 and 13). God wants us to use His *agape* love to reach out and spend time with those in need of friendship and attention. Church leaders should not allow themselves to become so busy they cannot minister to the needs of the lonely in their congregations and church communities. Doing this requires sacrifice and a death to selfishness.

The lonely should accept help from the Community of Faith in the way that the Community of Faith is equipped to supply help. To expect everyone in the church fellowship to focus on one person's needs is unrealistic. It is also inappropriate for individual members to try to dictate by whom and how they will accept help. Individual members should be willing to accept help from people other than the pastor.

A wise pastor or assistant pastor will meet with people to ascertain the problem and then assign the person to the appropriate deacon, deaconness or other acceptable person. These leaders should then accept the responsibility for providing ongoing fellowship for the lonely person. The pastor should make periodic calls to check on the progress of needy people, but he should not be expected to provide day-to-day support for everyone who needs it.

The entire Community of Faith is responsible. Jesus underscores the importance of the kingdom of heaven for believers (Matthew 25:34). He says the way we treat those in need is an indication of the way we feel about Him (25:35-40).

**Summary**. This chapter has focused on helping lonely people. Among the strategies for dealing with loneliness are: establishing a relationship with Christ, recognizing and understanding feelings of loneliness, becoming more aware of the presence of God, reaching out and helping others, using time productively and cultivating a positive attitude. Marriage was also presented as one of the ways the Lord has used to alleviate loneliness in humankind. The role of the church in helping lonely people was also emphasized.

We now turn our attention to applying these strategies to helping a lonely person, in the following case study.

## CASE STUDY

*INSTRUCTIONS: Mrs. Simpson, in the following story, is experiencing painful loneliness. The following exercises will lead you into an in-depth study of Mrs. Simpson's problem, and an opportunity to apply principles from the chapter to it.*

*The first five exercises consist of a series of "discovery" questions, followed by a summary question. The sixth exercise asks you to summarize and apply information you gained from the first five exercises. The seventh exercise asks you to make personal applications of the principles you learned in this chapter.*

240

## MRS. SIMPSON

*It was Tuesday night and Deacon Green was doing sick visitation in the senior citizens' complex, where many members of Beacon Street A.M.E. lived. When he reached 80-year-old Mrs. Belle Simpson's home, he knocked on the door, but no one answered. This seemed unusual, so Deacon Green rang the bell of Mrs. Adams, the floor captain on Mrs. Simpson's floor. Mrs. Adams came out and said that she had seen Mrs. Simpson earlier, and she believed that Mrs. Simpson was still in her apartment. Mrs. Adams rushed into her apartment and phoned security.*

*Mr. Bryant, the security guard, rushed over and opened the door. When the door was opened, Mrs. Simpson could be seen sitting by her window, staring into space. When they tried to talk to her, she was un-responsive.*

*Mr. Bryant immediately called an ambulance, and Mrs. Simpson was rushed to the nearby hospital. In the days that followed, Mrs. Simpson's son, who flew in from Mississippi, notified Deacon Green that Mrs. Simpson was successfully treated at the hospital, but had been suffering from a mild stroke and was in an acute state of malnutrition.*

*Raymond Simpson informed Deacon Green that his mother had been widowed 12 years ago, and for the past 10 years had been living alone in the seniors complex. During that time period, a number of her close friends had gone on to be with the Lord. Because she had stopped driving, she couldn't regularly attend church or be at meetings of the senior club at the church. She didn't want to be a bother to others.*

*Raymond informed Deacon Green that Mrs. Adams, the floor captain, had told him that Mrs. Simpson had*

**241**

*recently said she had lost her appetite. She had stopped cooking, saying that it was too much trouble to cook and eat alone. Most of her meals consisted of cereal and milk. Her only company, for days at a time, was the television. The telephone rarely rang.*

## 1. The role of the church

Mrs. Simpson had lost contact with her family and church.

a. Is it all right for Mrs. Simpson to worship the Lord alone, away from the church to which she belongs? (Hebrews 10:25)

b. Does the church have a responsibility to see that people such as Mrs. Simpson have a means for getting to church? (Acts 6:1-7; 1 Corinthians 12:23-26; Matthew 25:34-40)

c. Does Mrs. Simpson's family have a responsibility to see that her needs are met? (Exodus 20:12; Ephesians 6:2)

d. Can an 80-year-old woman really contribute anything to the Community of Faith? (1 Corinthians 7:7; 12:4-26)

e. What is one obvious gift that a Christian of Mrs. Simpson's age might bring to the body of Christ? (Hebrews 5:14)

f. SUMMARY QUESTION: Based on information from questions a-e above, summarize the biblical foundation for churches and families helping people such as Mrs. Simpson combat painful loneliness.

## 2. A relationship with Christ

One cannot rid oneself of painful loneliness without the Lord.

a. Does the fact that Mrs. Simpson once belonged to a church mean that she has made a personal commitment to Christ (i.e., is born again)? (John 10:1)

b. Can Mrs. Simpson be "born again" at her age? (John 3:3-5, 16)

c. If a person such as Mrs. Simpson has worked in the church all of her life, does this take the place of being born again?

(Ephesians 2:9)

d. If Mrs. Simpson is not born again, what does she need to do in order to be born again? (John 3:16; Romans 10:9, 10)

e. In what ways can salvation help Mrs. Simpson to handle loneliness better? (John 15:4, 5; Hebrews 13:5; 1 Kings 19:11-12)

f. SUMMARY QUESTION: How can a counselor, deacon or friend use the information in a-e above to lead Mrs. Simpson to Christ, if she is not already a Christian?

## 3. Helping others

One way of eliminating painful loneliness is to learn how to help others. Mrs. Simpson may have gifts or skills that can be used to help others in the Community of Faith.

a. What is the gift of wisdom? Can you think of a specific, concrete way that an 80-year-old woman with this gift might contribute to the Community of Faith? (1 Corinthians 2:6-12; 12:8)

b. What is the gift of faith? (1 Corinthians 12:9; Matthew 17:18-21) Can you think of a specific, concrete way that an 80-year-old woman with this gift might contribute to the Community of Faith?

c. Name at least three other gifts (not mentioned in a and b above) that a person such as Mrs. Simpson might bring to the Community of Faith. (1 Corinthians 12)

d. Is Black history important? (Deuteronomy 6:10-19; Judges 2:11-19) Can you think of a specific, concrete way that an 80-year-old Black woman can contribute to a Community of Faith, in the area of Black history?

e. What is another role (not mentioned in a-d above) that an older woman can play in the body of Christ? (Titus 2:4)

f. SUMMARY QUESTION: Based on the answers to a-e above, what are some ways that Mrs. Simpson can be encouraged to use her gifts to help others? What impact might these activities have on her painful experience of loneliness?

## 4. Using time productively

Some productive activities can be done alone. They are the types of "self-help" activities that counter the effects of loneliness.

a. What is one activity that Mrs. Simpson can carry out alone? (2 Timothy 2:15) What materials might she need to do this?

b. What is another activity, practiced by Anna in the New Testament, that can be done alone? (Luke 2:36-37)

c. What is another activity (not mentioned in a-b above) that Mrs. Simpson might carry out from her home, alone? (Matthew 25:36) What equipment might she need to do this? What supplies?

d. What is one "self-help" goal that Mrs. Simpson can set for herself? (Philippians 2:4-5)

e. What is another "self-help" goal that Mrs. Simpson can set for herself? (Hebrews 3:12)

f. SUMMARY QUESTION: How can a deacon, friend or counselor use the information in a-e above to help Mrs. Simpson learn to productively use the time that she spends alone?

## 5. Being grateful!

At 80 years of age, Mrs. Simpson has quite a bit for which to be thankful.

a. What is one thing for which Mrs. Simpson can be thankful? (Matthew 9:35)

b. For what else should Mrs. Simpson be thankful? (Philippians 4:13)

c. For what else should Mrs. Simpson be thankful? (Philippians 1:3-6)

d. For what else should Mrs. Simpson be thankful? (Psalm 23)

e. For what else should Mrs. Simpson be thankful? (John 14:16, 26; 15:26)

f. SUMMARY QUESTION: How can a counselor, friend, deacon or minister use the information from questions a-e above to comfort Mrs. Simpson?

## 6. SUMMARY EXERCISE

What types of ministries can be created, within the Black church, which can help seniors with some of the following? How can already existing programs be improved?

a. Transportation

b. Food

c. Fellowship

d. Health Care

e. Education

f. Meeting Potential Mates

## 7. PERSONAL APPLICATION

Are you lonely? What types of strategies, presented in this chapter, can you use to eliminate painful loneliness from your life?

# LOW SELF-ESTEEM

## Dr. LeRoy Yates

*When I was growing up in Alexandra it meant hate, bitterness, hunger, pain, terror, violence, fear, dashed hopes and dreams. Today it still means the same for millions of black children who are trapped in the ghettos of South Africa, In a lingering nightmare of a racial system that in many respects resembles Nazism. In the ghettos black children fight for survival from the moment they are born. They take to hating and fearing the police, soldiers and authorities as a baby takes to its mother's breast.*

*In my childhood these enforcers of white prerogatives and whims represented a sinister force capable of crushing me at will; of making my parents flee in the dead of night to escape arrest under the Pass laws; of marching them naked out of bed because they did not have the permit allowing them to live as husband and wife under the same roof. They turned my father--by repeatedly arresting him and denying him the right to earn a living in a way that gave him dignity--into such a bitter man that, as he fiercely but in vain resisted the emasculation, he hurt those he loved the most.*

In his autobiography, *Kaffir Boy*, Mark Mathabane describes Black people who experience low self-esteem. They are victims of the racism and apartheid of the South African government.

Racism and apartheid, when practiced by a group in power, foster low self-esteem in members of the groups being oppressed. Understanding the problem of low self-esteem is complex--especially as it relates to Black people of the United States. Though some Black people are naive about it, none have escaped the racism that is directed at Blacks in particular and at all American minorities in general.

This chapter deals with low self-esteem among Black people. It presents guidelines for helping people with low esteem to develop healthier self-images under God and combat the effects racism has had on their self-images.

## A Biblical Example of Low Self-Esteem

Gideon is an example of a person in Scripture who had low self-esteem, due to the circumstances of his birth. Gideon saw himself as the society around him projected him. His image of himself was entirely out of sync with the image that God had of him.

## from Scripture

**Judges 6:11** And there came an angel of the Lord, and sat under an oak which was in Ophrah, that pertained unto Joash the Abiezrite: and his son Gideon threshed wheat by the winepress, to hide it from the Midianites.

**12** And the angel of the Lord appeared unto him, and said unto him, The Lord is with thee, thou mighty man of valour.

**13** And Gideon said unto him, Oh my Lord, if the Lord be with us, why then is all this befallen us? and where be all his miracles which our fathers told us of, saying, Did not the Lord bring us up from Egypt? but now the Lord hath forsaken us, and delivered us into the hands of the Midianites.

**14** And the Lord looked upon him, and said, Go in this thy might, and thou shalt save Israel from the hand of the Midianites: have not I sent thee?

**15** And he said unto him, Oh my Lord, wherewith shall I save Israel? behold, my family is poor in Mannasseh, and I am the least in my father's house.

**16** And the Lord said unto him, Surely I will be with thee, and thou shalt smite the Midianites as one man.

## What Is Low Self-Esteem?

Self-esteem is how one feels about oneself. As a man thinks in his heart, so is he (Proverbs 23:7). Moreover, what one does is often based upon the way one feels about oneself. Bad feelings about oneself equals low performance. Feelings are related to productivity and quality of performance. This is true, regardless of the task to be performed.

High self-esteem, on the other hand, results in good performance. A good self-image is related to high self-esteem. In his excellent book, *The Sensation of Being Somebody*, Maurice Wagner, a professional Christian counselor, explains that there are three essential components of a healthy self-image. The first is a sense of belongingness. It is an awareness that one is accepted, wanted, cared for, enjoyed and loved. The second component of a healthy self-image is an inner sense of worth. It is the notion that: "I count. I am valuable. I have something to offer."

Gideon is an example of a person who lacked a healthy self-image. Gideon noticeably lacked a sense of his value, and he was convinced that he did not have anything to offer. In that sense, he did not have a healthy self-image. Instead, he had low self-esteem (Judges 6:15).

The third component of a healthy self-image is a sense of being competent. It is a feeling that: "I can do it. I can cope with the situation. I am able to meet the challenges of life." Because Gideon lacked a healthy self-image, due to his feelings about the circumstances of his birth and those of his people, he also lacked a sense of being competent to perform the task that the Lord had given him to do (6:14-15).

The story of Gideon shows that all three components of a healthy self-image can be destroyed by racism. If a person is exposed to the types of experiences that condition him/her to feel inadequate, these ideas eventually impregnate the mind itself and impregnate the personality with fear and a feeling of inferiority.

Black people who are not from strong, affirming and loving families are usually ill-equipped to handle racism. They are not able to understand racism well enough to cope with it and transcend it. Racism, to them, becomes traumatic and life threatening. It leaves emotional scars and memories which are difficult to ignore, even when the circumstances which evoked them have changed for the better.

People with low self-esteem, due to racism, are common in our churches, in the communities surrounding our churches, on our jobs, and in our families. Often people suffering from this type of low self-esteem reach out for help. As Christians carrying the Gospel into the world, and as church leaders who bear the responsibility for shepherding the flock, it is important to understand low self-esteem and how it affects Black Americans and other minorities. It is also important to understand how low self-esteem relates to racism of the dominant society.

The terrible disease of racism has shown its evil and monstrous head in our schools, communities, churches and places of employment. Anywhere a Black person goes, the monster of racism is already there. This is true throughout the world. In reading *Kaffir Boy* by Mark Mathabane, I was surprised to see that the racism in South Africa so closely resembles racism as it exists in the United States.

Similar to the South African situation, African Americans have been enslaved and abused by America and the white Christian church. In fact, today, American Christians are still divided along racial lines. Some of the major consequences of racism can be seen in the distorted images, incorrect teachings, and bad treatment which Black people have received at the hands of white people in America.

In fact, large numbers of white Christians have participated in discrimination against Black people and this fact has driven large numbers of Black people away from considering the Christian faith. While Black people are not the only ones having trouble with low self-esteem that results from racism, they, unlike whites who suffer various forms of discrimination, must face the daily added burden of constantly having to respond to bigotry and racism.

Black people, individually and collectively, are very similar to Gideon in this respect (6:15). Gideon, living at a time when Midianites were oppressing Israelites, looked at certain characteristics of the Abiezrites (6:11, 15), the clan of Manassites to which he belonged (6:15). He then concluded that, based on who his clan was, they did not have what it took to conquer the Midianites.

A modern example of the effects of racism on performance is the story of Debi Thomas, former international figure skating champion. The story of Debi Thomas is just one example of the effects of racism on self-esteem. Not long ago, Debi, former world champion, once again skated in the crucible of international Olympic competitions. It was obvious she was "head and shoulders" above the other participants in ability. However, she was Black. The fact of her color caused the entire world to watch. The white media blitz leading up to the Debi Thomas match was extreme, placing excessive racial pressure on her, until the young lady cracked under the pressure. In that moment, the self-esteem needed to fight the monster racism apparently was not high enough.

However, it is possible that, if the Black community and the Black church had been more visible and rallied around Debi Thomas and provided an alternative source of esteem, this could have been the very thing to help her face the monster racism. In any case, this type of visible display of support would have been essential if the situation had any possibility of being turned around. How one feels about oneself as a Black person affects performance.

Debi Thomas is a good example of how racism affects self-esteem and then performance. She is just one among so many gifted African Americans. She is one of many who have tremendous potential but so often fail to see their dreams come true. Unfortunately, most of their dreams of high achievement get aborted by others and sometimes by members of the Black community itself.

The source of racism and its resulting low self-esteem is not always from outside. Oppression can also come from within. Many times Black people themselves internalize self-hatred and that results in a distorted image of Black people. If a Black person accepts and believes the message of racism, then he or she believes that Black people are inferior, dumb, ugly, lazy, etc. Such distorted self-images can result in Black people mistreating other Black people.

Another example of how racism can affect self-esteem is an incident experienced by my wife, Beverly. Beverly was born and raised in a small town in Michigan. There were only a few Black families in the town. When Beverly was a child, she recalled a little white girl asking her teacher why some children were Black. The teacher answered, ''Oh, God forgot and kept them in the oven too long.''

Such a thoughtless and simple-minded comment left young Beverly very perplexed. The explanation had come from her teacher, someone she was taught to respect. As a child, one of her immediate responses was helplessness. She began to feel as though she were the victim of an absent-minded God. Incidents similar to this have happened to hundreds of African American children.

However, today my wife's teacher's comments seem mild compared with those of Dr. C. Scoffield in the *Scoffield Reference Bible*. Dr. Scoffield's comments have resulted in misinformation being transmitted to hundreds and thousands of Black people and this, too, has been the source of low self-esteem for many.

Dr. Scoffield attempted, under the guise of scholarship, to explain the notion that Black people are inherently inferior. He went on to justify the enslavement of Blacks in America by referring to some ancient curse, a curse which has no biblical grounds. By planting this terrible error within the context of the Bible itself, Dr. Scoffield paved the way for racists to believe they had a divine sanction for the terrible sin of slavery. He also created a colossal stumbling block for many Black people, who looked to him as an authority on the Bible. He provided the basis for many Black people to consider Christianity "the white folks' religion."

Racism has been used in this way by Satan to damage and destroy Christianity's credibility among many Black people, thereby attempting to rob them of the major source of a healthy self-image. Racism among Christians can be very destructive. Evidence of its effects can be seen, for example, in the fact that today, hardly any white missionary organizations consider Black Americans to be worthy subjects of their missionary enterprise.

## Building a Good Self-Image

Following are steps that one can take to build a healthy self-image and combat the damage of racism. Counselors and others can lead people through these steps as they help them build healthier self-images.

**Establish a relationship with God.** God is the source of good self-images. If a person hasn't accepted Jesus Christ as his/her personal Saviour, there really isn't any basis for attacking racism. One must begin there. Then God's Word, rightly divided, can help to correct erroneous information from the larger society. It can help to eliminate feelings of low self-esteem and build a healthy self-image.

A personal plan of salvation (deliverance) is basic to properly dealing with the problems of low self-esteem. The need for new directions, a new value system, guidance, support, a new identity and truth gives us a new awareness and a new reality. Salvation, however, is not an end in itself. Like physical birth, it is a means to an end which involves growing and learning. It involves constantly dropping old patterns and learning new patterns of belief and behavior.

As we learn better, we do better. As we learn and grow, we can assist others in their needs and struggles. God blesses us and then makes us a blessing to others. All who come to Christ find a new hope, a new way of life, and a new model to emulate. Such is the basis of a revolutionized life-style! Low self-esteem must give way to a new acceptance, a new assurance and the power to believe and become all that God wills for the redeemed personality.

In helping someone develop a better self-image, counselors must consider whether the person has accepted Jesus Christ as his/her Saviour. By leading the person to Christ, the counselor opens a new resource for the person (Matthew 28:18; 2 Corinthians 12:9).

**Reflect on oneself.** Once one has come into a relationship with the Lord, one must be open to developing an opinion of oneself that is separate from those held by others. Personal awareness of oneself is very important. Self-reflection releases us from being slaves to others' opinions. We must begin by asking ourselves why we think the way we do. Why do we do or not do certain things?

This is the first step towards developing an independent value system--one that gives meaning and direction to one's identity. Jesus said, ''ye shall know the truth, and the truth shall make you free'' (John 8:32). The Bible also says that as a man ''thinketh in his heart, so is he'' (Proverbs 23:7).

The Bible points out the importance of transforming our internal thoughts about ourselves, so that we think of ourselves as Jesus thinks of us (Romans 12:2). He made Himself available to ordinary folks (Luke 4:18) who were poor, oppressed, and powerless, and He said to one impotent man, "Wilt thou be made whole?"(John 5:6) From the man's response it is apparent that he was aware of his powerless condition but was not aware of what Jesus was talking about (John 5:1-9). Jesus was talking about being well or delivered.

The man thought an explanation was the only solution to his problem. However, explanations alone will not change one's condition. Christ ignored the man's explanation, and instead commanded him to "take up (his) bed and walk" (5:8).

This story teaches us that our inner thoughts about ourselves must change before we can change outer circumstances. Christ comes into our experiences and changes us inwardly and then we begin to change our situations outwardly. Second Corinthians 5:17 says: "Therefore if any man be in Christ, he is a new creature: old things are passed away; behold, all things are become new." Faith in Jesus Christ allows one to become aware of the spiritual dimensions and reality of God's promises and provisions. This helps us to build better self-esteem, as we see ourselves as God sees us.

Counselors, friends, church leaders and others can guide people into self-reflection exercises designed to discover who they are in Christ and the talents and gifts that the Lord has given to them (2 Corinthians 12; Exodus 19:3-6; 1 Peter 2:9-10; Matthew 25:14-30). Then they are well along the way toward a new self-image.

**Begin an affirmative action plan**. An affirmative action plan can be based on God's Word. It can be designed to foster love, promote healing, remove low self-esteem, and develop wholeness. Jesse Jackson, founder of Operation PUSH in Chicago, often challenges his audiences with the words, "I am somebody! I may be poor. I may be on welfare, but I am somebody!" This is an excellent way to help people become aware of their true potential.

God's word states that he "has made of one blood all nations of men for to dwell on all the face of the earth'' (Acts 17:26). God is no respecter of persons (Acts 10:34). To be delivered from low self-esteem, one must cooperate with God's Word. That involves reprogramming as God's renewal process takes place (Romans 12:2). Everything will not happen overnight.

Changing requires a continuous growth process. It means being "transformed by the renewing of your mind" (Romans 12:2). The verbs in this verse suggest continuous action, and the word ''mind'' is there to indicate the way you learn to think, and the way you learn to see life as a daily process of renewal.

The affirmative action plan requires reprogramming ourselves with the Word of God. God's Word is like a wonderful mirror that is able to let us see ourselves as we are, but it also gives us an image of what we can become by God's grace (James 1:22-25; 1 Corinthians 13:12; Matthew 4:4). Without God's Word, we are blind and sinful and unable to change or help ourselves.

The transforming and liberating work of the Gospel in the believer's life is the secret solution for low self-esteem. To develop a healthy self-image, one can and must change by growing in grace and in the knowledge of our Lord and Saviour Jesus Christ (1 Peter 2:2; 2 Peter 3:18).

Counselors, friends, family members, and others can help people with low self-esteem by encouraging them to develop goals and objectives (an affirmative action plan) for themselves based on the Word of God and His promises.

**See adversity as a blessing in disguise.** The history of the Children of Israel suggests that adversity can be a blessing in disguise. Historically, Black people have studied this and drawn a parallel between the struggles of Black people and those of people of God in the Old Testament. Dr. Martin Luther King saw this parallel. Often called a Moses in our times, Dr. King taught us to sing the song of deliverance and hope, "We shall overcome someday." The parallels between the Children of Israel and those of Black people have shown us that ''all things work together for good to them that love God, to them that are the called according to his purpose'' (Romans 8:28).

It is important to remember that God Himself, in the midst of our struggles, must be recognized and followed if we are to experience deliverance and obtain blessings. Counselors can encourage people with low self-esteem based on the circumstances in which they find themselves, to look ahead to the deliverance of the Lord!

**Have dreams!** Dreams are very important. Remember Joseph, the dreamer, in the Old Testament? Joseph was the dreamer who rose from the dark dungeon of imprisonment and became the wise prime minister of Egypt. He was used of God to save the then known world from starvation (Genesis 41:53-57; 47:14-26). In Dr. King's speech, presented in Washington D.C. in 1963, he said, "I have a dream."

Again, dreams are important! For God's word says, ''where there is no vision (dream), the people perish'' (Proverbs 29:18). One of the sad facts about our Black youth today is that many of them have lost contact with our past history as a people, and many have no vision for the future. Presently they are being consumed in a state of lost identity and confusion. Most have no direction and most have no specific plans for the future. Lacking dreams, goals, models and examples to emulate, many fall prey to drugs, prostitution and other crimes.

Many end up rotting away in jails or trapped in other forms of slavery. However, dreams can provide hope for the future. As families and communities, we must begin early to spend quality time with our children, helping them to develop their dreams. We must teach them. We must tell them stories and share our dreams so that their minds are shaped and their spirits are renewed.

Crime works against dreams! Black-on-Black crime, in particular, is an indication of self-hatred, self-rejection and worthlessness. Rather than tearing down dreams, we must learn how to build them up. Whatever happened to the "Black is Beautiful" saying of the '60's?

**Be optimistic and positive!** Counselors should encourage people with low self-esteem not to become pessimistic and negative. Negative thinking damages the personalities of young people. God's word tells us in Philippians 4:8 to think and speak to others in a positive manner. We must recognize the tremendous influence on others of both good and bad words (James 3:2-13). Remember the story of the 10 spies in Numbers 14? Ten out of the 12 spies brought back a negative report. They discouraged the Israelites and they were destroyed under God's judgment, because they believed the evil report of the 10 spies.

**Ignore peer pressure!** Peer pressure often contributes to low self-esteem. Victims of peer pressure often allow themselves to do things that aren't in their best interest. Such people do things because "everybody else is doing it." However, usually, everyone cannot be doing anything that anyone can imagine.

People with low self-esteem must be encouraged to resist peer pressure. This is particularly important for young Black people who are often pressured by peers to avoid studying, pursuing careers and developing their talents, so that they can be accepted by the negative peer group. Such thinking tells Black young people that Blacks who try to achieve are either ''nerds'' or they are ''trying to be white.''

When a young person accepts this line of thinking, s/he is accepting a low self-image. Negative self-esteem results in young people not studying, not planning for the future and not developing their talents--all of which, sooner or later, will come to contribute to the person's overall sense of self-worth.

**Train the children!** God's Word says to "train up a child in the way he should go and when he is older, he will not depart from it" (Proverbs 22:6). However, we must ask ourselves: What is the correct direction to train up a child? Some parents want the child to go in the directions about which the parents dream. However, such lofty dreams, no matter how noble, may not happen in the child's life. Other parents are too permissive and allow children to do whatever they wish.

**258**

However, the Bible says that a child must be brought up in the nurture and admonition of the Lord (Ephesians 6:4). This means that parents should be careful not to try to relive their lives through their children. On the other hand, they should allow the child to live out God's plan according to the child's abilities. In time, the child will begin to reckon with certain values, develop goals, and become autonomous. This process should begin before the birth of the child--and should continue throughout one's lifetime.

With God's help, anyone can become a new creation (2 Corinthians 5:17). One can choose, learn, grow, and become whatever God wants him or her to become. This is the best road to travel on life's highway. Being transformed and conformed to the image and likeness of Christ, God's image, is the ultimate for all humankind (Genesis 1:26, 27).

Our history, vision and dreams must not be forgotten or allowed to die. We must transmit them to the oncoming generation of young people and they must also pass such important information on to future generations. Otherwise, a people become lost, confused and eventually extinct.

In dealing with problems of low self-esteem, if all else fails, the teacher or counselor should remember to refer persons to a professional Christian counseling ministry for further help. One such example is the Westside Holistic Family Center in Chicago, Illinois.

What a wonderful vision God provides in His Word of God's people, with their renewed self-images! In God's beautiful plan, "they shall come from the east, and from the west, and from the north, and from the south, and shall sit down in the kingdom of God'' (Luke 13:29).

**Summary.** This chapter has focused on helping people with low self-esteem. Some of the causes of low self-esteem among Black people were presented along with guidelines for helping people with low self-esteem. The guidelines include: 1) establishing a relationship with God; 2) engaging in positive self-reflection; 3) developing an affirmative action plan; 4) viewing adversity as a blessing in disguise; 5) dreaming; 6) being optimistic and positive; 7) ignoring peer pressure; and 8) training the children.

Following is a case study which provides the opportunity to apply principles presented in this chapter.

## CASE STUDY

*INSTRUCTIONS: James, in the following story, is experiencing low self-esteem that is in part due to reactions against racism that he has encountered in society. The following exercises will lead you into an in-depth study of James' problem, and will provide the opportunity to apply principles covered in this chapter to helping people with similar problems.*

*The first five exercises consist of a series of "discovery" questions, followed by a summary question. The sixth exercise asks you to summarize and apply information you gained from the first five exercises. The seventh exercise allows you to make personal applications.*

## JAMES

*Late one Saturday afternoon, Brother Fraser, the newly appointed youth pastor, was preparing his Sunday School lesson, when his telephone rang. It was Mrs. Young, the mother of Neesha, one of the students in his class.*

*Mrs. Young was in tears. James, her 20-year-old son, had fallen 14 stories to the ground outside of the building where he was working as a window washer. He had been in a coma for several days and today had awakened for the first time. Mrs. Young openly thanked God that, while James was cut and bruised and had some internal injuries, he had no broken bones, was not paralyzed, and was not brain damaged.*

*Mrs. Young asked Brother Fraser if he would visit her son in the hospital. Brother Fraser agreed and visited him several times. It was during these weekly visits that James opened up to Brother Fraser. He told him he had a damaged past that only recently he had begun trying to repair.*

*He said that, by the time he was 13 years old, he had stopped attending church with his mother and sister and had dropped out of school. This led to arguments with his mother, so he left home and started living on the streets. He joined a gang near the housing projects where his family lived and dropped out of the magnet trade school he had been attending.*

*He said that he dropped out of school because of racism. He had once been very excited about the courses he was taking in electrical wiring, but he noticed some of the white male teachers did not like answering his questions. They paid much more attention to the white male students and seemed to ignore James.*

*The "straw that broke the camel's back" happened when James attempted, through the school, to find a part-time summer job working with an electrical wiring company. He was ignored by the employers who recruited for part-time help at the school. Instead, he was offered a job washing windows, at a rate that was much lower than the money being paid to white students.*

*James got angry and quit both school and church, believing that, if God loved Black people, He would not allow racism to exist. Before long, he began snort-*

**261**

*ing cocaine. He had nearly overdosed several times. Soon he began to rob homes, stores and other places to get the money he needed for cocaine. This is what started his brushes with "the law."*

*He had been in and out of juvenile homes and jails throughout his teenaged years. He deeply resented some of the white people who ran these places and the white police officers who, once he had a record, regularly harassed him on the streets. He was currently on probation and had promised the probation officer that he would accept a part-time job washing windows and pay room and board at his mother's home, as a condition of being released on probation. It hadn't been a month since he had been making a new start that the accident took place.*

*Over and over again, James said he had been held back by racism. While he acknowledged there were many Black men who had been successful in spite of racism, Brother Fraser could see that James did not feel he was one who could make it, against the odds.*

## 1. A relationship with God

James left church because he felt that God favored white people over Blacks.

a. Are Black people excluded from God's plan of salvation? (John 3:16; Acts 10:34; Psalm 139:12; James 2:1-5)

b. Does Jesus know how it feels to be discriminated against? (John 1:46)

c. What was the likely complexion of Jews in biblical times? (Genesis 15:13; Genesis 9)

d. In whose image is James made? (Genesis 1:26)

e. What does God promise James? (Isaiah 26:3; Luke 2:14)

f. SUMMARY QUESTION: How would you use the information from questions a-e to lead a Black person with low self-esteem (as a result of discrimination they have experienced) to Christ?

## 2. Self-Reflection

To develop self-esteem, James must be open to developing an opinion of himself that is separate from the opinions held by others.

a. Study James' life again, in the above story. What are some of the talents and abilities that God has given to him? (1 Corinthians 12)

b. What potential does James have? (1 Peter 2:5, 9)

c. Once James accepts Jesus Christ as his Saviour, who is he? How is this the basis of a new self-image? (2 Corinthians 5:17; James 1:9-11)

d. What are some characteristics which come along with salvation? How can these become a part of James' new self-image? (2 Corinthians 12)

e. What evidence is there, in Scripture, that "God didn't make no junk?" (Genesis 1:27)

f. SUMMARY QUESTION: How could a counselor use the information from questions a-e to guide James into meaningful and productive self-reflection?

## 3. An affirmative action plan

James needs to develop an affirmative action plan for himself, based on the Word of God.

a. What is the biblical basis for this plan? (Romans 12:2)

b. What is the biblical basis for setting goals? (Genesis 1:1-5)

c. Once James accepts Christ, does he have what it takes to achieve his goals? (Psalm 23; Acts 1:8)

d. How should James go about preparing for a career? (2 Timothy 2:15)

e. What should James do about his old friends? (2 Corinthians

6:17)

f. SUMMARY QUESTION: How could a counselor use the information from questions a-e in helping James to set new goals for his life?

## 4. Dealing with adversity

James can be shown that adversity is a blessing in disguise.

a. What is one basic fact about adversity? (Romans 8:28)

b. From the life of David, what do we learn about adversity? (1 Samuel 17:37, 45, 47, 50, 54)

c. What is another fact about adversity? (Ephesians 6:10-18)

d. What will be the outcome of adversity for the Christian? (James 1:12)

e. What is the source of power to overcome adversity? (Matthew 28:18; Acts 1:8)

f. SUMMARY QUESTION: How can a person use the information from questions a-e above to demonstrate to James that some of the things that happened to him are blessings in disguise?

## 5. Mrs. Young

It is usually very difficult for a single Black woman to raise a young Black man who has low self-esteem. However, the Bible does contain guidelines, promises and models for Christian women in this situation.

a. Does the Lord care about the problems encountered by women raising sons alone? (Luke 7:11-15; Hebrews 11:35)

b. What promise can Mrs. Young claim from the Lord, based on Isaiah 66:6-14?

c. What does 1 Corinthians 3:1, 2 and 1 Thessalonians 2:7 suggest about Mrs. Young's approach to James?

d. How can a woman such as Mrs. Young use Psalm 139:13-19 to help her son develop a healthy self-image?

e. Was Ephesians 6:9 intended for men only? What applications are there for single-parent women?

f. SUMMARY QUESTION: Thousands of Black women are attempting to raise Black sons whose self-images have been damaged, due to effects of racism. What specific guidelines can be developed from the above Scriptures, and applied in this difficult situation?

## 6. SUMMARY EXERCISE

How can the Black church develop and improve ministries to Black families that foster healthy self-images?

a. In what ways can the church develop educational opportunities (such as G.E.D. acquisition), job training skills (such as vocational programs), and legal counseling for young men such as James? How can existing programs be improved?

b. Are there specific ways that the men of the church can teach young men such as James to become reliable and responsible? Explain.

c. What types of substance abuse programs should the church offer? How can existing ones be improved?

d. What would constitute a good home environment for James? How can the church assist Black families (and extended families) in creating such environments?

e. Does the Black church require resources, literature and methods for attacking the problem of low self-esteem, that are different from the materials and methods used by white Christians? Explain your answer.

f. How can the church determine when James or Mrs. Young should be referred for professional counseling that is beyond the scope of church-based ministries?

## 7. PERSONAL APPLICATION

Reflecting on oneself with principles from the Word of God is a good way to develop healthy self-esteem. Use some of the Scriptures referenced above to identify your gifts, talents and potential as a child of God. Then pray that God will give you the courage you need, to be all that you can be!

# CHAPTER TWELVE

# POWERLESSNESS

## Rev. Pellam Love

*Sister Bailey walked up the steps and rang the door-bell of Mrs. Adams, the mother of some children who had come to Vacation Bible School last year. As she rang the bell, she could hear Mrs. Adams cursing and hollering over the sounds of children screaming and crying. Then she heard what sounded like a shoe crash against the wall. Finally, Mrs. Adams came to the door, looking exhausted, and asked Sister Bailey to come in.*

*Immediately Mrs. Adams started talking nonstop. "These bad kids got me in trouble with the A.D.C. people," she said. "They told those people over at the school that I beat 'em and curse 'em all the time." Soon she began to cry, saying that she couldn't get two steps forward without being pushed two steps back-ward. Everyone was against her--her children, the A.D.C., the nosy social worker at the school, and her teacher. "She's flunking me in this course that the A.D.C. is paying for," she added.*

*Mrs. Adams went on to say that, with all that she had to deal with, Sister Bailey couldn't expect her to take the time to get the children ready for Sunday School. She hoped that Sister Bailey understood.*

Mrs. Adams, like so many single parents today, feels powerless. She feels that she is a victim of people, of agencies, and of time itself. People and circumstances seem to be controlling her. Frequently people like Mrs. Adams, who feel powerless reach out to people like Sister Bailey for help. This chapter provides guidelines for helping people who feel powerless. It illustrates how to lead such people to their reservoir of power in Jesus Christ.

## An Example of Powerlessness in Scripture

At the trial which preceded the crucifixion of Jesus Christ, Pilate, the governor, faced Jesus Christ, on one hand, and the Jewish Sanhedrin on the other. Caught up in the ''system,'' Pilate surfaces in Scripture as a man who felt powerless.

## from Scripture

**John 18:29** Pilate then went out unto them, and said, What accusation bring ye against this man?

**30** They answered and said unto him, If he were not a malefactor, we would not have delivered him up unto thee.

**33** Then Pilate entered into the judgment hall again, and called Jesus, and said unto him, Art thou the King of the Jews?

**34** Jesus answered him, Sayest thou this thing of thyself, or did others tell it thee of me?

**38** Pilate saith unto him, What is truth? And when he had said this, he went out again unto the Jews, and saith unto them, I find in him no fault at all.

**19:1** Then Pilate therefore took Jesus, and scourged him.

**4** Pilate therefore went forth again, and saith unto them, Behold, I bring him forth to you, that ye may know that I find no fault in him.

**7** The Jews answered him, We have a law, and by our law he ought to die, because he made himself the Son of God.

**8** When Pilate therefore heard that saying, he was the more afraid;

**9** And went again into the judgment hall, and saith unto Jesus, Whence art thou? But Jesus gave him no answer.

**10** Then saith Pilate unto him, Speakest thou not unto me? knowest thou not that I have power to crucify thee, and have power to release thee?

**11** Jesus answered, Thou couldest have no power at all against me, except it were given thee from above: therefore he that delivered me unto thee hath the greater sin.

**Matthew 27:19** When he was set down on the judgment seat, his wife sent unto him, saying, Have thou nothing to do with that just man: for I have suffered many things this day in a dream because of him.

**20** But the chief priests and elders persuaded the multitude that they should ask Barabbas, and destroy Jesus.

**22** Pilate saith unto them, What shall I do then with Jesus which is called Christ? They all say unto him, Let him be crucified.

**23** And the governor said, Why, what evil hath he done? But they cried out the more, saying, Let him be crucified.

**24** When Pilate saw that he could prevail nothing, but that rather a tumult was made, he took water, and washed his hands before the multitude, saying, I am innocent of the blood of this just person: see ye to it.

## What Is Powerlessness?

Powerlessness is an emotion that is connected to a person's perception of other people and a person's perception of circumstances. Pilate experienced powerlessness related to both. People like Pilate, who feel powerless in their relationships with others, usually experience this feeling because of contact with other people either directly, via family relationships and jobs, or indirectly, through a system of which they are a part. People who feel powerless may be in contact with the people who evoke these feelings every day. They may be divorced from them or they may feel that such people have rendered them powerless following someone's death.

The person who feels powerless in relationships with others often asks him/herself some of the following questions:

What are they doing to me?

How are they bothering me?

What is my status with them?

This is one reason that Pilate had so many questions for Jesus regarding Jesus' conception of Pilate's status and power compared to that of Christ (John 19:10-11).

The person who feels powerless could probably diagram his/her relationships with others in one of the following ways:

| superior | creditor | jailer |
|----------|----------|--------|
| inferior | debtor | prisoner |

In other words, the person who feels powerless sees others as having power over him or her in some way. Others are seen by the person as having power over the person's opinions, actions, and even emotions. In the case where others are seen as superior, the person who feels powerless relates to others as though he is indebted to them and these are debts he will never be able to pay. Frequently such people operate from a sense of deficit that is similar to guilt. That is why Pilate felt it necessary to wash his hands (Matthew 27:24). The powerlessness such people feel is painful and can cause a person to feel "numb" and useless.

In many cases, the feeling of being a debtor may lead to feelings of being a "jailer." In other words, communications are "locked up." There is no progress in relationship to those who cause them to feel powerless. There is little emotional expression and relationships with the intimidating person(s) generally "drag." This can be seen in Pilate, as he travels back and forth from Jesus to the Sanhedrin Council, attempting to communicate, but to no avail (John 27:22-24). Such people feel "stuck" in these relationships. There is the feeling of "I'm the prisoner and they're holding the key."

When people who feel powerless express feelings of powerlessness about a specific person, they often confess that they have had these feelings for a long time. They accuse others as having held the keys which control them for a long time. Frequently they say they haven't been able to focus on anything other than these intimidating relationships. Thoughts about others having power over them seem to govern everything, including other relationships.

Some people who feel powerless express these perceptions of systems, rather than specific people. They feel that systems or agencies are controlling them. Examples are: welfare agencies, courts, billing agencies, and for Pilate, the Sanhedrin Council. In other words, the person who feels powerless usually feels that someone or some agency (or system) outside of him/herself holds the keys to well-being. People who link such feelings of powerlessness to agencies and systems are people who are usually facing seemingly unbeatable odds and a long ''uphill battle'' to fight in order to overcome the odds. Usually the situations in which they find themselves are not entirely of their own making.

Powerlessness for many is like a long, deep valley in which they are walking. Many cannot remember the last peak and the next peak stretches beyond their view.

## Dealing With People

The basic goal of many powerless people is to be able to deal with those who seem to be controlling them. Such people need to be shown how to bring their feelings of success closer together and to stretch their feelings of failure farther apart. They must be shown that they must deal with people and circumstances in order to survive. In order to achieve these goals with a client, the counselor might use some of the following techniques:

**Sorting.** Start by asking the person to sort through the layers of perceived problems to discover whether the source seems to be people or circumstances. This type exercise can be done with individual clients or in group counseling. To guide them through the sorting exercise, ask such questions as:

When did your feelings of powerlessness begin?

When did you become aware of the problem?

Who or what is involved?

Why does this person (or situation) bother you?

What would happen if you didn't do anything about this?

With your clients, "play detective" so that you can discover the source of the problem. Encourage them to explain whether they believe the feelings of powerlessness are unavoidable, were unforeseen, or uncontrollable. Engage the counselees or group in an exercise to "zero in" on the kinds of dominant/submissive relationships they might be experiencing. What person or groups of people, or systems overwhelm them?

Query them as to whether they feel outranked, indebted (a real sense of guilt) or ''jailed,'' with someone or some system holding the key. Have them identify the grip or hold the other person has. What bill must they pay, or what key is needed to unlock the ''jail'' so they can be released from ''prison?''

Strategies for dealing with powerlessness related to people are different from strategies for dealing with powerlessness related to systems.

**Leveling the "enemy."** If it is discovered that the root of the problem seems to be that other people are controlling, then the person who feels powerless needs to discover who is doing what for whom or to whom, and who is on top. Then the person needs to learn how to "level" this person so that the person no longer intimidates. The key to "leveling" such people is the awareness that all power belongs to God, not humankind.

The person who feels powerless needs to know to whom it is that s/he feels inferior, or a debtor or prisoner. Then the person who feels powerless must be taught how to "level" that person. The person needs to learn how, *at a mental level*, to get the intimidating person "eyeball to eyeball." They must learn to see the intimidating person as powerless, too. God is the only One who has all power (Matthew 28:18).

Once this is realized, the person who feels powerless is in a position to assess his/her strengths and weaknesses and those of the opponent. Jesus did this to Pilate (John 19:11). Jesus proved to Pilate that next to God's power he was unranked and, in that respect, was just another man (19:11).

Daniel's dealings with Nebuchadnezzar is another biblical example of the use of this technique (Daniel 2:14). Nebuchadnezzar was the most powerful autocrat the world had ever seen. Yet, Daniel knew that Nebuchadnezzar's unconscious mind had been invaded with a frightening dream that revealed him as powerless in the face of spiritual power. Daniel's gift of dream interpretation leveled Nebuchadnezzar "down to Daniel's size" and, in a sense, lifted Daniel to Nebuchadnezzar's lofty perch. Daniel was able to see that both of them were just flesh and blood in relationship to God.

The person who feels powerless must be encouraged to see life as Daniel saw it. Daniel knew that everyone has gifts, and that these gifts place everyone on the same level. In God's sight, the person who feels powerless stands on the same ground as those who, in the mind of the person who feels powerless, seem to tower over them as a superior, a creditor and a jailer.

The most powerful men in Scripture were all leveled by God. Pharaoh, of the exodus, was considered a god in Egypt, but the Lord told Moses that He had made Moses a god to Pharaoh (Exodus 7:1). Moses, at first, felt powerless before Pharaoh and before the situation Pharaoh had caused (Exodus 3:11). However, right before Moses' eyes, God leveled Pharaoh and raised Moses. God arranged it so that Pharaoh, not Moses, felt powerless before God.

Certainly it must have been a helpless feeling for the leader of the most powerful nation on earth to be caught in such a divine vice, with no options, no appropriate orders to give and no explanations. No explanations. No, not even to his wife for the loss of their firstborn son, and for the loss of all of the firstborn of Egypt. He was even leveled to the point of compliance with Moses' request to let Israel go (Exodus 12:30). Certainly Moses must have been able to see life differently after observing how the Lord worked.

This is true of all people. Everyone, at some point, proves to be powerless and can be equalized and leveled, causing the feelings of powerlessness to go away. Once the person who feels powerless learns to attribute all power to God, then that person can learn to look at him/herself in a different way, as having access to God's riches.

**Accepting unmet needs.** Powerless people must learn to accept themselves. The first step towards acceptance is accepting the reality of unmet needs. People who feel powerless often feel overwhelmed by unmet needs. However, the person who feels powerless must be shown that s/he is not unusual in having needs that are unmet. All people have unmet needs. In that sense, all people are equal. The knowledge of this fact can help the powerless person to feel less intimidated by seemingly "controlling others." They become aware that these people, too, have unmet needs.

**Accessing God's riches.** The powerless person must be shown that s/he has access, as a child of God, to all of God's riches. The Bible says that God will supply all of our needs (Philippians 4:19). When the Bible speaks of God's riches, it is speaking of God's ability to meet our unmet needs. God is rich in goodness, glory, grace, mercy, understanding, gifts and talents.

Whereas riches, in Scripture, refer to needs that can be met, when the Bible refers to gifts, it refers to God's capacity to meet needs. Everyone has been given gifts, and everyone has at least a capacity to meet the needs of others. Most of us have multiple gifts (1 Corinthians 12). The New Testament speaks of manifold grace and wisdom over which we are managers (Matthew 25:14-30). It is important that the person who feels powerless know that s/he has an abundance of gifts and talents which God has given.

Encourage such persons to identify at least five riches and five gifts or strengths that God has given to them. If counseling a group of such people, allow members of the group to help the person identify his or her gifts, talents and riches in Christ. There is no harm in allowing them to "bombard one another" with this information. This can prove to be a pleasant discovery for everyone. Some will discover jewels in their lives they didn't know were there. In addition, whether in one-on-one counseling or counseling in groups, an amazing sense of rapport will develop between the participants.

The powerless person must be shown that s/he is at the same time equipped to meet personal needs and the needs of others. The person must be shown that s/he may be praying about needs that have already been met, through the gifts and talents that God has provided. Once the person who feels powerless realizes this, then he or she is in a position to deal in an entirely different way with intimidating people.

**Handling others.** Equipped with the correct attitude toward those who seem intimidating, equipped with a knowledge of one's gifts, and aware of God's abundance of riches for every situation, the person who once felt powerless is ready to deal with those who once intimidated him or her. This person is now ready to demonstrate mutual, potential gains and shared interests.

The person is in a position now to highlight personal needs in terms of God's riches, and the capacity to meet another person's needs (gifts God had given). In other words, the person can say, "I need you and you need me. We won't make it without each other. If I win, you win! We can share interest and power."

People who once felt powerless can learn to tell this to their foremen, work leaders, social workers, teachers, children, husbands, wives and others. However, people who once felt powerless, like David, might need to start with smaller game, like the lion or the bear, before taking on the big prize, Goliath.

Everyone will need to work at leveling, finding mutual sharings of power. The use of the term "target" might sound aggressive, but that's what a powerless person has to learn to be. The term "target" also denotes strategy and those who are helpless need that too!

## Dealing With Circumstances

The overall goal of people who feel powerless due to circumstances is to be in control or, as God ordered the first human, "take dominion of yourself and the world around you" (Genesis 26:30). However, many people feel that they are unable to do this because they are faced with seemingly unbeatable odds and circumstances that are beyond their control.

Probably the best scriptural example of a person overwhelmed by odds is Job. The Book of Job is probably the oldest book in the Bible. Job was beset by an ongoing cluster of problems, of whose origin he was unaware (Job 1:13-22). However, the Bible shows us the other side of the picture, in which God and Satan contest Job's integrity. Satan's argument is, "he will curse you (God) to your face." God's response is, "all he has is in your power" (1:11).

Then in rapid succession, Job's animals are rustled, his sheep are destroyed, his camels are stolen, his servants are killed and finally his children are wiped out. However, Job did not succumb. He did not curse God. So Satan came back with more ammunition, since the first onslaught didn't "break" Job (1:22).

Next, Job's body is overcome by hideous boils. Pressure is applied by Mrs. Job, who is overcome with grief and loss. She urges him to curse God and die. She is overwhelmed by the circumstances, not the least of which is watching her husband diseased and in pain and grief (Job 2:9-10).

Following is a discussion of basic truths, imbedded in the story of Job, which can be used to help people who feel powerless due to overwhelming odds and circumstances.

**God is for us.** It is important for the person who feels powerless to know that God is for him/her. A counselor can show such people, from the story of Job, that God thinks well of them and is confident of them. It is God who first boasts of Job, "Have you considered my servant Job"(1:8). God is proud of all of His children.

The counselor can point out to the person who feels powerless that God sees His church (God's people) as a golden candlestick (Exodus 40:24). Gold symbolizes deity. In God's sight, we are not only valuable and precious, we reflect the image of God. All of this is evidence that God is for us and sees us in the best light.

In turning Job over to Satan's wiles, God indicates that Job is ready for testing and He could trust Job in this overwhelming situation. Point out that Satan did not get Job to curse God. God proved that He could in fact trust Job with a challenge.

So often, people who feel powerless due to circumstances feel as though God is working against them for some reason. However, whatever the overwhelming circumstance, they need to know that God is leaning toward them. God is in favor of them. They should know that, even when they feel guilty, God favors them. John says, in his first epistle: "if our heart (conscious) condemn us (makes us feel guilty), God is greater than our heart" (1 John 3:20). God knows the entire scope of a situation. The person who feels powerless needs to know that, not only does he need to trust God, God trusts him, too.

**Bad circumstances are not necessarily punishments for sin.** Often, when facing seemingly overwhelming odds, people feel that God is punishing them because they have sinned--even when there is no real evidence to support this notion. Often people who feel powerless are very hard on themselves. The counselor can use the story of Job to show that punishment from God in no way played a part in Job's circumstances. Job is not guilty of anything. Counselors need to help people see this, even when their friends try to take them on a "guilt trip." This does not mean that they should become self-righteous, as Job did during his monologue (Job 31).

Bad circumstances and guilt should not be automatically connected. People who feel powerless need to see that God is with them, working for them, and "boasting" about them. Guilt is not always from God. Show such people verses like Romans 8:33-34: "Who shall lay any thing to the charge of God's elect? It is God that justifieth. Who is he that condemneth? It is Christ that died..." And, as stated in 8:31, "If God be for us, who can be against us?"

**Be positive and grateful!** Ephesians 4:29 says, "Let no corrupt communication proceed out of your mouth, but that which is good to the use of edifying, that it may minister grace unto the hearers." People who feel powerless need to stop communicating with people who cause them to think bad things about themselves. They need to ignore communications that "smack of guilt trips." If they allow people close to them to browbeat them, they automatically are engaging in this themselves, throwing sticks and stones at themselves in their subconscious mind. By listening to others' negativity, they are really repeating and therefore reinforcing corrupt communications. Instead, the person needs to know how to administer grace to him/herself.

They need to become aware of God's grace and meditate on it. They need to remain positive! Encourage them to communicate to themselves (both silently and out loud) more than they communicate to anyone else. Encourage them to tell themselves that which is good and edifying and true (Philippians 4:8). A good exercise would be to ask the person to uncover things that are good and truthful. Encourage them to communicate these things to themselves so that they can offset bad communications they hear coming from others.

278

**Keep God's hedge in mind.** People who feel powerless need to know that they are secure in God. God has a hedge of protection around them just as He had one around Job. The counselor can point out to the powerless person that, interestingly enough, it is Satan that points out the hedge. Satan sees the hedge and needs permission from God to throw his fiery darts at Job (Job 1:10). The hedge symbolizes that God's children are in His care and protection, and that their security needs are already met in Him.

In other words, God has set boundaries of righteousness wherein we should remain focused. We should not venture beyond the boundaries God has set. If God has us hedged in, He Himself is our Protector and He is protecting us from the world and its devastation. If we keep in mind God's protection, and we stay within the boundaries of righteousness that He has set for us in His Word, then God will protect us.

**Know the parameters of the problem.** Once the person who feels powerless is aware of God's hedge of protection, then circumstances that seem unmanageable begin to be reduced to a manageable size. The counselor should help the person who feels powerless to see the parameters of the problem, by asking the following types of questions:

How long has this problem existed?

How bad is it?

Whom does it affect?

Who knows about it?

Who needs to know about it?

In discussing the last two questions, it is important to encourage the person to use discretion. Everyone can't be told everything all of the time because varying levels of maturity won't allow for everyone to handle sensitive issues sensitively.

Parameters alert a person to how far spread the problem is, and what steps must be taken in order to cover all the "open holes." If a person knows where the parameters are, goals can be identified and a timetable can be outlined concerning when to tackle the situation.

**Set goals.** Goals can serve as a road map. Every problem, regardless of its size, can be broken down into parts. The person who once felt powerless can be shown how to treat the individual parts of a problem like individual boundaries. The same questions can be asked about problem parts as were asked about parameters, in order to identify the parameters of parts of the problem as well as the whole. If necessary, ask the client to number the parts of the problem (1, 2, 3, etc.). Each part, then, represents an individual parameter.

For example, Mrs. Adams in the story at the beginning of this chapter, has a problem that can be broken down into the following parts:

1) the children

2) the children's school

3) her future career

4) A.D.C.

5) her education

Goals can be set for each part of the problem. Each goal has its own road map toward solving the overall problem. Over time, Sister Bailey could guide Mrs. Adams into setting goals as follows:

| Problem | Goal |
|---|---|
| 1) the children | Communicate without cursing and beating |
| 2) the children's school | Eliminate their fears that she is a child abuser. |
| 3) her future career | Satisfy educational and other requirements for a good job that is a part of a career. |
| 4) A.D.C. | Eliminate their fears that she is a child abuser, and |

|  |  |
|---|---|
|  | eliminate her dependence on them. |
| 5) her education | Complete assignments that are behind schedule, complete future assignments on time, pass final exams. |

**Change behavior.** In order to accomplish any goal, one must change one's behavior. There will always be something that the person needs to do differently from the previous routine. This doesn't necessarily mean that there will need to be drastic changes. Changes usually come slowly and must be plotted in relationship to goals.

In working with the person who wants to gain power over circumstances, it is important to identify each goal (related to each part of the problem) and identify the changes in behavior that will be necessary if the person is to achieve any individual goal. Encourage the person to think of a large problem as parallel to a mouse and a large chunk of cheese. The mouse can't eat the entire piece of cheese at one time. It must eat one piece at a time. Any oversized problem must be faced in this way. One part must be "knocked out" at a time. When enough have been "knocked out", the whole problem will be solved.

**Establish a calendar.** Encourage the person, while knocking out "holes in the cheese," to set some dates for solving each part of the overall problem. This will ensure that the parts that make up the problem will be tackled frequently enough so that the problem will begin to diminish before the person gets weary of the struggle.

Remind the person who feels powerless that, at the end of Job, God restores everything to the point of doubling what Job had at the beginning. This starts among his relatives with each giving a piece of money and one earring of gold (Job 42:11-12). Think of it, one piece at a time. There are specific steps and steadily increasing progress in God's process of restoration. No problem ends instantly, but after breaking down the problem into individual goals, making changes in behavior and setting a timetable, the overall problem can be solved, one piece at a time.

**Summary.** This chapter has dealt with the subject of helping people who feel powerless. The most frequent sources of powerlessness are perceptions of people, agencies and situations. The counselor can help people who feel manipulated and overwhelmed by teaching them to sort through their problems to locate the source, learn to see the ''enemy'' in a different way ("leveling"), accept the reality of personal unmet needs and unmet needs of the intimidating person, see oneself in a different way (by accepting God's riches, gifts and talents), and then deal with others on an entirely different, more equalitarian basis.

The counselor can help people who feel overwhelmed by circumstances by alerting them to the fact that God is for us, He has a hedge of protection around us, and bad situations are not necessarily punishments from God. Counselors can also help such people to identify the parameters of the problem, set goals, and establish realistic time lines for solving each individual problem involved in the overall problem.

## CASE STUDY

*INSTRUCTIONS: Drake, in the following story, is a person who feels powerless. The following exercises will lead you into an in-depth study of Drake's problem, based on the principles that were introduced in this chapter.*

*The first five exercises consist of a series of "discovery" questions, followed by a summary question. The sixth exercise asks you to summarize and apply information you gained from the first five exercises. The seventh exercise asks you to make personal applications of the principles you learned in this chapter.*

# DRAKE

*Drake, a veteran of the Marine Corps who once served in Vietnam, made an appointment with the counseling ministry at his church. During the session, he informed Brother Wilson that he had recently been laid off from his job at the plant. He had three small children. He was visibly upset because his marriage was unstable. He described how he and his wife had separated and then reunited, off and on, in cycles over the past few years, due to his drinking problem.*

*He was currently trying to earn a G.E.D. (General Educational Equivalency Diploma), but he was distracted by his problems at home. He was receiving veterans' educational benefits but was afraid that he might lose them because his grades were bad and his attendance was irregular.*

*What was of immediate concern to Drake was a situation that had arisen at the company from which he had been laid off. The company had offered to give him a large sum of money to purchase the seniority that he had accumulated over the past 10 years at the automobile factory. Drake felt a sense of powerlessness in relationship to the big company. He felt pressured to take the money, even though he knew that it was not enough to pay for tools, uniforms and other expenses that he would have.*

*Another problem that Drake discussed with the counselor was his relationship with his mother. His mother would, regardless of his successes or failures, always compare him with his older brother and say that he did not measure up. She also manipulated him, insisting that he should be loyal to her and that he was obligated to take care of her. Drake felt powerless in relationship to his mother, and he felt manipulated by her.*

**283**

## 1. Drake's marriage

a. In what ways can Matthew 28:18 influence the way that Drake approaches his marriage?

b. In what ways can John 19:11 help Drake to "level" his wife?

c. What might be some of Drake's unmet needs in relationship to his marriage? How can God meet these needs?

d. What might be some of Drake's wife's unmet needs in relationship to her marriage? How can God meet these needs?

e. What are some of the riches that God offers to Drake as he tries to improve his marriage? (1 Corinthians 12; Galatians 5:22)

f. SUMMARY QUESTION: What are some of the goals that Drake can set for his marriage? How can the information in exercises a-e be used to help remove the sense of power-lessness in Drake's marriage? How can this information be used by church leaders to improve Black marriages in general, at various stages of the life cycle?

## 2. Drake's mother

a. In what ways can Matthew 28:18 influence the way that Drake approaches his relationship to his mother?

b. In what ways can John 19:11 help Drake to "level" his mother?

c. What might be some of Drake's unmet needs in relationship to his mother? How can God meet these needs?

d. What might be some of Drake's mother's unmet needs? How can God meet these needs?

e. What are some of the riches that God offers to Drake as he tries to improve his relationship with his mother? (1 Corinthians 12; Galatians 5:22)

f. SUMMARY QUESTION: What types of goals can Drake

set for his relationship with his mother? How can the information in exercises a-e be used to remove the sense of powerlessness in his relationship to his mother? How can this information be used to improve other relationships between adult, married children and overbearing parents?

## 3. Drake's job/career

a. In what ways can Matthew 28:18 influence the way that Drake approaches his career planning?

b. What evidence is there that God is on Drake's side, during his career development? (Job 1:18; Romans 8:31)

c. What is one step that Drake should take in order to remain positive about the world of work? (Ephesians 4:29) What are some possible sources of negative thinking that Drake should avoid, when it comes to the world of work? (Philippians 4:8)

d. Does Drake have reason to worry? (Job 1:10) Why? Why not?

e. What types of changes in behavior need to take place if Drake is going to obtain meaningful and secure employment?

f. SUMMARY QUESTION: Using the information from exercises a-e, what are some ways that a counselor can help Drake to remove a sense of powerlessness as he plans a career? What are some ways that this information can help counselors minister more effectively to other Black men who are unemployed and feeling powerless?

## 4. Drake's company

a. In what ways can Matthew 28:18 influence the way that Drake approaches those who want him to sell his seniority?

b. In what ways can John 19:11 help Drake to "level" the big company?

c. What might be some of Drake's unmet needs in relationship to the company? How can God meet these needs?

d. What might be some of the company's unmet needs in relationship to Drake? How can God meet these needs?

e. What are some of the riches that God offers to Drake as he negotiates with his company? (1 Corinthians 12; Galatians 5:22)

f. SUMMARY QUESTION: What types of goals can Drake set for his relationship with the company? How can the information in exercises a-e be used to remove the sense of powerlessness in his relationship with the big company? How can counselors use this information to help people cope when their companies lay them off or relocate?

**5. Drake's problem with alcohol**

a. In what ways can Matthew 28:18 influence the way that Drake approaches his problem with alcohol?

b. In what ways can John 19:11 help Drake to "level" alcohol?

c. What might be some of Drake's unmet needs that alcohol seems to be meeting? How can God meet these needs?

d. How can Drake's problem with alcohol be broken down into parts? What types of goals should he set?

e. What are some of the riches that God offers to Drake as he removes his dependency on alcohol? (2 Corinthians 12:9; Philippians 4:13)

f. SUMMARY QUESTION: How can Drake use the information from exercises a-e to set goals for overcoming his dependency on alcohol? How can counselors use the information from exercises a-e to help those who escape through drugs and alcohol in response to being unemployed?

## 6. SUMMARY EXERCISE

How would you help Drake to complete the following planning form?

| PROBLEM | GOAL | DEADLINE |
|---------|------|----------|
| _____ | _____ | _____ |
| _____ | _____ | _____ |
| _____ | _____ | _____ |
| _____ | _____ | _____ |
| _____ | _____ | _____ |

## 7. PERSONAL APPLICATION

Ask yourself the following questions to apply what has been presented in this chapter to your personal life.

a. Do I ever feel powerless?

b. What is the primary source of my powerlessness--people? Circumstances?

c. How would I describe my relationship with the source of my powerlessness? Superior/inferior? Creditor/debtor? Jailer/prisoner? Do I feel debts or guilt?

d. How did the problem start? When did it start? Why am I stuck there?

e. What personal needs can be met through God's riches? Through my talents? Through God's gifts to me?

f. What challenges do I face within the next two weeks?

g. How can the big problem be broken down into parts?

h. What goals can I set?

i. What changes in behavior must I make?

j. Will I encounter any pitfalls packaged as attractive temptations?

k. Is there an opportunity, in this situation, to negotiate with "the enemy" by demonstrating shared interest? Mutual gains? Win-win? Mutual sharing of power?

# BIOGRAPHIES

**Patricia Beason** is a licensed clinical social worker, specializing in resume development, family therapy, substance abuse, sexual abuse, incest, and treating persons with multiple emotional and psychological problems. She is in private practice, and also works with the Central Baptist Family Services In-Home Counseling Center of Chicago. She is chairperson of the Counseling Ministry at Trinity United Church of Christ in Chicago. She earned a Bachelor of Arts in social work from the University of Missouri, and a Master of Arts in social work from Loyola University of Illinois.

**Rev. Zenobia Brooks** is an ordained minister, serving at Trinty United Church of Christ, in Chicago. She is a professional guidance counselor with the Malcolm X Westside Learning Center of Chicago and with Serenity Counseling Services of Chicago. She is also a chaplain for the St. Jude Chapter of the Chicago Police Department. She has served as a counselor for the Management Planning Institute of Chicago and is currently serving on the Board of Trustees of Community Supportive Systems, Inc. She earned a Bachelor of Arts from the National College of Education in behavioral sciences, and a Master of Divinity from Chicago Theological Seminary. She is married to Edward Brooks and has three children.

**Rev. William Butler** is a practicing pastoral psychotherapist at Parkside Pastoral Care Center at Lutheran General Hospital in Park Ridge, Illinois, and at the Black Pastoral Care Center in Chicago, Illinois. He is also the director of Black Campus Ministries for Intervarsity Christian Fellowship in the Chicago metropolitian area. He has earned a Master of Divinity from Chicago Theological Seminary and is completing a Doctorate of Ministry specializing in religion and psychology at Chicago Theological Seminary. He is an ordained United Church of Christ minister at Trinity United Church of Christ.

**Delores Holmes** is director of Family Focus, Our Place of Evanston, Illinois. It is a drop-in center for young people, teenage parents, their children and their families. She is also the director of Family Focus' Family Community Center which houses ten other community services. She is a member of the board of directors of the National Organization on Adolescent Pregnancy and Parenting, Inc. She has made numerous presentations on adolescent parenting and pregnancy prevention. She earned a Master of Arts in education from the National College of Education in Evanston.

**Rev. Pellam Love** is pastor of River Rouge Bible Assembly in Detroit, and is a professional guidance counselor at Wayne State University in Detroit. He specializes in servicing veterans. He is also an instructor at William Tyndale College Evening School. He has ministered to people in prison camps, children in Bible camps, students in middle and senior high schools, and veterans. He earned a Bachelor of Religious Education from William Tyndale College, a Bachelor of Arts in history from Spring Arbor College and a Master of Arts in counseling from the University of Detroit. He is also a veteran of the Vietnam War. He is married to Marion Love and has three children.

**Dr. Dwight Perry** is the national coordinator of Black Ministries of the Baptist General Conference. He is former midwest regional coordinator of the Moody Bible Institute Evening School. He is the founder of Chicagoland Bible Church and served as its pastor for eight years. He has served as a conference presenter on topics of missions, marriage and leadership development. He earned a Bachelor of Arts in education and a Master of Arts in educational psychology from the University of Illinois. He earned a Doctor of Ministry from Covington Theological Seminary. He is married to Cynthia Perry and has four children.

**Dr. Pauline Reeder** is the Director of Christian Education in the Progressive Baptist Convention for New York State. She is the former national dean and president of the Progressive Baptist Convention Congress of Christian Education. She is the first and only woman to have held this position. She has served in the field of Christian Education for 30 years. She has worked as a public school teacher in special education. She earned a Bachelor of Science in special education from the University of Maryland, a Master of Arts in sociology and psychology from Brooklyn College in New York, a Doctor of Humane Letters from Virginia Seminary and College and is currently completing a Doctorate in sociology and the study of religion from City College of New York. She is married to Dr. James T. Reeder, pastor of Mount Ararat Baptist Church. They have four children.

**Dr. Loretta Adams Reid** is an ordained minister in the African Methodist Episcopal Church, serving at Grant Memorial A.M.E. Church in Chicago. She has served as teacher and administrator in the Chicago public school system. She has served as a counselor for Parental Stress Services and as a volunteer chaplain for the Literacy Council of Chicago. She earned a Bachelor of Science degree in education from Northern Illinois University, a Master of Education degree from National College of Education, a Master of Divinity degree from Chicago Theological Seminary, and the Doctor of Ministry degree in pastoral counseling from Trinity Theological Seminary of Newburg, Indiana. She is married to Dr. Wilfred Reid.

**Rev. Paul Sadler** is pastor of Central Congregational United Church of Christ of New Orleans, Louisiana. He is the host and executive producer of a Christian talk show in New Orleans. He has served as a pastor and as a minister in several churches in Washington, D.C. and Chicago, Illinois. He earned a Bachelor of Arts and a Master of Divinity from Howard University. He is married to Kim Sadler and has two children.

**Bertha Swindall** is currently a private practitioner in psychotherapy, specializing in family adjustment and the welfare of children. She has served as Assistant Professor on the faculty of the University of Chicago School of Social Science Administration. She also served as the Assistant General Secretary and as the International Consultant for Children and Family Services Board of Global Ministries of the United Methodist Church. She has served as Vice President of the Board of Child Serve, and as Assistant Director of the Illinois State Department of Mental Health Subzone #6. She is currently a member of the board of Beatrice Caffrey Youth Services, and a member of the Board of Directors of Evanston Church Women United. She earned a Bachelor of Arts in sociology from the University of Illinois, and a Master of Arts in social work from the University of Chicago School of Social Science Administration.

**Dr. Jeremiah A. Wright, Jr.** is pastor of Trinity United Church of Christ in Chicago, the fastest growing church in the United Church of Christ. Its membership has grown from about 100 in the 1970's to more than 5,000 members.

**Beverly Yates** is a registered nurse. She worked for the University of Illinois Hospital for 20 years, specializing in critical care nursing. She is currently vice president of the board of the Westside Holistic Family Center, and president of the Chicagoland Christian Women's Conference. She has presented workshops at such conferences as the National Christian Education Conference, the National Conference on Pioneering Black America, the Decade of Promise, and the Christian Working Women Conferences. She graduated from the University of Illinois Cook County School of Nursing. She is married to Rev. Leroy Yates, and is the mother of five children and grandmother of six children.

**Dr. Leroy Yates** serves as one of the three co-pastors of Westlawn Gospel Chapel of Chicago, Illinois. He is a professional Christian counselor at the Westside Holistic Family Center, and is executive director of Circle Y Ranch, a summer youth camp for children. He has also served as a microbiologist at the Chicago Medical School. He is a graduate of Moody Bible Institute and earned Bachelor of Science and Master of Science degrees from Chicago State University. He has an honorary doctorate from Detroit Bible College. He is married to Beverly Yates, and they have five children.

# BIBLIOGRAPHY

Abatso, George and Yvonne. *The Black Christian Family* (Chicago: Urban Ministries, 1985).

Adams, Jay. *The Christian Counselor's Manual* (Phillipsburg, New Jersey: Reformed Publishing Company, 1983).

_____. *Competent to Counsel* (Ada, Michigan: Baker Books, 1970).

_____. *Marriage, Divorce and Remarriage* (Grand Rapids: Zondervan, 1980).

Akbar, Na'im. *Chains and Images of Psychological Slavery* (Tallahassee, Florida: New Mind Press, 1984).

Applewhite, Barry. *Find Yourself - Give Yourself* (Wheaton: Victor Books, 1980).

Backus, William and Marie Chapian. *Telling Yourself the Truth* (Bloomington, Minnesota: Bethany Fellowship, Inc., 1980).

Bauer, David G. *The "How To" Grants Manual* (New York: Macmillan Publishing Company, 1984).

Baum, Gregory. *"An Invitation to Mourning, Not Guilt,"* Touchstone, Volume 6:4-9, January, 1988.

Becker, A. H. *Ministry with Older Persons* (Columbus: Augsburg, 1986).

Black, David. *"Jesus on Anger: The Text of Matthew 5:22a Revisited,"* Nov Test, Volume 30, January, 1988, pp. 1-8.

Bowlby, John. *Loss: Sadness and Depression* (New York: Basic Books, 1980).

Briscoe, Stuart. *What Works When Life Doesn't* (Wheaton: Victor Books, 1976).

Brothers, Joyce. "Why Husbands Walk Out," *Reader's Digest,* July 1987, pp. 27-32.

Bustanoby, Andrea. "Sharing a Sensitive, Sensible Heart: A Counselor Tells What to Do When Your Child is Depressed," *Fundamental Journal,* Volume 5, No. 4, April, 1986, pp. 30-32.

Carter, Velma Thorne and J. Lynn Leavenworth. *Caught in the Middle: Children of Divorce* (Valley Forge: Judson Press, 1985).

Chicago Tribune Staff, *The American Millstone* (Chicago: Chicago

Tribune, 1986).

Christopherson, Victor A. *Childrearing in Today's Christian Family* (Valley Forge: Judson Press, 1985).

Clark, Reginald. *Black Family Achievement in School* (Chicago: University of Chicago Press, 1983).

Crabb, Lawrence. *Basic Principles of Biblical Counseling* (Grand Rapids: Zondervan Press, 1975).

Crabb, Lawrence. *Effective Biblical Counseling* (Grand Rapids: Zondervan Press, 1977).

Davis, Ernest, Jr., D. Min. *Utilizing the Local Church as a Non-Traditional Setting for the Delivery of Mental Health Services* (Drew University, 1983). Dissertation Abstracts International, Volume 44/11-A, p. 3411 (Order No: AAD84-02915).

Davis, Robert. "Black Suicide and Social Support Systems: An Overview and Some Implications for Mental Health Practitioners," *Phylon,* Volume 43, No. 4, December, 1982, pp. 307-314.

Dennis, Ruth E. "Social Stress and Mortality Among Non-white Males," *Phylon,* Volume 38, No. 3, September, 1977, pp. 315-328.

Doering, Jeanne. *The Power of Encouragement* (Chicago: Moody Press, 1982).

Eng, Eugenia, John Callan, and Anne Callan, "Institutionalizing Social Support through the Church and into the Community," *Health Education Quarterly,* Volume 12, No. 1, Spring, 1985, pp. 81-92.

Estadt, B. K., Siang-Yang Tan, Emerson, James Gordon. "Lay Pastoral Counseling: Thought and Response," *Journal of Pastoral Care,* Volume 40, No. 4, December, 1986, pp. 291, 304-309.

Fagan, Ronald. "Skid-Row Rescue Missions: A Religious Approach to Alcoholism," *Journal of Religion and Health,* Vol. 26, Summer, 1987, pp. 193-171.

Flesch, Rudolf. *Why Johnny Can't Read* (New York: Harper & Row, 1955).

Freidman, Maurice. "Healing Through Meeting," *Tikkum,* Volume 3, March-April, 1988, pp. 33-35, 85-87.

Fryling, Alice. *An Unequal Yoke* (Downer's Grove: Intervarsity Press, 1979).

Gaulke, Earl H. *You Can Have a Family Where Everybody Wins* (St. Louis: Concordia Press, 1987).

Gee, Arizona Langston. *Viewpoints of a Black Senior Citizen* (Seminole: Open Door Ministries, 1986).

Gilkes, Cheryl Townsend. "The Black Church as a Therapeutic Community: Suggested Areas for Research into the Black Religious Experience," *Journal of the Interdenominational Theological Center,* Volume 8, Fall, 1980, pp. 29-44.

Gillespie, Bonnie. "The Black Church and the Black Elderly: A Bibliographical Historical Essay," *Journal of Religious Studies* (Ohio), Volume 10, No. 2, 1983, pp. 19-31.

Goba, Bonganjalo. "The Role of the Black Church in the Process of Healing Human Brokenness: A Perspective in Pastoral Theology," *Journal of Theology of South Africa,* No. 28, September, 1979, pp. 7-13.

Gray, Cleo Jones, Ph.D. *Attitudes of Black Church Members Toward the Black Elderly as a Function of Denomination, Age, Sex and Level of Education* (Howard University, 1977). Dissertation Abstracts International, Volume 38/11-A, p. 6396 (Order No: AAD78-05433).

Green, Garey. "The Black Church and the Criminal Justice System: A Pilot Project Designed to Train Black Clergy and Laymen in Pastoral Care and Counseling." *Lutheran Theological Southern Seminary,* 1982.

Gregory, Howard. "Bereavement: A Parish-Based Approach for the Jamaican Situation," *Caribbean Journal of Religious Studies,"* Vol. 6, No. 2, September, 1985, pp. 24-38.

Griffin, J. H. *Black Like Me.* Sepia Publishing Co., 1960.

Grindall, Harold. *Telecare Ministry* (Columbus: Augsburg, 1983).

Hale-Benson, Janice. *Black Children* (Baltimore: John Hopkins University, 1982).

Hare, Julia and Nathan. *Bringing the Black Boy to Manhood* (San Francisco: Black Think Tank, 1984).

Hare, Nathan and Julia. *Endangered Black Family* (San Francisco: Black Think Tank, 1985).

Harris, James Henry. *Expectations of Ministers in the Black Urban Church: A Study of Political and Social Expectations in the Context of Ministry to Community and World* (Old Dominion University). Dissertation Abstracts International, Volume 46/06-A, p. 1733.

Harris, Thomas A. *I'm OK, You're OK* (New York: Harper and Row, 1973).

Hawk, Gary. *Building Bonds Between Adults and Their Aging Parents* (Nashville: Convention Press, 1987).

Heath, Daryl. *Counseling Children About Christian Conversion and Church Membership* (Nashville: Southern Baptist Sunday School Board, 1975).

Henning, Lawrence H. "The Emotional Aspect of Treating Child Abuse," *Journal of Religion and Health,* Vol. 26, Spring, 1987, pp. 37-42.

Hodge, Serchal Wilfred. *Assisting Members of a Rural Black Church Develop Their Christian Faith and Realize Their Potential to be More Effective Christians* (Wesley Theological Seminary, 1979). Dissertation Abstracts International, Vol. X.

Hodges, Norman. *The Senior Years: Getting There/Being There* (Nashville: Southern Baptist Convention Publishing Board, 1983).

Hollyday, Joyce. "The Nightmare of Abuse," *Sojourners,* Volume 17, February, 1988, pp. 5-6.

Howe, Leroy. "Pastoral Care and the Healing of Guilt," *Quarterly Methodist Review,* Vol. 7, Fall, 1987, pp. 38-53.

Howe, Leroy T. "Theological Foundations of Civic Intervention," *Modern Churchman,* Vol. 29, No. 4, 1987, pp. 20-22.

Jackson, Jacquelyne Johnson. "Contemporary Relationships Between Black Families and Black Churches in the United States: a Speculative Inquiry," in *Families and Religions,* edited by W. D'Antonio and J. Aldous, 1983, pp. 191-220.

James, John W. and Frank Cherry. *A Step-by-Step Program For Moving Beyond Loss* (New York: Harper and Row Publishers, 1988).

Johnson, Otis Samuel. *The Social Welfare Role of the Black Church* (Brandeis University, The F. Heller Graduate School for Advanced Study in Social Welfare, 1980). Dissertation Abstracts International, Volume 41/05-A, p. 2293 (Order No: AAD80-24554).

Jones, R. L. *Black Psychology* (New York: Harper & Row, 1972).

Jourard, Sidney M. *The Transparent Self* (D. Van Nostrand Co., Inc., 1964).

Kantzer, Kenneth S. and Paul Fromer. "Nightmare of the 80's: Despite Its Disastrous Effects, The Use of Cocaine is Skyrocketing," *Christianity Today,* Volume 30, No. 4, March 7, 1986, pp. 14-15.

Kearney, John Henry, D. Min. *The Development of a Lay Ministry of Visitation to the Hospitalized and Shut-in Members of the Mount Calvary Missionary Baptist Church* (Drew University, 1982). Dissertation Abstracts International, Volume 43/09-A, p. 2950 (Order No: AAD83-02407).

Kimble, Melvin A. *"Pastoral Care for the Elderly,"* Journal of Pastoral Care, Vol. 41, September, 1987, pp. 270-279.

Kliewer, Dean. "Management of Feelings: Anger, Sex and Depression," *Journal of Psychiatry and Christianity,* Volume 5, No. 4, Winter, 1986, pp. 2-70.

Knight, George W. *When Families Hurt, Deacons Can Help* (Nashville: Southern Baptist Sunday School Board, 1976).

Koll, Karla. "The Fear of Fear Itself," *Christianity in Crisis,* Volume 48,

June 6, 1988, pp. 202-203.

Kunjufu, Jawanza. *Countering the Conspiracy to Destroy Black Boys* (Chicago: African American Images, 1985).

_____. *Developing Positive Self-Images and Discipline in Black Children* (Chicago: African American Images, 1984).

_____. *Lessons from History: A Celebration in Blackness* (Chicago: African American Images, 1987).

_____. *Motivating and Preparing Black Youth to Work* (Chicago: African American Images, 1986).

_____. *To Be Popular or Smart: The Black Peer Group* (Chicago: African American Images, 1988).

La Haye, Timothy F. and Beverly LaHaze. "Help Your Teen Avoid Suicide," *Fundamentalist Journal,* Volume 5, No. 1, January, 1986, p. 59.

Larson, Jim. *A Church Guide for Strengthening Families* (Columbus: Augsburg, 1986).

Lawson, William B. "Chronic Mental Illness and the Black Family," *American Journal of Social Psychiatry,* Volume 6, No. 1, Winter, 1986, pp. 57-61.

Lewis, Mary C. *Herstory: Black Female Rites of Passage* (Chicago: African American Images, 1988).

Lincoln, Eric C. "The Black Family, Black Church, and the Transformation of Values," *Religious Life,* Volume 47, Winter, 1978, pp. 486-496.

Livezey, Louis Gehr. "Sexual and Family Violence: A Growing Issue for the Churches," *Christian Century,* Vol. 104, October 28, 1987, pp. 938-942.

Lloyd, Anthony Frazier, D. Min. *The Black Church's Role in Community Mental Health Care* (School of Theology at Claremont, 1985). Dissertation Abstracts International, Volume 46/06-A, p. 1650 (Order No: AAD85-16146).

Lorch, Barbara. "Church Youth Alcohol and Drug Education Programs," *Journal of Religion and Health,* Vol. 26, Summer, 1987, pp. 106-114.

Lundberg, Sherry. "Ministering to Victims of Domestic Violence," *Christian Ministry,* Vol. 18, March, 1987, pp. 25-27.

Luther, Erwin. *Managing Your Emotions* (Wheaton: Victor Books, 1983).

Lyles, Michael R. and James H. Carter. "Myths and Strengths of the Black Family: A Historical and Sociological Contribution to Family Therapy," *Journal of the National Medical Association,* Vol. 74, No. 11, Nov., 1982, pp. 1119-1123.

Mace, David and Vera Mace. *Letters to a Retired Couple* (Valley Forge: Judson Press, 1985).

Martin, Francis A. *Facing Grief with Faith* (Nashville: Southern Baptist

Convention Publishing Board, 1976).

Mathabane, Mark. *Kaffir Boy* (New York: MacMillan Press, 1986).

McCray, Walter. *Reaching and Teaching Young Black Adults* (Chicago: Black Light Fellowship, 1985).

McDowell, Josh. *Building Your Self-Image.* (Wheaton: Tyndale House Publishers, 1987).

Wedel, Leonard E. *Making the Most of Retirement* (Nashville: Southern Baptist Convention Publishing Board, 1976).

Nabi, Gene. *Ministering to Persons with Mental Retardation and Their Families* (Nashville: Convention Press, 1985).

Mitchell, Kenneth R. and Herbert Anderson. *All Our Losses, All Our Grief: Resources For Pastoral Care,* (Philadelphia: The Westminister Press, 1983).

Mowbray, Thomas L. "The Function in Ministry of Psalms Dealing with Anger: The Angry Psalmist," *Journal of Pastoral Counseling,* Vol. 21, No.1, Spring-Summer, 1986, pp. 34-39.

Murray, Robert G., D. Min. *The Black Alcoholic In and Out of the Black Church* (Boston University School of Theology, 1981).

Narramore, Bruce. *The Psychology of Counseling* (Grand Rapids: Zondervan Press, 1960).

Narramore, Clyde M. *The Compact Encyclopedia of Psychological Problems* (Grand Rapids: Zondervan Publishing House, 1984).

Neer, Tom. "Neighbors Without Shelter in the Trauma of Homeless Families," *Sojourner,* Vol. 17, June, 1988, pp. 34-35.

Norwood, Robin. *Women Who Care Too Much* (New York: Pocket Books, 1985).

Nowen, Henri. *The Wounded Healer* (New York: Image Books, 1979).

Ogilvie, Lloyd J. *You are Loved and Forgiven* (Ventura, California: Regal Books, 1987).

Oglesby, William B. "Referral as Pastoral Care," *Journal of Pastoral Care,* Vol. 41, June, 1987, pp. 43-52.

Olander, E. A. "Amends: Abusive Men Exploring New Directions," *Military Chaplain's Review,* No. 2, Spring, 1986, pp. 43-52.

Olson, Richard, and Carole Della Pia-Terry. *Help for Remarried Couples and Families* (Valley Forge: Judson Press, 1985).

Pannell, William. *My Friend the Enemy* (Waco, Texas: Word Publishers, 1968).

Patterson, George W. "The Pastoral Care of Persons in Pain," *Journal of Religion and Aging,* No. 1, Fall, 1984, pp. 17-30.

Perkins, John. *A Call to Holistic Ministry* (Seminole, Florida: Open Door Ministries, 1975).

Peterson, J. Allen. *The Myth of the Greener Grass* (Wheaton: Tyndale House Publishers, 1983).

Pipe, Virginia. *Live and Learn with Your Teenager* (Valley Forge: Judson Press, 1985).

Powell John. *Why Am I Afraid to Tell You Who I Am* (Saratoga Springs: Argus Communications, 1987).

Pressley, Arthur L., Jr. *A Study in the Use of Consumer Marketing Theory to Develop Entry Systems for Pastoral Counseling Centers* (Northwestern University, 1986). Dissertation Abstracts International, Volume 47/06-A, p. 2202.

Monroe, Doris D. *Reaching and Teaching Mentally Retarded Persons* (Nashville: Convention Press, 1980).

Richardson, Bernard Lester, Ph.D. *The Attitudes of Black Clergy and Parishioners Toward Mental Illness and Mental Health Professionals* (Michigan State University, 1981). Dissertation Abstracts International, Volume 43/02-B, p. 512 (Order No: AAD82-16583).

Rodgers, Augustus and Edward D. Hayes. "Development of a Counseling and Referral Service in a Black Church," *Psychiatric Forum,* Volume 12, No. 2, Spring, 1984, pp. 48-52.

Ross, Sharon Zanter. "A Pastoral Response to Incest: Theological Resources for Those Who Care for Victims and Victimizers," *Lutheran Forum,* No. 2, February 21, 1987, pp. 12-18.

Sabra, George. "God's Love Casts Out Fear," *Theological Review* (Near East) No. 1, 1988, pp. 81-88.

Saint George, Arthur and Patrick H. McNamara. "Religion, Race and Psychological Well-Being," *Journal for the Scientific Study of Religion,* Volume 23, December, 1984, pp. 351-363.

Sally, Columbus and Ronald Behem. *Your God Is Too White* (Downer's Grove: Inter-Varsity Press, 1970).

Schaper, Richard. "Pastoral Care for Persons with AIDS and Their Families," *Christian Century,* Vol. 104, August 12-19, 1987, pp. 691-694.

Schlesinger, Benjamin. "Abuse of the Elderly Is the Silent Crime," *Grail,* Vol. 4, March, 1988, pp. 53-61.

Seamands, David A. *Healing for Damaged Emotions* (Wheaton: Victor Books, 1981).

Sebastian, Ssempija L. "Pastoral Counseling and Depression: A Psychological Perspective," *African Editorial Review,* Vol. 29, April, 1987, pp. 108-116.

**301**

Sedore, Marva. *To Walk and Not Faint,* (Chappagua, New York: Christian Herald Books, 1980).

Simmons, Richard. *The Crucial Element* (Chicago: Richard Simmons, 1985).

Simms, Claudette. *Don't Weep for Me* (Houston: Impressions, 1989).

Sindos, Louise King, D.S.W. *Service Needs and Use Among a Population of Single Black Men and Women* (City University of New York, 1986). Dissertation Abstracts International, Volume 47/04-A, p. 1505 (Order No: AAD86-14703).

Smith, Archie. *The Relational Self: Ethics and Therapy from a Black Church Perspective* (Abingdon, 1982).

Smith, Fred. "How to Give Good Advice," *Leadership,* Vol. 8, Winter, 1987, pp. 70-76.

Smith, J. Alfred, Sr. *For the Facing of This Hour* (Elgin: Progressive Baptist Publishing House, 1981).

Smith, W. C. *The Church in the Life of the Black Family* (Valley Forge: Judson Press, 1987).

Solomon, Charles. *Handbook to Happiness* (Detroit: Tyndale Press, 1989).

Sontag, Frederick E. "Evil, Being Black, and Love," *Journal of the Interdenominational Theological Center,* Volume 10, No. 1-2, Fall-Spring, 1982-83, pp. 15-19.

Stoner, Thomas K. "Family Life Education in the Local Church," *Christian Education Journal,* Volume 5, No. 2, 1984, pp. 53-56.

Strunk, Orlo, Jr. "The Therapeutic Use of Devotional Reading in Working with the Aging," *Journal of Religion and Aging,* No. 2, Winter, 1984, pp. 1-8.

Tarkenton, Fran. *Playing to Win* (New York: Harper & Row, 1984).

Tatum, Beverly Daniel, Ph. D. *Life in Isolation: Black Families Living in a Predominantly White Community* (The University of Michigan, 1984). Dissertation Abstracts International, Volume 45/07-B, p. 2365 (Order No: AAD84-22337).

Themes, Roberta, Dr. *Living With An Empty Chair: A Guide Through Grief* (New York: Irvington Publishers, Inc., 1980).

Thomas, Robert, D. Min. *Alternative Strategies for Inner-City Black Churches in Ministry to the Black Youth Job Crisis* (San Francisco Theological Seminary, 1973). Dissertation Abstracts International, Volume X1973.

Timmerman, John H. "Shedding Light on the Darkness of Depression," *Christian Century,* Volume 105, March 2, 1988, pp. 213-216.

Van Meter, Mary Jane S. and Patricia Johnson. *"Family Decision-making and Long-Term Care for the Elderly,"* Journal of Religion and Aging, No. 4, Summer, 1985, pp. 59-72.

Vann, Fred Herbert, D. Min. *Developing a Functional Program for the Black Church in Pastoral Care Through Working Together of the Clergy and the Laity* (Boston University School of Theology, 1985).

Walker, Curtis. "A Christian Perspective of God and Suffering, Particularly in Family Violence/Spouse Abuse," *AME Zion Quarterly Review,* October, 1987, pp. 22-37.

Wiggen, Cooper. "The Male Minister and the Female Rape Victim," *Christian Ministry,* Vol. 18, May, 1987, pp. 24-26.

Williams, Charles, Jr. "Contemporary Voluntary Associations in the Urban Black Church: The Development and Growth of Mutual Aid Societies," *Journal of Voluntary Action Research,* Volume 13, No. 4, Oct-Dec, 1984, pp. 19-30.

Wilson, Amos. *Developmental Psychology of the Black Child* (New York: Africana Research, 1978).

Wilson, Earl D. "Ministering to Victims of Incest," *Leadership,* Vol. 9, Winter, 1988, pp. 127-129.

Wimberly, Edward P. "The Healing Tradition of the Black Church and Modern Science: A Model of Traditioning," *Journal of the Interdenominational Theological Center,* Volume 11, Fall, 1983-Spring, 1984, pp. 19-30.

_____. *Pastoral Care in the Black Church* (Nashville: Abingdon Press, 1979).

_____. *Pastoral Counseling and Spiritual Values* (Nashville: Abingdon Press, 1982).

Woods, John Henry, Jr. *The Black Church in the Ministry of Housing* (American Baptist Seminary of the West, 1981). Dissertation Abstracts International, Volume X1981.

Worthington, Everett L. *How to Help the Hurting* (Downer's Grove: Intervarsity Press, 1985).

Wright, H. Norman. *Crisis Counseling: Helping People in Crisis and Stress* (San Bernadino, California: Here's Life Publishers, 1985).

Wyatt, Lawrence Paul. *Developing a Premarital Guidance Program within a Group of Black Local Churches of God in the Detroit, Michigan Area* (Drew University, 1982). Dissertation Abstracts International, Volume 43/10-A, p. 3280.

Yancy, Philip. *In His Image* (Grand Rapids: Zondervan Press, 1984).

Urban Ministries, Inc., of Chicago, Illinois is an independent Christian publishing company formed in 1970. UMI is the first predominantly Black-owned publisher to produce interdenominational Sunday School and Vacation Bible School curriculum.

In addition to the UMI curriculum, various books, supplies, and other resources are available from UMI. All the materials have been carefully selected from a number of publishers with your needs in mind. Call today, for a FREE sample packet of UMI's Sunday School curriculum. 312/233-4499.